REASSESSING 'ABILITY' GROUPING

Presenting original quantitative and qualitative data from a large-scale empirical research project conducted in British secondary schools, *Reassessing 'Ability' Grouping* analyses the impact of attainment grouping on pupil outcomes, teacher effectiveness and social equality.

Alongside a comprehensive account of existing literature and the international field, this book offers:

- Rigorous conceptual analysis of data
- A view of wider political debates on pupils' social backgrounds and educational attainment
- A discussion of the practicalities of classroom practice
- Recommendations for improved practice to maximise pupil outcomes, experiences and equity
- Vignettes, illustrative tables and graphs, as well as quotes from teacher interviews and pupil focus groups

Addressing attainment grouping as an obstacle to raising pupil attainment, this book offers a distinctive, wide-ranging appraisal of the international field, new large-scale empirical evidence, and 'close to practice' attention to the practicalities and constraints of the classroom. *Reassessing 'Ability' Grouping* is an essential read for any practitioners and policymakers, as well as students engaged in the field of education and social justice.

Becky Francis is Director of the UCL Institute of Education, UK.

Becky Taylor is Senior Research Fellow in the Centre for Teachers and Teaching Research, UCL Institute of Education, UK.

Antonina Tereshchenko is Research Fellow in the Centre for Teachers and Teaching Research, UCL Institute of Education, UK.

REASSESSING 'ABILITY' GROUPING

GROUPING

Improving Practice for Equity
and Attainment

*Becky Francis, Becky Taylor and
Antonina Tereshchenko*

Routledge
Taylor & Francis Group

LONDON AND NEW YORK

First published 2020
by Routledge
2 Park Square, Milton Park, Abingdon, Oxon, OX14 4RN

and by Routledge
52 Vanderbilt Avenue, New York, NY 10017

Routledge is an imprint of the Taylor & Francis Group, an informa business

British Library Cataloguing-in-Publication Data
A catalogue record for this book is available from the British Library

Library of Congress Cataloging-in-Publication Data
A catalogue record has been requested for this book

ISBN: 978-1-138-34865-3 (hbk)
ISBN: 978-1-138-34883-7 (pbk)
ISBN: 978-0-429-43651-2 (ebk)

Typeset in Bembo
by Swales & Willis Ltd, Exeter, Devon, UK

CONTENTS

FIGURES

TABLES

ACKNOWLEDGEMENTS

This book reports the work of a much wider team of colleagues, who have variously been involved with the Best Practice in Grouping Students study. Firstly there is the project team, which has included a range of colleagues over the four-year study. Many of these colleagues have been variously involved in analysing and writing up the data which is reported in this book. In addition to ourselves, the team included: Jeremy Hodgen, Louise Archer, Paul Connolly, Nicole Craig, Anna Mazenod, John Barlow; and contributions from Seaneen Sloan, Mary-Clare Travers, Sarah-Jane Miller, David Pepper, Richard Sheldrake and Nicola Bretscher. It has been an absolute pleasure working with these talented individuals and friends, with such diversity of skills, theoretical perspectives and methodological expertise brought to bear on the project. We extend this also to Ben Style and Palak Roy from NfER.

Then there are those that have been integral in supporting and facilitating the project. The project would not have been possible without the funding – but also invaluable advice along the way – from the Education Endowment Foundation, including Kevan Collins, Emily Yeomans and Robbie Coleman. We benefitted from the wisdom of advocates like Christine Gilbert, who chaired our Advisory Board, the various board members, and of course the headteachers that encouraged and facilitated our pilot work – especially to Rachel McGowan and Gary Philips who also sat on our Advisory Board. We want to thank all these, as well as the teachers from the pilot schools who gave up their time to help us design and test the intervention, pilot research instruments, and lend us their practitioner expertise: Coombe Girls' School, Hinchley Wood School, Islington Arts and Media School, Kings Norton Girls' School, Langdon Park School, Lilian Baylis Technology School and Plashet School. We are also grateful to the pupils from these schools who participated in pilot interviews, focus groups and surveys.

Then of course there are the schools that participated in the main project: the senior leaders who signed up to our project, and the teachers and administrators who participated. Often, we recognise, this added an administrative burden in responding to the research, and demanded additional time to engage the intervention, in an already very pressurised environment for teachers. And we mustn't forget the pupils, who agreed to participate and shared their opinions and experiences with us. We are very grateful to all participants.

We acknowledge and thank the journals that have agreed for us to draw on material published in journal articles: *British Educational Research Journal, British Journal of Educational Research, Cambridge Journal of Education, International Journal of Education Research, Pedagogy, Culture & Society* and *Research Papers in Education.*

And we want to thank Alison Foyle, Ellie Wright, and all at Routledge, as well as our anonymous referees, for supporting the publication of the book.

Finally, we want to thank our family and friends, for their patience, love and support as always. Especially from Becky (F) to Dan, Ben and Louis. Becky (T) wishes to mention Marc, Hester and Anja. And Antonina thanks her sister Valentina.

AUTHOR BIOGRAPHIES

Professor Becky Francis is Director of the UCL Institute of Education (IOE). Her research focuses on education and social justice, particularly on the impact of gender, ethnicity and social class on educational attainment and experiences; and education policy for school and system improvement, and equity. She has incorporated policy work through her career, for example in her previous roles as Director of Education at the RSA, and as Standing Advisor to the Parliamentary Education Select Committee, and currently as an advisor to governments.

Dr Becky Taylor is Senior Research Fellow in the Centre for Teachers and Teaching Research at the UCL Institute of Education. Previously she was Researcher Practitioner and Project Manager for the 'Best Practice in Grouping Students' study. Prior to this, she taught in English secondary schools for 11 years. Her research interests include how schools and teachers engage with research and social justice.

Dr Antonina Tereshchenko is Research Fellow in the Centre for Teachers and Teaching Research at the UCL Institute of Education, and was Research Associate on the 'Best Practice in Grouping Students' study discussed in this book. She previously held two research fellowships at King's College London and at the University of Porto. Her research interests centre on social identities and inequalities in education.

1
INTRODUCTION

Cast your mind back to your first day at secondary school. Do you remember? The cacophony of noise and bigger children, and the feeling that everyone else knew what they were doing? A time of excitement and expectation, but also, of trepidation, vulnerability and anxiety. Imagine, then, that on arrival in your new school you found you had been separated from many of your friends from primary school, and placed for most of your classes with a particular group of students. You quickly learn from other pupils and teachers that this is the 'low ability group'. What does that do to your self-perception, your feelings about school, and your expectations of the future?

You might think that this could dampen self-esteem, and even demotivate young people from learning. Whereas the converse might be true of those placed in top groups – their placement might affirm their achievement and boost self-perception. We shall show you in this book that this does indeed tend to be the case. However, in fact the scenario we have painted – of experience of attainment grouping for the first time at secondary school – is increasingly unusual. This is not because segregation by attainment has become less common. Quite the reverse. It is because the growing prevalence of 'ability grouping' in primary schools means that children will frequently have experienced it long before arrival in secondary school. In the UK, setting is now common for maths and English in the later primary years, and 'ability tables' are frequently employed from as early as Year 1: that's five to six year olds. Often, teachers believe that young children don't understand the significance of their 'ability tables' – sadly, the research shows that this is not the case.[1]

Our research interests have focused on elements of social inequality in education, and their impacts on young people's educational experiences, attainment, and constructions of self. A series of governments in England have sought to narrow the very large socio-economic gap for educational attainment – but with relatively scant effect. One of the well-evidenced reasons for this is the strong level of wealth inequality in England which provides young children with very different starting points on entry to school, for which schools will struggle to compensate. But gaps are shown to widen, rather than to narrow, through schooling. This is again partly explained by cumulative effects of the differential access to financial, social and cultural capital relating to education that families can mobilise. However, educational research has shown how these differing family resources and products of social background interact with the school system and classroom practice to impact pupil experiences and outcomes. And, how schools' structures and classroom practices themselves can exacerbate such inequalities. Given that pupils from low socio-economic backgrounds are disproportionately concentrated in low 'ability' groups – and that pupils in these groups are shown to make less progress than their peers in higher attainment groups – could the prevalence of attainment grouping in the English education system be an example of a school practice that promotes social inequality?

Is segregation by attainment damaging our children and switching them off learning? Or is attainment grouping beneficial and necessary to facilitate the best learning outcomes? What does the research say? Does attainment grouping differentially impact different social and attainment groups? And why is it so prevalent?

This book seeks to answer these questions, providing a comprehensive, evidence-based account of the impact of attainment grouping on pupil attainment, confidence, and experiences at school; and its relative effects on different social groups. Drawing from the international research literature, and from our own large-scale study of different forms of pupil grouping practice, we will demonstrate how attainment grouping perpetuates social inequality in education, in relation to social background, 'race', and gender.

We also attend to mixed attainment grouping: a topic that has generated very little research attention. While some researchers have posited 'mixed ability' practice as the preferable alternative to militate against negative effects of attainment grouping, there has been little research into effective mixed attainment practice, resulting in a dearth of research evidence or teaching materials to support this approach. We feel that it is both unrealistic and irresponsible to expect teachers to adopt new practices with little evidence; and one of aims of the study reported in this book was to address that gap.

But before we proceed further, a note on language. You may already have noticed how we are placing inverted commas around the word 'ability'. We do not subscribe to conceptions of 'ability' as ascribed and fixed: rather we see it as malleable, and prior attainment to reflect a range of societal factors that impact educational progress and outcome. This is not to deny that pupils may have different competencies and affinities in relation to the school curriculum, but these differ across and within curriculum topics, and may be explained by a raft of different factors. To ascribe categories to pupils at a single time point, and to imply that these accurately express a fixed and inherent level of 'ability', flies in the face of logic and science. Hence our use of inverted commas, and our reference where possible to 'attainment grouping' rather than 'ability grouping'.

The different methods of attainment grouping will be elaborated in the next chapter.

Background

Grouping by 'ability' within education – or 'tracking', as it is called in the United States – has been a longstanding topic of controversy. Whether segregating students by school type, or within schools via different streams, sets or 'ability tables', segregation by prior attainment remains prevalent internationally. In England, the tripartite[2] system that overtly segregated pupils by school type largely gave way to comprehensivisation during the 1970s.[3] The desirability or otherwise of between-school segregation is now back on the political agenda, given the Conservative Government's commitment to the expansion of grammar schools. However, even for the comprehensive school majority, the title 'comprehensive' often masked continuing practices of segregation by prior attainment *within* schools – arrangements which have been actively encouraged as 'good practice' by different governments (Dracup, 2014; Francis et al., 2017).

And segregation by attainment – or 'ability', as it is often conceived – also meant segregation by social background. Working class students, and those from particular minority ethnic groups, have been consistently shown to be over-represented in low sets and streams (as they were similarly over-represented in secondary modern schools under the tripartite system). This might be seen to be unremarkable: after all, on average children from disadvantaged backgrounds are shown to be significantly behind their middle-class peers on entry to schooling. Unsurprising, then, that they predominate in low attainment groups. However, crucially, a substantial body of international research shows that once *in* these 'low ability' groups, students make less educational progress than their counterparts in higher sets and streams. In other words, young people from disadvantaged backgrounds who are placed in 'low ability' groups face a double disadvantage.

As we will outline in more detail later in this book, research shows that grouping by prior attainment is both socially divisive, and detrimental to students with low prior attainment – and that both these elements increase socio-economic gaps for educational attainment. Research, especially from the United States, has highlighted the impact on racial segregation and attainment gaps. Moreover, international meta-analyses show that there is no significant benefit of attainment grouping overall.[4] Why, then, does 'ability grouping' remain so prevalent? We have argued that the reasons are partly political, and partly pedagogic (Francis et al., 2017). Previous research has been less good at disaggregating the various potential explanations for the lack of positive impact of attainment grouping, giving practitioners scant information with which to precipitate changes in practice. Moreover, as Taylor et al. (2017) show, teachers are impeded from developing mixed attainment practice by existing school cultures (including avoidance of risk, and overwork), lack of exemplars, and local factors (such as concerns for the views of middle-class parents).

It was these different controversies and our commitment to social justice – and therefore, to improving the educational experiences and attainment of young people from disadvantaged backgrounds – that motivated the large-scale study reported in this book. The 'Best Practice in Grouping Students' project, funded by the Education Endowment Foundation (EEF), sought to redress some of the challenges impeding impact in raising attainment for young people from disadvantaged backgrounds, and to fill existing gaps in the research literature on the topic of the impact of pupil grouping on outcomes. It is the most substantial and ambitious empirical project on attainment grouping on record, involving work with 139 secondary schools across England in a mixed methods study including two randomised control trials (RCTs). This book reports its findings, contextualised within broader political debates and research evidence on attainment grouping. We hope that it will be a valued resource for educationalists serious about educational improvement, pedagogical excellence, and social equality.

As a fundamental principle within our democratic national system, families from all backgrounds are supposed to have an equal stake in our public services; the vast majority of them paying the taxes that secure the continued provision of these services. On this basis, no one could argue that children ought not to be entitled to equality of access to quality education. Of course, many believe beyond this that society and schooling should involve an element of social redistribution that equalises life chances for young people fated to begin school with different material resources. In the UK, governments of all political colours have supported this latter principle to greater or lesser extents, the present government maintaining the socially redistributive Pupil Premium,[5] for example. But this aside, entitlement to equality of access to (high) quality education should in any case be a fundamental assumption. Yet, attainment grouping ('tracking') has a bearing on provision, experiences and outcomes of schooling; and in a way that impacts particular pupil groups differently. This book is intended to show how, to what extent, and why; and to investigate how we might do better.

The structure of the book

The book begins with an extensive chapter providing the background on attainment grouping, and reviewing the existing research literature in relation to key questions, including:

- Why attainment grouping is adopted
- The different forms of attainment grouping, and associated terminology
- The international picture on segregation by attainment
- The effectiveness or otherwise of attainment grouping
- The effectiveness or otherwise of mixed attainment practice

- Attainment grouping and social in/justice (the impact of attainment grouping on social in/equality)
- Unanswered questions about attainment grouping

Building on the final section of Chapter 2 (unanswered questions), Chapter 3 presents a brief account of what our project set out to do and why; and the methodology. The explanation of the study includes detail on the two student grouping interventions that we applied in schools, the various sources of data, and other details of the study, including its limitations.

Chapter 4 will elaborate further the prior research findings on the impact of segregation by attainment on pupil outcomes and self-confidence, and present our findings from the study with regard to the two key trial measures of attainment and self-confidence in learning (for pupils subject to an intervention on setting). We discuss the research findings in relation to pupil social background. And where Chapter 4 focuses on the impact of attainment grouping on pupil outcomes (attainment and self-confidence), Chapter 5 looks at student perspectives, and the effect of grouping practices on pupils' experiences of school. It will compare pupils' experiences of attainment grouping and mixed attainment practice; and explore the impact of attainment grouping for pupils' enjoyment of school. It will also present findings on pupil preferences for attainment grouping or mixed attainment practice, and the impact of pupil grouping on social relations within school. Again, findings will be discussed in relation to pupil social background.

Chapter 6 turns to teachers and teaching, exploring the impact of attainment grouping on pedagogy and practice. It analyses research findings concerning the challenging issues of teacher effectiveness, teacher expectations, and quality of pedagogy, in relation to different attainment groups. It focuses especially on findings that low sets and streams tend to be offered poorer 'quality' teachers and teaching, stemming from low expectations and labelling of pupils, as well as from different structural dis/incentives within the school system. And having outlined these disturbing findings, we then turn in Chapter 7 to investigate the question of why better practice in setting appears difficult to achieve. One of our study interventions aimed at improving practice in setting, based on research evidence (designed to mitigate some of the elements of setting practice that have been identified as detrimental by the research). This chapter will explore our study findings that schools found these 'best practice' stipulations, aimed at improving setting practice, difficult to implement. We will provide details of the differing levels of schools' subscription to our intervention requirements, and examine the various structural, political, and practical impediments we discovered via our classroom observations and data from teachers.

In Chapters 4 to 7 the attention has been on segregated attainment practice; especially setting. Chapter 8 turns to mixed attainment practice, exploring the existing research in this field, highlighting gaps, and elaborating the findings concerning elements of effective practice. We explore the challenges of implementation, and suggest principles of best practice in mixed attainment grouping.

Chapter 9 summarises and reflects on what we have learnt from the 'Best Practice in Grouping Students' study, and the prior literature. It discusses theoretical accounts that help explain the findings, and explores implications for practice. Especially, it draws out implications for social in/justice, and for the ongoing socio-economic gaps for attainment. It will consider what we know and have found out about best practice in mixed attainment grouping and setting, and what we need to do on order to improve practice further and support pupil outcomes and experiences. Finally, building on the implications for practice developed in the previous chapter, Chapter 10 will make recommendations for practitioners in terms of ensuring best practice in grouping students, and for policymakers in terms of promoting good outcomes for young people. We will propose ways for schools to address the constraints identified in previous chapters, as well as improving practice; offering recommendations for both mixed attainment grouping and improved setting practice, to maximise pupil outcomes, experiences, and equity.

Notes

1 See, for example, Marks (2016, 2013). In our own research in secondary schools we have also frequently been told by teachers that pupils are not aware of the significance of their set placement (for example, due to the use of less transparent labels for these attainment groups); yet the briefest of interviews with the young people concerned reveals the opposite to be true. For discussions of attainment grouping in the early years, see Bradbury & Roberts-Holmes (2017).
2 The system in which there were three types of schools: academic 'grammar schools'; technical schools (there were few of these in practice); and less academic 'secondary moderns' (the majority of schools). Children were sorted into these schools by a selective test called the 'Eleven Plus' at age 11.
3 Albeit grammar schools survive in some areas of the country, and regular political uproar is still provoked by suggestions they be revitalised or extended.
4 See e.g. Slavin (1990); Kutnick et al. (2005), Steenbergen-Hu et al. (2016), EEF (2018).
5 The Pupil Premium is a funding mechanism employed in England, 'designed to help disadvantaged pupils of all abilities perform better, and close the gap between them and their peers' (DFE, 2018). Schools receive a sum of money for each pupil registered as eligible for free school meals (FSM) at any point in the last six years (the 'Ever FSM' measure). The money is intended to be spent directly on these pupils, to raise their attainment.

References

Bradbury, A. & Roberts-Holmes, G. (2017). *Grouping in early years and Key Stage 1: 'A necessary evil'?* London: National Education Union.
DFE. (2018). Pupil premium: funding and accountability for schools. Retrieved from www.gov.uk/guidance/pupil-premium-information-for-schools-and-alternative-provision-settings.
Dracup, T. (2014). The politics of setting. Retrieved from https://giftedphoenix.wordpress.com/2014/11/12/the-politics-of-setting/.
EEF. (2018). *The Sutton Trust – Education Endowment Foundation teaching and learning toolkit.* London: Education Endowment Foundation.

Francis, B., Archer, L., Hodgen, J., Pepper, D., Taylor, B., & Travers, M-C. (2017). Exploring the relative lack of impact of research on 'ability grouping' in England: a discourse analytic account. *Cambridge Journal of Education*, *47*(1), 1–17.

Kutnick, P., Sebba, J., Blatchford, P., Galton, M., Thorp, J., MacIntyre, H., & Berdondini, L. (2005). *The effects of pupil grouping: literature review*. London: DFES.

Marks, R. (2013). 'The blue table means you don't have a clue': the persistence of fixed-ability thinking and practices in primary mathematics in English schools. *FORUM: for Promoting 3–19 Comprehensive Education*, *55*(1), 31–44.

Marks, R. (2016). *Ability grouping in primary schools: case studies and critical debates*. Northwich: Critical Publishing.

Slavin, R. E. (1990). Achievement effects of ability grouping in secondary schools: a best-evidence synthesis. *Review of Educational Research*, *60*(3), 471–499.

Steenbergen-Hu, S., Makel, M. C., & Olszewski-Kubilius, P. (2016). What one hundred years of research says about the effects of ability grouping and acceleration on K–12 students' academic achievement: findings of two second-order meta-analyses. *Review of Educational Research*, *86*(4), 849–899.

Taylor, B., Francis, B., Archer, L., Hodgen, J., Pepper, D., Tereshchenko, A., & Travers, M-C. (2017). Factors deterring schools from mixed attainment teaching practice. *Pedagogy, Culture & Society*, *25*(3), 327–345.

2

'ABILITY GROUPING' – WHAT IS IT, AND WHY DO WE DO IT?

Why do education systems and the schools within them segregate pupils by attainment? The basic premise is that different students function at different levels of 'ability', and/or have different talents and attributes. Therefore, they will benefit – and/or their teachers will benefit – by being grouped and taught with others like them.

Already, we can see the complexity and contestability of these premises. In terms of pupil 'ability' or levels of attainment, these are clearly difficult to categorise, both conceptually and practically. Indeed, later in this book we will show the difficulties schools have with these delineations. For example, when all humans develop learning throughout the life course, and perhaps especially in childhood and adolescence,[1] is it meaningful or legitimate to apply measurement at a single point in time to predict future achievement, and determine a young person's attainment group, pathway or school type accordingly? And what exactly is to be measured – we know that young people's attainment often differs significantly between different subjects and skills – and even between different competencies within a subject. Fundamentally, there are two key questions at stake – firstly, whether children and young people *can be* effectively (accurately and fairly) categorised according to prior attainment; and secondly, whether they *should be*. As we shall see, matters of equity and social in/justice pertain to both. And if we peel back a further conceptual layer, we find that understandings of 'aptitude' – or 'ability' as it is most frequently termed – underpin all debates and practice in this area.

Some educational supporters of attainment grouping reject premises of attainment as fixed, or as expressing a student's innate potential. Rather, they maintain that attainment grouping is a practical response to a pedagogic challenge – it is beneficial to students to learn with others presently at a similar attainment level, and such groups are easier for teachers to teach. Let us call this the *pragmatic argument*. And it is possible to subscribe to this without subscribing to notions of 'ability' as inherent or fixed. Indeed, although rarely articulated as such, such pragmatic perceptions may be seen to underpin 'high integrity' versions of attainment grouping such as setting[2] by individual subject, wherein students are grouped for each distinct subject strictly according to their performance in that subject, in contrast to streaming (tracking)[3] or 'blended' versions of attainment grouping. However, as we shall see, such approaches are practically very difficult to implement, as well as having other implications for social in/justice. And meanwhile, a more prevalent view that infuses debate and practice in this area is that of 'fixed ability' thinking. It is no coincidence that what we are referring to as 'attainment grouping' is usually referred to as 'ability grouping' – and different groups (tables, sets, streams, or 'tracks' as they are called in the US) referred to as 'high ability', 'middle ability' and 'low ability' groups respectively. Underpinning the practice of attainment grouping, and especially manifest in systems of between-school grouping such as the tripartite system,[4] is an assumption that students are 'naturally' different from each other, and have different predispositions, including inherently different ability levels, which their educational attainment reflects.

This chapter will explore, then, some key questions in this field concerning the prevalence and nature of attainment grouping, and what the prior research literature has said about them. But before we turn to these questions, it is worth noting that this field is rife with often confusing and competing labels: even in the above introductory paragraphs we have made allusion to practices which may be opaque. Here we present a 'key' to grouping in relation to prior attainment (albeit it must be highlighted that in practice some of these approaches may be blurred together, and/or operated in quite different ways, within individual schools).

The different forms of within-school attainment grouping

As Figure 2.1 indicates, different forms of grouping by attainment tend to be used in different sectors, and are applied in diverse ways between schools. Primary schools in England often use *within-class grouping*, in the form of 'ability tables': pupils of similar attainment levels are seated with others deemed to share their level, either throughout the school day, or for particular topics. Such practices have burgeoned in recent decades, with 'ability tables' being applied as early as Year 1 (age five to six) (Davies et al., 2003; Hallam & Parsons, 2013a, 2013b) and in early years education (Bradbury & Roberts-Holmes, 2017; Bradbury, 2018). As we observed in Chapter 1, research has found that primary school teachers often believe children are too young to understand the implications of these grouping practices; whereas in fact even very young primary pupils are usually highly aware (Marks, 2013). This awareness is likely accentuated by the crass practices sometimes applied in the *naming* of these tables: Marks (2016) found names given to different tables to often evoke a hierarchy; for example, a moped used to label a low attainment group, a Ferrari for a high group. We ourselves have come across examples of symbolic distinction in the naming of tables in ways that elevate higher

Streaming (tracking)	Grouping students according to their perceived general 'ability' across all or most subjects, such that students are taught in the same, streamed groups for all lessons. Hence irrespective of subject, students will be sitting in class with the same students.
Setting (tracking by subject)	Grouping based on attainment in individual subjects, so a student might be in a high set for mathematics and a lower set for English.
Within-class 'ability' grouping	Most commonly practiced in primary schools. Children are organised at 'ability tables' within a class containing a wide range of prior attainment.
Banding	A rather vague term that usually indicates streaming, but may also apply to school admissions, whereby pupils are categorised into 'ability bands' to ensure a diverse school population.

FIGURE 2.1 Different forms of within-school attainment grouping

'ability tables', including: names of carnivorous animals for high 'ability' tables and herbivores for low 'ability'; and names of broadsheet newspapers for high 'ability' tables and tabloids for low 'ability'.

Hallam and Parsons (2013a) also found that practices of setting and streaming are increasingly practiced in primary schools, often in addition to within-class grouping. Streaming and setting are forms of *between-class grouping*, in which pupils are divided into different whole-class groups according to attainment levels. In the US, between-class grouping is referred to as tracking (see Gamoran & Nystrand, 1994). But between-class grouping includes a potential range of quite distinct practices. In the UK, we refer to the practice wherein pupils are divided into classes by a proxy for 'overall ability' and sit with the same class of pupils for all subjects as *streaming*. If we see attainment grouping as a spectrum, with hard forms of segregation at one end, and mixed attainment grouping at the other, streaming sits near the 'hard' end. It is based on a premise that pupils can be divided into these groups irrespective of curriculum subject: as such it is fundamentally based on a concept of overall inherent 'ability' (rather than, for example, prior attainment, and recognition of fluidity of such across subjects).

By contrast, the practice of setting divides pupils into classes based on prior attainment for particular subjects. Hence setting practice can recognise that a pupil may be low attaining in one subject area, but high attaining in another. In this sense, the practice has higher conceptual integrity than streaming, and these more diverse practices also somewhat mitigate (or at least narrow to subject-level) the labelling element found to be associated with grouping by attainment. It also ensures social mixing in some classes (see Deunk et al., 2018). Setting practice varies between schools: in some schools it is applied just to one or two subjects; in others to all subjects. And in some schools setting practices either combine elements of streaming, or are added to streaming. To elaborate: it is quite often the case that secondary schools use pupil prior attainment and subsequent set level at one key subject, to determine the set level for others. For example, set level at maths is quite commonly used to determine set level for all of the sciences. And we have also found examples of prior attainment and set level in English being used to determine set level in Modern Foreign Language (MFL). Clearly, the conceptual justification for setting is diluted in such practices (given that the association and assumption for similar achievement across such subjects is not evidenced). Finally, many schools that apply streaming also apply setting additionally to further delineate pupils by attainment in key subject areas. So pupils might sit in a particular stream or 'band' across the curriculum (typically three different levels), but then are additionally subject to an extra element of hierarchical grouping for maths and/or other subjects. In our project we found that the number of set levels that secondary schools applied ranged between two and ten, with the majority of schools having between three and five set levels.

Aside from within-class and between-class grouping, the other key practice of attainment grouping is *between-school* segregation. This practice is at the 'hard end' of the spectrum, premised as it is on the assumption that children can be legitimately delineated and segregated by overall 'ability' based on a test at a particular moment in their lives, and be consequently placed in different types of school 'suited' to different levels of achievement and disposition. It is not an overstatement to say that such systems seek to identify different 'kinds' of pupil and steer them towards different 'appropriate' futures – indeed this is precisely the rationale for such systems.

In England, the former 'tripartite system' (academic grammar schools, secondary moderns for 'the rest', and the few technical schools) was largely dismantled in the 1970s and 80s following the 1968 Education Act. However, grammar schools remain in some local jurisdictions, either forming a local system (as in Kent), or with just a few grammar schools remaining within a local authority area. There are 163 state-funded grammar schools across England with a total of 167,000 students (around 5% of all pupils). These students are much less likely to have Special Educational Needs or be eligible for free school meals than average (Bolton, 2017; Sullivan et al., 2018). Supported as part of present Conservative Party policy, grammar school provision is again on the rise; albeit given the levels of controversy and contestation, and the fragility of the present Government, this expansion is being done 'by the back door' rather than by statute (Jeffreys, 2018). Nevertheless, grammar schools and others that select by attainment remain a small minority within the state education system[5] in England. The grammar school system remains prevalent in Northern Ireland, while the other UK countries of Scotland and Wales are fully comprehensive. The focus of this book is on within-school grouping practices rather than between-school grouping practices: nevertheless, between-school grouping practices are clearly relevant – and indeed shape the cultural assumptions and material experiences that inform grouping practices within schools.

We hope to have captured the complexity of terminology here, and of the practices that sit behind the labels. Understanding this complexity is vital in approaching the topic of attainment grouping, as it hampers communication

'Hard'				'Soft'	None
≤					>
Between-school segregation	Streaming (including streaming and additional setting)	Setting with elements of streaming	Setting	Setting for just one or two subjects	Mixed attainment grouping
	fixed 'ability tables' consistent across school day		'ability tables' just for certain subjects		

FIGURE 2.2   Attainment grouping spectrum

and research on the issue in a range of ways. In relation to research, much of the prior research on this topic has been conducted in the United States (US). Yet as we noted above, in the US all between-class grouping is referred to as tracking (see Gamoran & Nystrand, 1994). Indeed, some authors refer to between-school segregation as 'tracking by school'. Clearly then, 'tracking' includes wildly diverse practices. Generalising findings on its impact can therefore be problematic. And this problem is compounded by meta-analyses, which frequently draw conclusions from studies of quite distinct practices that were imposed with diverse intentions. In relation to practice, in a large secondary school, it is often the case that different practices may be being adopted by different subject departments, and that the headteacher (and teachers in different parts of the school) is unaware of the nature and diversity of these practices. Specificity and care in labelling these practices is therefore fundamental in facilitating accuracy, and thereby in encouraging rigor and efficacy in research and practice.

The international picture

In comparison with many other countries, England has a highly inclusive education system. This point is often received with surprise by English practitioners, partly due to widespread awareness of the large gap for educational achievement according to socio-economic background. Indeed, educational attainment in the UK is unusually tightly correlated to family wealth, in comparison to many other European countries (Jerrim & Macmillan, 2015). Moreover, the English system is unusually diversified in terms of a proliferation of different types of school, and complexity of systems of school autonomy and accountability (Francis, 2017). The education press regularly highlights exclusionary practices operated by schools, that often disproportionately impact pupils from vulnerable groups. And the continuing support for selective grammar schools by the Conservative Party, combined with high levels of popular and professional contestation, means that this topic features prominently and disproportionately in the media. Nevertheless, the English education system remains predominantly comprehensive at entry, and maintains this comprehensive approach until relatively late in pupils' educational trajectory (age 16, which remains the end of mandatory schooling in England, albeit the vast majority of pupils stay in education or training until at least age 18). And within this the English education system is also relatively inclusive of those children designated physically disabled and/or as having Special Educational Needs (SEN) (D'Alessio & Watkins, 2009).

In the majority of education systems around the world, some kind of stratification by 'ability' is employed within secondary schooling, but its nature and extent differs between countries. In many cases, this takes the form of explicit between-school tracking where, at a point somewhere between age ten and 16, students are sorted into overarching education programmes offering more vocational versus more academic curricula. Across the OECD, the mean age of selection is 14, but in the majority of OECD countries it is mainly applied at age 15 or 16 (see Table 2.1). Among the countries that begin to select students into different types of programmes or schools at the end of primary phase are Austria, Germany, Turkey, and Central European countries Czech Republic, Slovakia, and Hungary (Woessmann, 2009b; OECD, 2016b).

As we can see from Table 2.1, national education systems broadly adopt one of three different approaches to between-school segregation. The group of countries listed above select early, at the end of primary education. It is interesting to note that these are all European nations, with the exception of

TABLE 2.1 First age at selection in the OECD and partner countries

Age at selection	10	11	12	13	14	15	16
	Austria	Hungary	Netherlands	Luxembourg	Slovenia	Albania	Australia
	Germany	Czech Republic	Belgium	Bulgaria	Croatia	Brazil	Canada
		Slovakia	Switzerland		Italy	B–S–J–G (China)	Chile
		Turkey	Singapore		Romania	Chinese Taipei	Denmark
						Colombia	Dominican Republic
						Costa Rica	
						France	Estonia
						Georgia	Finland
						Greece	Iceland
						Hong Kong (China)	Jordan
						Indonesia	Latvia
						Ireland	Lithuania
						Israel	Malta
						Japan	New Zealand
						Korea	Norway
						Macao (China)	Peru
						Mexico	Poland
						Montenegro	Qatar
						Portugal	Russia
						Thailand	Spain
						UAE	Sweden
						Uruguay	UK
						Vietnam	USA

Source: adapted from OECD (2016b), p. 167; Woessmann (2009b), p. 26

Singapore. A second, large and geographically diverse group, select as pupils begin the final stage of mainstream secondary schooling (at age 14 or 15). And a final (again, large and diverse) group maintain comprehensive education to the end of mainstream secondary education at age 16. Whether this is at the end of mandatory education provision differs between countries. However, the similarity remains that the following stage for this group is generally preparation for different onward routes; either vocational skills training or academic preparation for university. It is worth noting that in spite of comprehensive inclusivity to this point, pathways at this stage still tend to be highly socially classed, whether in Sweden or the UK (Fjellman et al., 2018). Also, that university selection practices have become near universal, and can be seen to drive selective practices in post-16 education (or indeed earlier) (Blackman, 2017).

According to OECD (2016b), the number of state school types or education programmes available to 15-year-olds ranges from one in Australia, Denmark, Estonia, Finland, Iceland, New Zealand, UK, and USA to five and more in Czech Republic, Latvia, the Netherlands, and Slovakia. However, here we can see the 'broad brush' approach of OECD reporting obscuring important information that undermines the meaningfulness of analysis. Not only does it hide complexity of school governance and provision types that may impact school quality across these countries, but it also overlooks ongoing (albeit minority) selective schooling in these countries (e.g. the UK and US).

The second popular type of sorting adopted by national education systems is between-class grouping, which consists of grouping students by attainment into different classes within a school. As we have seen, this 'tracking' may be on a subject-by-subject basis (setting), or irrespective of curriculum (streaming). Some systems offer distinct courses at varying levels of difficulty in one or more subjects (see Domina et al., 2016 for an account in US high schools). According to a PISA 2015 survey of school principals regarding how 15-year-olds are grouped for learning, the following OECD countries combine late *between-school* selection with high levels of *between-class* attainment grouping: United Kingdom, USA, Israel, Ireland, Australia, Canada, New Zealand. The practice is also widespread in Singapore, Hong Kong, Malta, Thailand, and Vietnam. In these countries, at least three in four students receive instruction in at least one subject in a class grouped by attainment (OECD, 2016b). In the UK, around 99% of students participating in PISA 2015 attended schools that grouped by attainment, into different classes, for some or all subjects – the highest proportion across OECD countries (Jerrim et al., 2018). By contrast, the OECD countries where less than 20% of students were grouped by attainment into different classes within schools are Austria, Portugal, Greece, Norway, Denmark, Latvia, Italy, as well as OECD partner countries Brazil, Uruguay, Georgia, and Moldova. If we cross-reference with Table 2.1, we can see that for some of these countries this reflects especially highly comprehensive practice (e.g. Denmark, Latvia, Norway), where for others it reflects a reliance on between-school sorting rather than within-school sorting (e.g. Austria, Italy).[6]

The third type of grouping that the OECD is concerned with is *within-class* grouping by attainment. Overall, attainment grouping within classes was found to be more common than between classes (OECD, 2016b). In the following countries between 70% and 80% of students were said to attend schools that group students within classes, for some but not all subjects: Denmark, Hong Kong (China), Hungary, Israel, the Netherlands, New Zealand, Poland, Singapore, and the United Kingdom. However, this type of grouping is notoriously ambiguous and data hard to interpret: for one thing, practices are highly diverse, with some in-class grouping reflecting attainment grouping, but other instances reflecting other purposes; and in some cases practice may be consistently maintained while in others practice is more partial. Moreover, these practices will in many cases be applied in addition to (rather than instead of) the between-school and between-class approaches we have discussed.

More fine-grained recording and analysis of different national practices is clearly needed. Nevertheless, what we can see is that a very wide range of practices of segregation and grouping by attainment are adopted by different international education systems, representing both ends of our spectrum (see Figure 2.2). And that it is very rare for countries not to apply some kind of delineation by attainment – indeed only a very small group of countries are listed by the OECD (2016b) as maintaining comprehensive education to 16, and limiting between or within-class segregation (Norway, Spain, Iceland, Estonia, and Sweden). Indeed, some systems have institutionalised multiple layering of distinction by attainment. But is there research evidence to support these practices?

Why is attainment grouping adopted? The assumptions behind the concept

It needs to be acknowledged that in fact there has been little actual research on educationalists' motivations for implementing practices of attainment grouping – or, indeed, where these discussions and decisions take place. Some countries and/or local jurisdictions have overt policies on the issue (and even school systems built around these decisions). However, for most schools in England, schools have autonomy on pedagogic issues and as such this is a school-level decision.[7] In this case, the practices adopted may be promoted by a school leadership team across the school, or, in the case of secondary schools, potentially in particular curriculum areas; they may be adopted and developed under the impetus of particular subject departments; or they could be promoted 'bottom up' by teachers advocating for particular practices. In some schools, practices instigated historically have become part of the longstanding institutional culture, and simply go unquestioned.

In terms of what motivates these decisions, the predominant focus emerging in the research literature and in policy discussions of attainment grouping, is that of attainment outcomes for pupils. In other words, which practices best support pupil attainment? Those who favour segregation by attainment argue that this approach enables teachers to stretch and challenge 'able' learners, and to provide support to those who are struggling (DfES, 2005). It is claimed that when groups are more homogeneous, it better enables teachers to direct appropriate resources and to design learning activities to meet the needs of students in a group, and so maximise progress and attainment (Hallinan & Sorenson, 1987; Dar & Resh, 1994; Cahan et al., 1996). As Slavin (1990) observes, advocates of 'ability grouping' maintain it allows teachers to adapt instruction to the needs of a diverse student body, giving them the opportunity to provide more difficult material to high achievers, and more support to low achievers. As we shall see, these assumptions do not have foundation in research evidence. And indeed, we have analysed the way in which policymakers, especially, make assumptions about attainment grouping practices supporting pupil attainment *without* evidence (Francis et al., 2017a). We showed how a succession of British governments, individual ministers, and governmental organisations (including the schools inspectorate, Ofsted), have promoted attainment grouping without supporting evidence, or recognition that the evidence is lacking. Doubtless such interventions, especially that of Ofsted, have influenced the thinking of practitioners and lent attainment grouping credibility and overt endorsement. Elsewhere we have discussed the genealogy of the discourses and assumptions that underpin such unevidenced assertions of attainment grouping as 'common sense' and reflecting 'natural' distinctions between pupils (Francis et al., 2017a). Nevertheless, the rationale presented in such advocacy is on promoting pupil attainment outcomes.

Ironically, the evidence presented in the next section will demonstrate that it would be just as – if not more – legitimate for proponents of mixed attainment grouping to advocate for 'de-tracked' (mixed attainment) practice on the basis of pupil attainment outcomes. However, arguments for mixed attainment grouping tend to be focused on equity and social justice (see e.g. Alvarez & Mehan, 2006; Welner & Burris, 2006; Boylan & Povey, 2012; Peacock, 2016). Advocates of mixed attainment grouping tend to focus on social inclusion and the benefits of social mixing, or the dangers of 'fixed ability thinking' (Bradbury, 2019; Yarker, 2019).

There are also other arguments for attainment grouping that focus on ease for teachers, and these were evident in teachers' fears expressed in our study that mixed attainment practice would increase workload (Taylor et al., 2017). We attend to some of these concerns further in Chapters 7 and 8.

As we shall see, in spite of the assertions that attainment grouping practices positively impact pupil progress and outcomes, not only is there scant evidence to support these claims, but also the very premises of attainment grouping are subject to contestation.

Is attainment grouping effective?

This topic has been subject to a huge amount of research. However, in spite of the quantity of research, the impact of attainment grouping on pupil outcomes remains a contested research domain. The body of research to date has tended to be somewhat polarised in focus and methodology, indicatively with small-scale qualitative research focusing on experiences of grouping practices; and with large-scale quantitative, experimental and/or meta-analytical work focused on pupil outcomes. The latter has tended to be the most influential, and also the least conclusive. We consider that this lack of clarity may be explained by various factors, as follows:

- The complexity and frequently overlapping nature of the attainment grouping practices included within meta-analyses (for example, setting and streaming included as 'tracking', and different forms of these various practices also taken together, etc). This lack of nuance and rigorous specificity in categorisation and documentation is heightened by the need for large-scale quantitative data in order to facilitate generalisation on pupil progress and outcomes – yet the methodology necessary to produce such data is usually unable to precisely capture the complex practices (or their fidelity) underpinning pupil outcomes.
- The research often focuses on different sub-groups, and different audiences, but the findings of which are then inappropriately applied out to broader populations (the body of work on practice directed to 'gifted and talented' pupils is an example here; as is the conflation between practice and outcomes in primary and secondary education.)[8]
- As already noted, the methodological and reporting challenges in the previous two points are compounded within meta-analyses, which sometimes incorporate studies on and in different constituencies and of somewhat different practices. And it appears that different regression models and assumptions can sometimes lead to different conclusions, even from the same datasets.
- The topic is highly political, with strong avocation for and against attainment grouping, which can lead research findings to be 'spun' or interpreted in different ways.

Very broadly, it can be said that the conclusion of the extensive research literature on the impact of attainment grouping on pupil outcomes, is that *overall* these practices are not of significant benefit to attainment, with a negative impact for low attainment groups. (As we shall see, it is these lower sets and streams in which pupils from lower socio-economic groups are disproportionately represented). As Boaler and Wiliam (2001) summarise:

> bringing together the different research studies on ability grouping the general conclusion is that streaming has no academic benefits whatsoever, while setting confers small academic benefits on some high-attaining students, at the expense of large disadvantages for lower attainers.
>
> *(p. 179)*

Likewise, reviewing the evidence for primary schooling, Deunk et al. (2018) concur,

> In general, homogeneous whole-class ability grouping does not seem to be very effective for students in primary education, nor does it seem to positively influence the well-being of students of all ability levels.
>
> *(p. 33)*

To elaborate: a number of studies used meta-analytic techniques to synthesise a large body of available studies on the effects of grouping by attainment, compared to the outcomes for heterogeneously grouped students. Slavin's (1990) best evidence synthesis of secondary-level grouping reviewed 29 studies that used standardised or teacher-created tests to measure achievement of high-, average-, and low-achieving students taught the same curriculum in grouped and ungrouped classes. The analysis concluded that 'the effects of ability grouping on student achievement are essentially zero' (p. 484). In other words, despite some variations across the studies, Slavin found no evidence to conclusively point to positive effects of either tracking or heterogeneous ('mixed ability') grouping. Similarly, an earlier meta-analysis conducted by Kulik and Kulik (1982) found that grouping produced only insignificant effects on overall achievement. However, these authors determined that 'gifted and talented' students who were taught an enriched curriculum in grouped classes obtained benefits.[9]

Focusing on the evaluation of de-tracking reform, Rui (2009) reviewed 15 studies that had been conducted in North America and published since 1972, including four experimental studies, two quasi-experimental studies, seven observational studies, and two qualitative studies. He found overall positive effects of heterogeneous (mixed attainment) grouping on students' academic outcomes. Further analysis by student attainment level revealed statistically significant academic gains for low-attaining groups in de-tracked (mixed attainment) settings, but no effects for students at high and average attainment levels.

More recently, Steenbergen-Hu et al. (2016) conducted a second order meta-analysis integrating and synthesising the findings of the 13 meta-analyses conducted in the past 100 years on the effects of different types of attainment grouping on K-12 students' academic outcomes. In relation to between-class grouping (i.e. setting and streaming), their findings on achievement effects replicate those reported earlier – effects are negligible, regardless of students' initial attainment levels. These authors also conducted a mini meta-analysis of five randomised controlled trials with a view to re-examining the effects of attainment grouping reported earlier, at a more granular level. In this case, they found small, positive and statistically significant effects of between-class grouping on the attainment of middle and junior high students.

One of the challenges with these meta-analytical studies (in addition to the points we made at the beginning of this section) is the dates. Slavin's (1990) widely cited study is now very old, and in concluding their mini meta-analysis Steenbergen-Hu et al. (2016) also caution its being based on studies published before 1994.

Recent evidence from PISA 2012 suggests that at the system level only a weak relationship exists between grouping by attainment within schools and the share of low and top performers in an education system (OECD, 2016a). If there is an association, it is the opposite to that suggested by some studies within individual countries: the OECD concludes that 'more ability grouping within schools is related to a greater number of low performers in mathematics, and fewer top performers' (2016a, p. 186).

The Education Endowment Foundation Teaching and Learning Toolkit (Education Endowment Foundation, 2018) includes a meta-analysis of experimental studies of attainment grouping. The authors conclude that:

> On average, students experiencing setting or streaming make slightly less progress than pupils taught in mixed attainment classes.
>
> The evidence suggests that setting and streaming has a very small negative impact for low and mid-range attaining learners, and a very small positive impact for higher attaining pupils. There are exceptions to this pattern, with some research studies demonstrating benefits for all learners across the attainment range.
>
> Overall the effects are small, and it appears that setting or streaming is not an effective way to raise attainment for most pupils.
>
> *(Education Endowment Foundation, 2018)*

Several other reviews have concluded a lack of overall impact of between-class attainment grouping on pupil achievement (Ireson & Hallam, 2001; Kutnick et al., 2005; Nomi, 2009). Ireson et al. (2005) investigated the effect of setting in English, maths and science at GCSE, and found no significant effects for setting in either subject.

This overall finding could be read as suggesting that ability grouping neither helps nor hinders but, as we shall see, there are implications for pupils in particular attainment groups.

Comparing effects of placement in high/low attainment groups

Other studies measured effects of grouping by attainment within schools, comparing the effects of placement in high and low groups. Many have demonstrated the gains made by high achieving pupils at the expense of low achievers placed in bottom groups. One of the most cited studies on the topic of differential gains of students placed in high and low sets and streams is Kerckhoff's (1986) study, conducted in Britain. Analysing birth cohort data, Kerckhoff analysed school achievement data of the cohort of children born in 1958 who attended one of four types of secondary schools: private, grammar, secondary modern, and comprehensive. The divergence hypothesis that attainment grouping differentially affects performances of students in high and low groups was found clearly and consistently in comprehensive and secondary modern schools both in English and mathematics tests taken at age 16. The same, albeit weaker, patterns were observed for children grouped by attainment in grammar and private schools. Nothing warranted these differences other than attainment grouping.

Certainly there appear to be consequences for the attainment outcomes of those students placed in different groups. Linchevski and Kutscher (1998) looked at students who were borderline between different 'ability' bands. While the differences in attainment between the highest-scoring students in the lower band, and the lowest-scoring students in the upper band were very small, the *subsequent* attainment (post-grouping) differed greatly, with the students assigned to the higher groups attaining significantly more than students of a similar ability assigned to lower groups (see also Ireson et al., 2005). Linchevski and Kutscher concluded from this that the achievements of students close to the band cut-off points were largely dependent on their arbitrary assignment to either the lower or higher group. The study also showed benefits for lower achieving students of being taught with higher achieving students.

With a few exceptions (Betts & Shkolnik, 2000; Figlio & Page, 2002), similar patterns showing how between-class tracking increases inequality in outcomes have been indicated by both quantitative and qualitative studies of tracking in the US (Gamoran & Berends, 1987; Gamoran & Mare, 1989; Lucas & Gamoran, 2002).

In addition to these conclusions concerning the impact (or lack of it) of attainment grouping on pupil progress and achievement outcomes, there have been various other impacts of attainment grouping identified and debated in the literature.

Other impacts of attainment grouping

A range of research has suggested that the labelling involved in tracking – i.e. pupils being labelled as 'grammar school kids' (academic, 'bright') or 'secondary modern' (non-academic, 'dull'); or as 'high ability' (academic, 'bright') or 'low ability' (non-academic, 'dull') – has an impact on pupils' self-concept, their levels of self-confidence in learning, and their feelings about school. This literature is analysed and discussed in Chapter 4. However, it is important to highlight at this point that opportunity to experience different levels of attainment group are not equal, and hence these impacts of attainment grouping are not equally distributed.

Equity issues

It is well established that practices of within- and between-school attainment grouping have promoted social segregation (Ball, 1981; Cassen & Kingdon, 2007; OECD, 2016b), with working-class pupils – and those from some minority ethnic groups – disproportionately represented in low sets and streams (Cassen & Kingdon, 2007; Connolly et al., forthcoming; Dunne et al., 2007; Kutnick et al., 2005). This trend might of course be predicted given that children from socially disadvantaged families tend to arrive in the schooling system less 'school ready' (as it has been branded) than their more affluent peers (Wagdofel & Washbrook,

2010). For example, it has been found by the National Equality Panel that by the age of three, children from low socio-economic backgrounds have been assessed to be one year behind children from more affluent families in terms of communication (Hills, 2010), and in some disadvantaged areas, up to 50% of children begin primary school without the necessary language and communication skills (Hills, 2010). The better preparedness of middle class children for school reflects financial, cultural, and social capitals more available to middle class families (see e.g. Bourdieu & Passeron, 1977; Reay, 1998; Francis & Hutchings, 2013), and a home culture that is more in keeping with the middle class values of the school, ensuring familiarity for these children (Bernstein, 1971). For these reasons, some researchers have challenged the very concept of 'school readiness', asking whether instead the school ready for diverse children (Lupton, 2016). In any case, the point is that children from low socio-economic backgrounds tend to start their education from a point of disadvantage, and have fewer resources of educational support at their disposal – and as such, that where attainment grouping is applied, children from poorer backgrounds are likely to be over-represented in lower groups (the reverse being true for middle class children). This is amply and infamously illustrated by the remaining grammar schools in England, wherein the population of entrants taking free school meals (as a rough proxy indicator for relative poverty) is only 2.5%, compared to the 16% national average (Cullinane, 2016). The thriving shadow industry of private tuition to prepare for the Eleven Plus exam for access to grammar schools likewise provides a ready example of the way that financial capital can aid likelihood of placement in a high 'track'.

And indeed, research has consistently shown that where tracking is applied, these patterns do indeed manifest, with children from poorer families being concentrated in lower attainment groups/schools, and the reverse being true for pupils from more affluent backgrounds. Jackson (1964) identified this point back in the 1960s (we shall return to his important findings below). Likewise, conducting an ethnographic study of one secondary school ('Beachside comprehensive') at the beginning of the 1980s, Ball (1981) found students in the upper stream were more likely to have parents in non-manual occupations, while those in the lower stream were more likely to have parents in manual occupations. In a study of 44 English schools in areas of disadvantage, low socio-economic status was a strong predictor of lower set membership (Muijs & Dunne, 2010). Likewise, Bosworth's (2013) research on schools in North Carolina showed that 4th and 5th grade students from lower socio-economic background were over-represented in low sets. And our own findings have illustrated the continuity of this phenomenon in English schooling (Connolly et al., forthcoming).

Socio-economic background is not the only factor pertaining to in/equity in allocation to particular attainment groups or 'tracks'. Black students are frequently found to be more likely to be allocated to lower sets and streams both in England and the USA (Hallinan, 1996; Muijs et al., 2010; Moller & Stearns, 2012; Modica, 2015). White students, by contrast, are more likely to be allocated to higher sets (Muijs & Dunne, 2010; Moller & Stearns, 2012; Modica, 2015). In England,

Bangladeshi students are more likely to be in lower groups (Muijs & Dunne, 2010), while in the USA Asian–American students are more likely to be in college tracks (Moller & Stearns, 2012). Moller and Stearns (2012) note that their findings persist even when attainment is controlled for; and again, our recent research found the same (as we elaborate further in Chapter 5).

The evidence in relation to gender appears to be more mixed, with some studies finding that boys are more likely to be allocated to lower streams and sets than girls (Jackson, 1964; Van de Gaer et al., 2006; Hallam & Parsons, 2013a), other studies finding no notable differences (Muijs & Dunne, 2010), and others still suggesting that boys are more likely to be placed in high 'ability' tracks (Moller & Stearns, 2012). Charlton et al. (2007) suggest that in Australia, some 'low ability' streams are so dominated by boys that girls are moved down into these groups despite having higher attainment, reflecting teachers' belief or hope that they will provide a moderating influence on boys' behaviour – causing the authors to brand this discriminatory practice that of 'sacrificial girls'.

However, an important point to emphasise is that, in addition to these established trends wherein pupils from different backgrounds are more or less likely to be represented in particular attainment groups, research over the past half-century has consistently demonstrated *practices of allocation* to attainment groups to be biased (Jackson, 1964; Tomlinson, 1987; Dunne et al., 2007). In other words, research has found that allocation to attainment groups is not necessarily reflective of prior attainment (or 'ability'), but rather, is frequently influenced by other factors, including prejudice (Jackson, 1964; Dunne et al., 2007). Since Jackson (1964) found a stark picture of the segregation of students into streams according to their social backgrounds (wherein pupils with the same IQ results were placed in different streams, with those whose fathers were in middle class occupations placed in higher streams, and those with fathers in manual work placed in lower ones), there have been a number of studies suggesting that certain social groups are more likely to be allocated to lower sets and streams, even after prior attainment has been controlled for. The schools in Jackson's study reported using a range of sources to stream children, including internal and external assessment data as well as teacher judgements or recommendations. More recent research has found a similar range of strategies being applied, with similar outcomes of exacerbation of social distinction in allocation (Ireson & Hallam, 2001; Muijs & Dunne, 2010; Taylor et al., 2019); albeit these later studies did find schools placing a greater emphasis on attainment data than had been found by Jackson. Issues of misallocation to attainment groups are explored in more detail in Chapter 5.

All of this matters. As we have shown already, the research has found that when subject to attainment grouping, this impacts the respective outcomes of pupils placed in different attainment groups, including for attainment and in other related areas such as self-concept. There is also evidence that these practices result in increased social inequality. Parsons and Hallam (2014) found that, in primary schools, attainment grouping contributes to the widening of the gap in achievement between students from disadvantaged backgrounds and their peers.

Research based on international achievement studies such as TIMSS and PISA also shows that later between-school selection reduces the impact of students' socio-economic status and family background on their test scores (Woessmann, 2009b; OECD, 2013, 2016b). The equity concerns hold true in both cross- and within-country analyses. For example, research within countries that have devolved education systems but share a common set of characteristics such as language, legal system, general culture, and the like, has demonstrated that earlier tracking increases inequality. Woessmann's (2009a) analysis of attainment data from the 16 German states mirrors the cross-country evidence from PISA on the important links between institutional stratification and educational outcomes for disadvantaged learners. The study has found that the two states which delay between-school tracking by two years, are more equal than any of the other 14 German states. Within a similar logic, Bauer and Riphahn (2006) analyse the difference in the predicted probabilities of attending the college-bound track for children of high and lower educated parents and compare those differences between early and late tracking cantons in Switzerland. The results show that early between-school tracking greatly increases the relative advantage of children with highly versus mid-educated parents. In this case, the SES effects occur at the point of selection into different programmes. So both Woessmann (2009a) and Bauer and Riphahn (2006) have demonstrated that cross-country trends hold within the same country with slightly different tracking systems: greater equality of opportunity is associated with reduced tracking, just as cross-country analysis also demonstrates (OECD, 2012, 2016b).

More recently, Raitano and Vona (2016) have contributed to the literature by extending analysis of the PISA 2012 data to incorporate school-level attainment grouping practices. Their analysis shows that the positive influence of postponing between-school tracking appears weakened and not statistically significant in more complex models that include a full set of school level practices. Having jointly considered country- and school-level sorting policies, they found that *grouping students at school level* into different classes (between-class grouping) greatly amplifies the association between students' performance and parental background. They argue that considering only country-specific policies, especially the effect of the age of between-school tracking between general and vocational programmes, overestimates the effect of these practices on inequality in student outcomes, and that attention should also be given to the inequities precipitated by within-school between-class tracking. As they explain:

> We show that including sorting policies enriches the explanation of the socio-economic gradient, that is, the association between students' performances and parental background, with respect to previous studies including only country-level features. The negative impact of early tracking on equality of opportunity is overvalued without including other sorting policies, while grouping students' within-school by ability increases the socio-economic gradient and a greater students' heterogeneity in the school reduces the gradient.
>
> *(p. 3148)*

This consideration is particularly important given the increased popularity of between-class grouping around the world (Loveless, 2013; Johnston & Wildy, 2016) and the general decline in enrolment into vocational courses (Becker et al., 2016; OECD, 2016b).

Other international studies also found that the 'softer' segregation system of attainment grouping within schools is ridden with problems. Using PISA 2003 dataset, Chmielewski (2014) compares across 20 countries course-by-course tracking (i.e. setting) and academic/vocational streaming in terms of the level of socio-economic segregation between tracks, the size of achievement gaps between tracks, and the strength of socio-economic background as a variable in predicting achievement within tracks. The statistical modelling confirms findings from the prior literature that, even after accounting for student demographic characteristics, course-by-course tracking systems tend to have lower socio-economic segregation between tracks than academic/vocational streaming systems. As such, setting is a more equitable *system* (as well as having better conceptual efficacy). However, the size of attainment gaps appears similar across the two types of tracking systems. With respect to socio-economic disparities in achievement *within* tracks, Chmielewski finds that socio-economic status is more predictive of achievement in course-by-course tracking than in academic/vocational streaming. OECD's (2016a) analysis of PISA 2012 concluded that on the system level grouping by attainment within schools is even more harmful for low-attaining students than between-school segregation.

Thus far we have focused on individual attainment outcomes, but there is also evidence that the social segregation promoted by attainment grouping is detrimental to pupil attainment overall, and that social mixing in schools is associated with stronger system outcomes, including narrower socio-economic gaps for attainment. The OECD (2001) is clear that school systems that perform well and show below-average socio-economic inequalities 'provide all students, regardless of their socio-economic backgrounds with similar opportunities to learn', and have less segregated systems. As Douglas Willms (2006) observes from this international analysis,

> Countries with high levels of segregation along socio-economic lines tend to have lower overall performance and greater disparities in performance between students from high and low socio-economic backgrounds . . . In countries with high levels of socioeconomic segregation, policies that aimed to reduce socio-economic segregation through compensatory reforms would likely bring considerable gains in raising and levelling the learning bar.
>
> *(pp. 68–69)*

To summarise, longstanding concerns about the impact of attainment grouping in exacerbating existing educational inequalities in relation to social class, ethnicity, and gender appear justified. Clearly these practices illuminate *existing* social inequalities (by segregating pupils by prior attainment this also by default exacerbates social segregation within schools), but the evidence also suggests they further exacerbate them. In later chapters we will draw on our contemporary research to further explore and test these theses, as well as focusing on particular issues relating to attainment grouping, and on how to improve practice in support of equity and achievement.

Obviously these conclusions suggest that attainment grouping is socially unjust, and promotes further social inequality. As such, we may ask, to what extent attainment grouping can be ethically justified? This is an important question, which deserves serious consideration. At the 2018 American Educational Research Association conference in New York we attended a session in which tracking was branded racist, and as we shall show in more detail in Chapter 6, there is clear evidence to support such assertions. However, we are also mindful that teachers are working in challenging conditions and facing a range of institutional constraints, regarding available resource, capacity, and discursive/policy climate, within which decisions about pupil grouping are made (Francis et al., 2017b). Every day within schools, pragmatic compromises are made in the absence of preferable alternatives. We recognise that while it is easy for educational researchers to criticise practice, teachers and education leaders need research-evidenced solutions and resources in order to effect change. And these are notably lacking in the case of optimal pupil grouping practice, in spite of the vast array of research on the impact or otherwise of tracking and attainment grouping (Francis et al., 2017a).

Mixed attainment grouping

Some evidence suggests that mixed attainment grouping provides an equitable alternative to setting or streaming. Boaler found improved academic outcomes and self-confidence in mixed attainment mathematics classes, compared with attainment sets (Boaler et al., 2000; Boaler, 2008). Slavin (1990) found no advantage to 'ability grouping', when compared with heterogeneous classes, but a trend towards higher outcomes for heterogeneously grouped social studies classes. Linchevski and Kutscher (1998) found that low attaining students made better progress when taught with high attaining students. It therefore seems that mixed attainment grouping can be employed without detriment to academic outcomes, and potentially with improved outcomes for lower-attaining students.

We have elaborated elsewhere our surprise at the almost entire absence of research-based material on mixed attainment practice, and good practice therein (Francis et al., 2017a). In spite of the aforementioned evidence that low attaining pupils perform better in mixed attainment (heterogeneous) classes than in low attainment groups, we know strikingly little about why this is. It is one thing to criticise existing practices, but without evidence and exemplars of high quality alternatives, it is not reasonable to expect that practitioners will have confidence to experiment. Hence one of the intentions of this book is to provide a discussion of issues in deployment of mixed attainment practice, and an account of good practice in this regard. In doing so we also attempt to give due attention to the various reasons why many teachers and school leaders in our study were wary of mixed attainment practice, in order better to consider the conditions necessary to facilitate 'de-tracking'.

Conclusion

We have summarised the key issues at stake in debates on attainment grouping, and the findings of the prior research concerning the impact of these practices on student outcomes. Although there is a vast existing literature on grouping by attainment, developed over the last 60 years, controversy and many unanswered questions remain. The role of attainment grouping in exacerbating various forms of social inequality is clear, both in terms of illuminating existing inequalities (in allocation of pupils to attainment groups, and resulting segregation), and in terms of exacerbating these (in misallocation to attainment groups, and in the differential outcomes for different attainment groups, wherein pupils from different backgrounds are unequally distributed). Yet the *extent* of these impacts remains debated, as does the extent or otherwise of any positive impacts of attainment grouping (for example, on high prior attainers), and the trade-off of these in regard to different potential practices. And while a range of potential factors are posited by the research as explanations for the unequal outcomes resulting from attainment grouping, these factors have rarely been disaggregated (Francis et al., 2017a). As such, we know little about which factors make the most difference, and whether these could be remedied; or whether actually it is the simple act of labelling pupils by prior attainment that precipitates effects. Likewise, there is scant research on mixed attainment practice, in terms of its impact, or the constitution of good practice in mixed attainment grouping.

Our own research set out to try to address some of these unanswered questions. It sought to test whether these findings of socially iniquitous trends resulting from within-school grouping practices remain in the present in the British context; whether detrimental impacts of setting can be mitigated; and what are the characteristics of good practice in mixed attainment grouping. The next chapter explains the methods of our ambitious study.

Notes

1 See Blakemore (2018).
2 See next page for definition.
3 See next page for definitions.
4 See explanation in Chapter 1.
5 Private schools are largely selective (by attainment, as well as by ability to pay), but remain only 7% of schooling in England.
6 The picture is also complicated by different kinds of practice applied. For example, in 2015 PISA, Finland reported that just under half (47%) of students attended schools where there was no ability grouping at all, but only 2.5% of students were in schools which grouped into different classes for all subjects. This is very different from the UK.

7 Or potentially a school group level decision in the case of Multi-Academy Trusts (MATs) and so on; albeit in practice even MATs often defer autonomy on such issues to individual schools within the Trust.

8 Deunk et al. (2018) discuss this latter point in their systematic review and meta-analysis of students on differentiation in primary education.

9 It is important to note the existence of a significant research literature focused on practice to facilitate optimal outcomes for exceptionally high attaining students – those referred to in the UK as 'gifted and talented'. Studies within this literature have often focused on whether these pupils should be taught in mainstream classrooms or educated separately with other high attainers; hence there has sometimes been overlap with the broader literature on attainment grouping (see Dracup, 2014). Studies on exceptionally high attainers have often found benefits to these pupils being provided with curriculum material discrete from the mainstream curriculum, with an implication that setting will be of benefit to them (see Ireson et al., 2002); albeit the various options for effective extension provision are of course more diverse. Meanwhile, a recent study by Heller-Sahlgren (2018) challenges both the efficacy of methods of identifying these children, and of the assumptions of benefits of (discrete) grouping practices that have been claimed in prior research.

References

Alvarez, D. & Mehan, H. (2006). Whole-school detracking: a strategy for equity and excellence. *Theory Into Practice*, *45*(1), 82–89.

Ball, S. J. (1981). *Beachside comprehensive: a case-study of secondary schooling*. Cambridge: Cambridge University Press.

Bauer, P. & Riphahn, R. T. (2006). Timing of school tracking as a determinant of intergenerational transmission of education. *Economics Letters*, *91*(1), 90–97.

Becker, M., Neumann, M., & Dumont, H. (2016). Recent developments in school tracking practices in Germany: an overview and outlook on future trends. *ORBIS SCHOLAE*, *10*(3), 9–25.

Bernstein, B. (1971). *Class, codes and control. Volume 1: Theoretical studies towards a sociology of language*. London: Routledge and Kegan Paul.

Betts, J. R. & Shkolnik, J. L. (2000). The effects of ability grouping on student achievement and resource allocation in secondary schools. *Economics of Education Review*, *19*(1), 1–15.

Blackman, T. (2017). *The comprehensive university: an alternative to social stratification by academic selection*. Oxford: HEPI.

Blakemore, S.-J. (2018). *Inventing ourselves: the secret life of the teenage brain*. New York: Doubleday.

Boaler, J. (2008). Promoting 'relational equity' and high mathematics achievement through an innovative mixed-ability approach. *British Educational Research Journal*, *34*(2), 167–194.

Boaler, J. & Wiliam, D. (2001). Setting, streaming and mixed-ability teaching. In J. Dillon & M. Maguire (Eds.), *Becoming a teacher* (2nd ed., pp. 173–181). Maidenhead: Open University Press.

Boaler, J., Wiliam, D., & Brown, M. (2000). Students' experiences of ability grouping-disaffection, polarisation and the construction of failure. *British Educational Research Journal*, *26*(5), 631–648.

Bolton, P. (2017). *Grammar school statistics*. London: House of Commons Library.

Bosworth, R. (2013). What sort of school sorts students? *International Journal of Quantitative Research in Education*, *1*(1), 20–38.

Bourdieu, P. & Passeron, J.-C. (1977). *Reproduction in education, society and culture*. London: Sage.

Boylan, M. & Povey, H. (2012). Moving off track: mathematics teacher education for all attainment teaching. In L. Jacobsen, J. Mistele, & B. Sriraman (Eds.), *Mathematics teacher education in the public interest: equity and social justice* (pp. 117–158). Charlotte: Information Age Publishing.

Bradbury, A. (2018). The impact of the phonics screening check on grouping by ability: a 'necessary evil' amid the policy storm. *British Educational Research Journal*, *44*(4), 539–556.

Bradbury, A. (2019). Rethinking 'fixed-ability thinking' and grouping practices: questions, disruptions and barriers to change in primary and early years education. *FORUM: for Promoting 3–19 Comprehensive Education*, *61*(1), 41–52.

Bradbury, A. & Roberts-Holmes, G. (2017). *Grouping in early years and Key Stage 1: a 'necessary evil'?* London: National Education Union.

Cahan, S., Linchevski, L., Ygra, N., & Danziger, I. (1996). The cumulative effect of ability grouping on mathematical achievement: a longitudinal perspective. *Studies in Educational Evaluation*, *22*(1), 29–40.

Cassen, R. & Kingdon, G. (2007). *Tackling low educational achievement*. York: Joseph Rowntree Foundation.

Charlton, E., Mills, M., Martino, W., & Beckett, L. (2007). Sacrificial girls: a case study of the impact of streaming and setting on gender reform. *British Educational Research Journal*, *33*(4), 459–478.

Chmielewski, A. K. (2014). An international comparison of achievement inequality in within- and between-school tracking systems. *American Journal of Education*, *120*(3), 293–324.

Connolly, P., Taylor, B., Francis, B., Archer, L., Hodgen, J., Mazenod, A., & Tereshchenko, A. (forthcoming, accepted). The misallocation of students to academic sets in maths: a study of secondary schools in England. *British Educational Research Journal*.

Cullinane, C. (2016). *Gaps in grammar*. London: Sutton Trust.

D'Alessio, S. & Watkins, A. (2009). International comparisons of inclusive policy and practice: are we talking about the same thing? *Research in Comparative and International Education*, *4*(3), 233–249.

Dar, Y. & Resh, N. (1994). Separating and mixing students for learning: concepts and research. *Pedagogisch Tijdschrift*, *19*(2), 109–126.

Davies, J., Hallam, S., & Ireson, J. (2003). Ability groupings in the primary school: issues arising from practice. *Research Papers in Education*, *18*(1), 45–60.

Deunk, M. I., Smale-Jacobse, A. E., de Boer, H., Doolaard, S., & Bosker, R. J. (2018). Effective differentiation practices: a systematic review and meta-analysis of studies on the cognitive effects of differentiation practices in primary education. *Educational Research Review*, *24*, 31–54.

DfES. (2005). *Higher standards, better schools for all: more choice for parents and pupils*. London: HMSO.

Domina, T., Hanselman, P., Hwang, N., & McEachin, A. (2016). Detracking and tracking up. *American Educational Research Journal*, *53*(4), 1229–1266.

Dracup, T. (2014). *The politics of setting*. Retrieved from https://giftedphoenix.wordpress.com/2014/11/12/the-politics-of-setting/.

Dunne, M., Humphreys, S., Sebba, J., Dyson, A., Gallannaugh, F., & Muijs, D. (2007). *Effective teaching and learning for pupils in low attaining groups*. London: DfES Publications.

Education Endowment Foundation. (2018). *Sutton Trust-EEF teaching and learning toolkit*. London: Education Endowment Foundation.

Figlio, D. N. & Page, M. E. (2002). School choice and the distributional effects of ability tracking: does separation increase inequality? *Journal of Urban Economics*, *51*(3), 497–514.

Fjellman, A.-M., Yang Hansen, K., & Beach, D. (2018). School choice and implications for equity: the new political geography of the Swedish upper secondary school market. *Educational Review*, 1–22.

Francis, B. (2017). *The role of academies in English education policy*. London: Cambridge Whitehall Group.

Francis, B., Archer, L., Hodgen, J., Pepper, D., Taylor, B., & Travers, M-C. (2017a). Exploring the relative lack of impact of research on 'ability grouping' in England: a discourse analytic account. *Cambridge Journal of Education*, *47*(1), 1–17.

Francis, B., Mills, M., & Lupton, R. (2017b). Towards social justice in education: contradictions and dilemmas. *Journal of Education Policy*, *32*(4), 414–431.

Francis, B. & Hutchings, M. (2013). *Parent power? Using money and information to boost children's chances of educational success*. London: Sutton Trust.

Gamoran, A. & Berends, M. (1987). The effects of stratification in secondary schools: synthesis of survey and ethnographic research. *Review of Educational Research*, *57*, 415–435.

Gamoran, A. & Mare, R. D. (1989). Secondary school tracking and educational inequality: compensation, reinforcement, or neutrality? *American Journal of Sociology*, *94*, 1146–1183.

Gamoran, A. & Nystrand, M. (1994). Tracking, instruction and achievement. *International Journal of Educational Research*, *21*(2), 217–231.

Hallam, S. & Parsons, S. (2013a). The incidence and make up of ability grouped sets in the UK primary school. *Research Papers in Education*, *28*(4), 393–420.

Hallam, S. & Parsons, S. (2013b). Prevalence of streaming in UK primary schools: evidence from the millennium cohort study. *British Educational Research Journal*, *39*(3), 514–544.

Hallinan, M. T. (1996). Track mobility in secondary school. *Social Forces*, *74*(3), 983–1002.

Hallinan, M. T. & Sorenson, A. B. (1987). Ability grouping and sex differences in mathematics achievement. *Sociology of Education*, *60*(2), 63–72.

Heller-Sahlgren, G. (2018). *What works in gifted education? A literature review*. London: Centre for Education Economics.

Hills, J. (2010). *An anatomy of economic inequality in the UK – report of the national equality panel*. London: Centre for Analysis of Social Exclusion, LSE.

Ireson, J. & Hallam, S. (2001). *Ability grouping in education*. London: Paul Chapman.

Ireson, J., Hallam, S., Hack, S., Clark, H., & Plewis, I. (2002). Ability grouping in English secondary schools: effects on attainment in English, mathematics and science. *Educational Research and Evaluation*, *8*(3), 299–318.

Ireson, J., Hallam, S., & Hurley, C. (2005). What are the effects of ability grouping on GCSE attainment? *British Educational Research Journal*, *31*(4), 443–458.

Jackson, B. (1964). *Streaming: an education system in miniature*. London: Routledge and Kegan Paul.

Jeffreys, B. (2018). Grammar schools: thousands of new places created. *BBC News*. Retrieved from www.bbc.co.uk/news/education-44727857.

Jerrim, J., Greany, T., & Perera, N. (2018). *Educational disadvantage: how does England compare?* London: Education Policy Institute.

Jerrim, J. & Macmillan, L. (2015). Income inequality, intergenerational mobility, and the Great Gatsby curve: is education the key? *Social Forces*, *94*(2), 505–533.

Johnston, O. & Wildy, H. (2016). The effects of streaming in the secondary school on learning outcomes for Australian students – a review of the international literature. *Australian Journal of Education*, *60*(1), 42–59.

Kerckhoff, A. C. (1986). Effects of ability grouping in British secondary schools. *American Sociological Review*, *51*(6), 842–858.

Kulik, C.-L. C. & Kulik, J. A. (1982). Effects of ability grouping on secondary school students: a meta-analysis of evaluation findings. *American Educational Research Journal*, *19*(3), 415–428.

Kutnick, P., Sebba, J., Blatchford, P., Galton, M., Thorp, J., MacIntyre, H., & Berdondini, L. (2005). *The effects of pupil grouping: literature review*. London: Department for Education and Skills.

Linchevski, L. & Kutscher, B. (1998). Tell me with whom you're learning and I'll tell you how much you've learned: mixed-ability versus same-ability grouping in mathematics. *Journal of Research in Mathematics Education*, *29*(5), 533–554.

Loveless, T. (2013). *The 2013 Brown Center report on American education: how well are American students learning?* Washington, DC: Brookings Institution Press.

Lucas, S. R. & Gamoran, A. (2002). Track assignment and the black-white test score gap: divergent and convergent evidence from 1980 and 1990 sophomores. In T. Loveless (Ed.), *Closing the gap: promising strategies for reducing the achievement gap* (pp. 171– 198). Washington, DC: Brookings Institution Press.

Lupton, R. (2016). Re-thinking values and schooling in white working class neighbourhoods. In C. Timmerman, N. Clycq, M. McAndrew, B. Alhassane, L. Braeckmans, & S. Mels (Eds.), *Youth in education: the necessity of valuing ethnocultural diversity* (pp. 233–248). Abingdon: Routledge.

Marks, R. (2013). 'The blue table means you don't have a clue': the persistence of fixedability thinking and practices in primary mathematics in English schools. *FORUM: for Promoting 3–19 Comprehensive Education*, *55*(1), 31–44.

Marks, R. (2016). *Ability-grouping in primary schools: case studies and critical debates*. Northwich: Critical Publishing.

Modica, M. (2015). *Race among friends: exploring race at a suburban school*. New Brunswick, NJ: Rutgers University Press.

Moller, S. & Stearns, E. (2012). Tracking success: high school curricula and labor market outcomes by race and gender. *Urban Education*, *47*(6), 1025–1054.

Muijs, D. & Dunne, M. (2010). Setting by ability – or is it? A quantitative study of determinants of set placement in English secondary schools. *Educational Research*, *52*(4), 391–407.

Nomi, T. (2009). The effects of within-class ability grouping on academic achievement in early elementary years. *Journal of Research on Educational Effectiveness*, *3*(1), 56–92.

OECD. (2001). *Knowledge and skills for life: first results from the OECD Programme for International Student Assessment (PISA) 2000*. Paris: OECD Publishing.

OECD. (2012). *Equity and quality in education: supporting disadvantaged students and schools*. Paris: OECD Publishing.

OECD. (2013). Selecting and grouping students. In *Pisa 2012 results: what makes schools successful? Resources, policies and practices* (Vol. *IV*, pp. 71–92). Paris: OECD Publishing.

OECD. (2016a). *Low-performing students: why they fall behind and how to help them succeed*. Paris: OECD Publishing.

OECD. (2016b). *Pisa 2015 results (Volume II)*. Paris: OECD Publishing.

Parsons, S. & Hallam, S. (2014). The impact of streaming on attainment at age seven: evidence from the millennium cohort study. *Oxford Review of Education*, *40*(5), 567–589.

Peacock, A. (2016). *Assessment for learning without limits*. London: Open University Press.

Raitano, M. & Vona, F. (2016). Assessing students' equality of opportunity in OECD countries: the role of national- and school-level policies. *Applied Economics*, *48*(33), 3148–3163.

Reay, D. (1998). *Class work mothers' involvement in their children's primary schooling*. London: University College Press.

Rui, N. (2009). Four decades of research on the effects of detracking reform: where do we stand?—a systematic review of the evidence. *Journal of Evidence-Based Medicine*, 2(3), 164–183.

Slavin, R. E. (1990). Achievement effects of ability grouping in secondary schools: a best-evidence synthesis. *Review of Educational Research*, 60(3), 471–499.

Steenbergen-Hu, S., Makel, M. C., & Olszewski-Kubilius, P. (2016). What one hundred years of research says about the effects of ability grouping and acceleration on k–12 students' academic achievement. *Review of Educational Research*, 86(4), 849–899.

Sullivan, A., Parsons, S., Green, F., Wiggins, R. D., Ploubidis, G., & Huynh, T. (2018). Educational attainment in the short and long term: was there an advantage to attending faith, private, and selective schools for pupils in the 1980s? *Oxford Review of Education*, 44(6), 806–822.

Taylor, B., Francis, B., Archer, L., Hodgen, J., Pepper, D., Tereshchenko, A., & Travers, M-C. (2017). Factors deterring schools from mixed attainment teaching practice. *Pedagogy, Culture & Society*, 25(3), 327–345.

Taylor, B., Francis, B., Craig, N., Archer, L., Hodgen, J., Mazenod, A., Tereshchenko, A., & Pepper, D. (2019). Why is it difficult for schools to establish equitable practices in allocating students to attainment 'sets'? *British Journal of Educational Studies*, 67(1), 5–24.

Tomlinson, S. (1987). Curriculum option choices in multi-ethnic schools. In B. Troyna (Ed.), *Racial inequality in education* (pp. 92–108). London: Tavistock.

Van de Gaer, E., Pustjens, H., Van Damme, J., & De Munter, A. (2006). Tracking and the effects of school-related attitudes on the language achievement of boys and girls. *British Journal of Sociology of Education*, 27(3), 293–309.

Wagdofel, J. & Washbrook, E. (2010). *Low income and early cognitive development in the UK*. London: Sutton Trust.

Welner, K. & Burris, C. C. (2006). Alternative approaches to the politics of detracking. *Theory Into Practice*, 45(1), 90–99.

Willms, J. D. (2006). *Learning divides: ten policy questions about the performance and equity of schools and schooling systems*. Montreal: UNESCO Institute for Statistics.

Woessmann, L. (2009a). Institutional determinants of school efficiency and equity: German states as a microcosm for OECD countries. *Journal of Economics and Statistics*, 230(2), 234–270.

Woessmann, L. (2009b). International evidence on school tracking: a review. *CESifo DICE Rep*, 7(1), 26–34.

Yarker, P. (2019). Calling time on 'fixed-ability' thinking and practice. *FORUM: for Promoting 3–19 Comprehensive Education*, 61(1), 3–9.

3

THE BEST PRACTICE IN GROUPING STUDENTS STUDY

Explaining our methods

This chapter introduces the 'Best Practice in Grouping Students' study. The study was designed to address some of the prior gaps we had found in the literature, as outlined in the previous chapter, as well as to apply a range of different research techniques to the investigation of more equitable practice in grouping students. It involved a three-year investigation of effective approaches to grouping secondary students to improve educational engagement and attainment, with particular focus on the outcomes of students from disadvantaged backgrounds. The study aimed to explore the impact of an intervention on 'best practice in setting by attainment' (which attempts to remediate poor practices associated with setting) on the attainment outcomes and self-confidence of young people, and to conduct a feasibility trial on 'best practice in mixed attainment grouping' in relation to young people's outcomes. The project was funded by the Education Endowment Foundation in England and adopted a randomised controlled trial (RCT) design, including two educational interventions and a mixed methods research component. The use of RCTs allowed us to test the effectiveness of the interventions by measuring the progress of participating students against that of a control group of equivalent students, whereas the mixed methods approach added vital explanatory power in relation to the real-world settings and participants' experiences (Connolly, 2009; Francis et al., 2017).

The fully powered RCT evaluated the effect size of an intervention 'Best Practice in Setting' on the attainment outcomes and self-confidence of students taught in sets. The pilot trial 'Best Practice in Mixed Attainment', with an RCT design element, investigated the impact of mixed attainment teaching and grouping, but it was not statistically powered to detect an effect size. These interventions lasted two years, running from September 2015 to July 2017. As discussed below, they required schools to adopt specific grouping practices in the core curricular subjects of English and/or mathematics with a cohort of Year 7 students who were then followed into Year 8. The first two years of secondary education were chosen for the interventions as these years represent a fresh start for students, and schools perceive these years to be relatively 'low-stakes' compared to other key stages in so far as there is no statutory assessment in Year 7 or 8. The pilot research year before the beginning of the trials was used to develop and refine the content and delivery of the interventions with seven secondary schools, as well as to pilot our research methods (Taylor et al., 2017).

Our mixed methods research aimed to examine the perceptions and experiences of grouping practices among students and teachers. In order to generate both the breadth and depth of data, we used online surveys with students and teachers, and individual and group interviews with a sub-sample of students and teachers. The surveys were conducted at two key milestones: at the beginning of the intervention year, in autumn 2015, when students had just started at secondary school in Year 7 (age 11/12), and in summer 2017, when students reached the end of Year 8 (age 12/13). The qualitative data collection took place at the end of the first year of the 'Best Practice in Mixed Attainment' intervention and in the second year of the 'Best Practice in Setting' intervention.

These two interventions, and the RCT methods, are outlined in the next section. We then go on to describe the main datasets that we draw on in subsequent chapters, including the outcome measures, surveys, and interviews with teachers and students. We conclude with the reflection on the limitations of this research.

The Best Practice in Setting intervention

The 'Best Practice in Setting' (BPS) intervention was designed by the research team to remove or mitigate poor practices associated with attainment grouping that potentially have impact on the outcomes for students in low sets and streams (Francis et al., 2017). A total of 126 state secondary schools (with 24,742 Year 7 students on roll) took part in the trial assessing the effectiveness of the intervention. The trial was open to schools that already applied attainment grouping (either setting or streaming) in Year 7. Schools could take part in the trial for both English and mathematics or for one subject only, as we expected that more schools used setting in mathematics than in English. As a result, 73 schools took part for both maths and English, 48 schools took part for maths only, and six schools took part for English only. Of the total 121 schools taking part in the maths trial, 61 were randomly assigned[1] to the intervention group and 60 to the control group. Of the 79 schools taking part in the English trial, 43 were assigned to the intervention and 36 to the control group.

Schools in the control group continued with their attainment grouping practices as usual. Those in the intervention group received the intervention over a two-year period. This intervention consisted of two elements. First, schools had to commit to implementing the best practice principles of the intervention described below. Second, two teachers from participating departments were expected to participate in the professional development programme[2] designed to support schools with the implementation of the trial. The level of school engagement and compliance with the intervention was measured by implementation fidelity – the degree to which delivery of an intervention adheres to the original programme model (see Chapter 7 for further discussion).

The key principles of the setting intervention

The principles of the intervention were built from the existing research evidence on in/equality in attainment grouping. The stipulations were as follows:

Allocation of students to a maximum of three (or four) set levels

It is likely that a smaller number of set levels results in broader sets, aiming to reduce hierarchies and any negative impacts of misallocation. It has been established that student perceptions and experiences of hierarchical 'ability' grouping have a detrimental impact on their social and educational identities, engagement, and consequent outcomes (Ball, 1981; Kutnick et al., 2005; Education Endowment Foundation, 2018).

Allocation of students to sets by attainment only

To ensure that set allocation exclusively reflected attainment rather than other factors, students were allocated to sets strictly on the basis of their Key Stage 2 test results, the assessments carried out in all state primary schools in England at the end of children's primary schooling in Year 6. While Dunne et al. (2007) found that prior attainment was the *main* predictor of set placement, they also found it a relatively poor predictor, with for example over half the pupils with low prior attainment in English being placed in middle or high sets. They also found that social class is a significant predictor of set placement, with those pupils from higher socio-economic status backgrounds being more likely to be assigned to higher sets, and less likely to be assigned to lower sets (see Ball, 1981; Bosworth, 2013). Other research has also shown bias in set allocation according to variables such as gender and 'race'/ethnicity (Muijs & Dunne, 2010; Moller & Stearns, 2012).

Moving students between sets at fixed points

Previous research has shown that once placed in an 'ability group' pupils tend to remain there, irrespective of their progress or attainment (Flores, 1999; Dunne et al., 2007; Dunne et al., 2011). This undermines the premise of setting (i.e. the notion of homogeneity of attainment and 'meritocracy'), and also risks increasing social injustice given that working class students tend to be overrepresented in allocation to low groups. To address this issue, we instructed participating schools to review student progress and attainment three times across the two-year intervention period and to move students between sets accordingly.

Random or best practice allocation of teachers to sets

Schools were asked to submit to the independent randomisation of teachers across sets. This was in response to evidence that higher sets are more likely to be allocated highly qualified and experienced teachers, whereas lower sets are less likely to be taught by a subject specialist, and experience more changes of teacher (Boaler et al., 2000; Kelly, 2004; Kutnick et al., 2005; Papay & Kraft, 2015). However, during our pilot study we found that many of our schools were unwilling or unable to commit to this principle in the context of demanding school timetables and other accountability pressures (see Chapter 7). Therefore, where schools were not prepared to adopt this approach, they were asked to allocate teachers according to principles provided through the intervention to ensure equitable distribution both across year groups and year-on-year. These principles included placing some of their most experienced teachers with lower attaining sets and not assigning newly qualified and non-subject specialist teachers to low sets.

High expectations of all students

Teachers were encouraged to develop and maintain high expectations of all students' attainment, irrespective of their background, set level or perceptions of their 'ability'. There is a body of research evidence that suggests that teachers think about, and respond differently towards, pupils according to perceptions of their 'ability' (Jackson, 1964; Croll & Moses, 1985; Hacker et al., 1991; Sukhnandan & Lee, 1998). Teacher expectations also have a bearing on practice, with Hallam and Ireson (2005) and Boaler et al. (2000) showing that teachers of high sets convey high expectations through provision of fast-paced and challenging work, whereas pupils in low sets receive slow-paced teaching that covers less of the curriculum. Research also shows that pupils in higher sets are given more homework (Ireson & Hallam, 2001).

A rich curriculum for all

The curriculum experience of students in lower sets might be narrower and shallower than those in the top sets due to exposure to 'thinned' subject knowledge content and simplified activities (Page, 1989; Ireson & Hallam, 2001), as well as weak curriculum delivery (Ofsted, 2013). This compounds the 'lack of fluidity' problem because students who move up a set have difficulty catching up with the work (Macqueen, 2012). Setting can also produce an artificial ceiling, wherein pupils in lower sets are excluded from higher tier study and qualification routes (Gillborn & Youdell, 1999; Ireson et al., 2005; Gazeley & Dunne, 2007). Teachers in participating schools were therefore encouraged to reflect on the importance of a rich curriculum to support student movement between sets, as well as on how to make the common curriculum accessible to all students, for example, through differentiation.

The Best Practice in Mixed Attainment intervention

A pilot trial 'Best Practice in Mixed Attainment' (BPMA) investigated mixed attainment grouping and teaching across 13 schools (with 2,107 Year 7 students on roll). The scale of this trial was small for two reasons. First, it was specifically designed as a feasibility study due to the lack of prior research evidence on mixed attainment practice. Second, because so few schools in England practice mixed attainment in both English and maths, we wanted to establish whether it was possible to recruit schools to a large trial. To facilitate recruitment any school was considered eligible to take part regardless of their prior grouping arrangements as long as they were willing to implement mixed attainment grouping. Despite substantial recruitment efforts lasting five months, only 13 schools took part (rather than the target of 20). Chapter 8 discusses our struggle to recruit schools and explains why mixed attainment practice is seen as problematic.

Of the 13 schools in the trial, eight were randomly assigned to the intervention group and five to the control group.[3] We have distilled four principles of Best Practice in Mixed Attainment, as outlined below. The schools in the intervention group were instructed to follow these. The intervention also involved a substantial training component[4] led by the project team to facilitate the adoption of mixed attainment approaches to grouping students. The extent to which the intervention had been delivered as intended was explored by fidelity measures, including teacher attendance at training sessions and cascading training to colleagues within the department, and to what extent schools had followed our four key principles outlined below (see Chapter 8 for further details).

The key principles of the mixed attainment practice intervention

Broad range of prior attainment in each teaching group

Schools undertook to ensure that classes contained a full diversity of prior attainment, facilitating equitable resources to all, and social mixing.[5] This ensured that practice was genuinely 'mixed attainment' teaching and learning.

Flexible within-class grouping (not attainment-based)

The second principle is that, where used, within-class grouping should be flexible and established for specific activities, rather than inflexible and based on students' general attainment in a subject. It is likely that teaching students in flexible, balanced, carefully structured small groups for particular purposes can raise attainment, improve attitudes and lead to higher self-confidence (Slavin, 1987; Slavin, 1996; Lou et al., 1996; Education Endowment Foundation, 2018).

Differentiation, emphasis on 'by outcome' and 'by feedback'

Closely linked to the above is our third principle, that differentiation should mainly be by feedback (or response) and by outcome, avoiding any differentiation practices that encourage the labelling of students by 'ability' or which differentiate the curriculum accessed by students working from different levels of prior attainment. Practices that differentiate between students typically offer a range of tasks to a class (e.g. Tomlinson, 1995) but this risks increasing teacher workload (Delisle, 2015) and encouraging fixed labelling of students, in turn encouraging self-fulfilling prophecy. Instead, we advocate tasks that are accessible to all students, with a range of entry points and support and challenge provided through differentiated teacher responses (Hart, 1996). Combining rich classroom tasks with personalised questioning and feedback from peers and from the teacher creates opportunities for all students to be supported and challenged (Hodgen & Webb, 2008).

High expectations of all students

Our fourth and final principle of the intervention builds on this point: teachers should have high expectations of all students regardless of prior attainment and should take a flexible view of 'ability'. As pointed out in relation to the setting intervention, research suggests that teachers hold lower expectations of progress for students perceived as lower 'ability' (Sukhnandan & Lee, 1998; Boaler et al., 2000; Hallam & Ireson, 2005). There is also a tendency for teachers to regard ability as fixed (Dixon et al., 2002; Hamilton & O'Hara, 2011). A mixed attainment class group, wherein all students are expected to engage with one common task, enables the same high expectations to be held for all students. It also permits the teacher to expect that all students, including those with low prior attainment, can achieve at the highest levels.

Outcome measures of the trials

The trials tested whether the above described interventions could improve both the attainment outcomes and self-confidence in English and mathematics of low-attaining (and all other) students, compared to the students from the respective control schools, who continued as normal. The interventions were independently evaluated by the National Foundation for Educational Research (NFER) (Roy et al., 2018a; Roy et al., 2018b).

Primary outcome measure – attainment

The attainment outcome measure for the trials was GL Assessment's Progress Test in English (PTE13) and Progress Test in Mathematics (PTM13). These tests were administered by NFER at the end of Year 8 and marked by GL Assessment themselves.[6] To reduce the testing burden on schools, NFER randomly sampled 30 students per school to take each subject test. This meant that in a school taking part in both maths and English, 60 students would sit the GL tests. This selection was stratified by eligibility for free school meals (FSM) in the previous six years.

Due to the high attrition rate from the BPS trial over the two year period of the intervention (discussed further in Chapter 7), there were 79 schools (out of 126) that undertook the GL Assessment tests; 76 in maths and 37 in English. The final student sample for this outcome measure analysis included: 941 students from 32 intervention schools and 1,442 students from 44 control schools for maths; 410 students from 15 intervention schools and 529 students from 22 control schools for English.

In the BPMA trial, nine out of 13 schools took part in GL Assessment's maths test and eight schools took part in the English test. The student sample for the outcome measure analysis comprised 289 students from six intervention schools and 64 students from three control schools for maths; 262 students from five intervention schools and 66 students from three control schools for English.

Secondary outcome measure – self-confidence

The impact of two years' experience of different grouping arrangements on self-confidence in maths and English was measured by surveys, which we administered at baseline and at end-point. Pre-intervention self-confidence measures were collected during the first term of the school year. Post-intervention measures were collected close to the conclusion of the trials. Self-confidence composite measures were developed using factor analysis on seven items used in the baseline survey to measure self-confidence in each subject. These items included: 'Work in maths/English lessons is easy for me'; 'I am not very good at maths/English'; 'Maths/English is one of my best subjects'; 'I hate maths/English'; 'I do well at maths/English'; 'I get good marks in maths/English'; and 'I learn things quickly in maths/English lessons'.

The student sample for this outcome measure analysis in the BPS trial included: 2,445 students from 27 intervention schools and 3,584 students from 33 control schools for maths self-confidence; 972 students from 13 intervention schools and 2,074 students from 17 control schools for English self-confidence. In the BPMA trial, the analysis was based on a sample of 751 students from eight schools for maths self-confidence, and of 772 students from eight schools for English self-confidence.

The analysis of the outcome measures for the trials, discussed in Chapter 4, employed multi-level modelling, separately for maths and English outcomes. Effect size was calculated as the standardised mean difference between the control and intervention groups, using the pooled standard deviation. Subgroup analysis explored the differential impact of the interventions on attainment outcomes and self-confidence accounting for: prior attainment (i.e. Key Stage 2 national curriculum tests in maths and reading);[7] gender; household occupation; ethnicity; and, where applicable, set level; as well as whether or not the student was eligible for FSM in the previous six years.

Surveys with students and teachers

We conducted two large-scale student and teacher surveys over the course of the project. Student surveys provided a broad longitudinal picture of the impact of different grouping practices on young people's attitudes, self-confidence, feelings about school, etc. In the baseline phase, we received responses from 12,997 students. Of these, 11,608 students were from 86 schools in the BPS trial (40 intervention and 46 control schools) and 1,389 students from ten schools in the BPMA trial (six intervention and four control schools).[8] The final survey was completed by 9,501 students, including 8,653 from 76 BPS schools (32 intervention and 44 control) and 848 from seven BPMA schools (six intervention and one control).[9] 7,296 students who completed the final survey also completed the baseline survey.[10]

The student surveys were developed[11] and validated during the pilot year with ten students, using a cognitive interviewing approach (Willis, 2005). The reliability and validity of the specific items were enhanced by amending the wording of some questions that had been commonly misunderstood by students. The surveys were then piloted with 680 students from five pilot schools.

We collected a range of socio-demographic data on the surveys. And students were asked about their school's grouping practices in English and maths. Although we collected data about students' group position through official school channels, we also asked students in the BPS trial which set they thought they were in for English and maths; the number of sets in school for English, maths, and science; frequency of movement between English and maths sets and how many students usually moved. Students in the BPMA trial were asked to rank their position in the class in terms of achievement in English and maths. The majority of questions in the surveys used a Likert scale to elicit attitudinal responses: disagree/slightly disagree/neither agree nor disagree/slightly agree/strongly agree. Both baseline and outcome surveys followed the same topics to allow for data comparison. We asked students about a wide range of topics: their self-confidence in English/maths; their self-efficacy in English/maths; perception of teaching in English/maths; general self-confidence and liking for school; perceptions of setting; reasons for GCSE subject choices; and university aspirations. The survey data was linked using the student name, date of birth, and school name to students' prior attainment data from the National Pupil Database, as well as data on set or class allocation, which we obtained from schools.

As with the students, all teachers in English and maths departments in participating schools were offered a survey. The aim was to collect teachers' beliefs about different forms of attainment grouping, their expectations of students and information on actual classroom practices. At the beginning of the trials, the survey was completed by 667 teachers who were from 92 schools (82 in BPS and ten in BPMA trials). Of the 597 teacher respondents in the BPS trial, 248 were from the intervention and 349 from the control groups. Of the 70 teacher respondents in the BPMA trial, 37 were from the intervention and 33 from the control groups. The second survey was administered at the end of the trials. Some 471 teachers from 72 BPS schools (28 intervention and 44 control) and 81 teachers from nine BPMA schools (six intervention and three control) completed the questionnaire. Our longitudinal teacher sample was smaller: 138 teachers from 50 schools in the BPS trial and 22 teachers from seven schools in the BPMA trial completed both surveys.

Most of the questions we asked teachers remained the same in both surveys. Teachers were asked about their attitudes to setting by attainment; attitudes to mixed attainment grouping; beliefs about ability and attainment; practices with young people from different attainment groups; perceived departmental grouping practices; and, where relevant, attitudes to the BPS or BPMA interventions. To explore relationships between 'teacher quality' and set allocation, we also asked teachers about their academic and teaching qualifications, subject teaching specialism and level of qualification therein, length of tenure, position at the school (e.g. classroom teacher, head of department), and subject/s which they are presently teaching.

The regression analyses based on the comparison of students' and teachers' core characteristics in the baseline survey determined that a good balance had been achieved between the control and intervention groups of the trials. The validity and reliability analyses were also conducted to determine internal consistency of survey scales. All scale items were subjected to factor analysis using principal axis factoring. The analyses revealed that the key components in the surveys (for example, 'general self-confidence in learning', 'self-confidence in English/maths', 'liking for school', 'attitudes to setting') had 'acceptable' to 'good' internal consistency (Cronbach's alpha values $0.6 \leq \alpha < 0.9$). Following these initial analyses, on data used in this book, the project team conducted multi-level modelling with students (level 1) clustered within individual subject sets (level 2) and then within schools (level 3) to estimate the adjusted mean self-confidence scores for students in the three set levels (i.e. top, middle, and bottom), controlling for a series of other covariates representing gender, FSM eligibility, family occupation, ethnicity, and total number of sets within the school (Chapter 4). This approach ensured sufficient consideration of the potentially differential effects of the intervention across students (Connolly et al., 2007). To analyse differences in student attitudes towards setting by trial, set level and Key Stage 2 test results, the one-way analysis of variance (ANOVA) and Bonferroni post-hoc tests (multiple comparisons following the ANOVA) were used (Chapter 5). Frequency analyses were applied to examine the item-level differences between groups of students and teachers (Chapters 6, 7, and 8).

Interviews with students and teachers

In addition to surveys, we wanted to explore young people's views, experiences, and identities in greater depth. To this end, we conducted lesson observations and student focus groups in five schools in the BPMA trial, and student focus groups in ten schools in the BPS trial. These schools (see Table 3.1) were purposefully sampled from the schools participating in the trials with the aim of representing a variety of geographic contexts and student demographics (e.g. rural, suburban, and urban; multi-ethnic and predominantly white, deprived, and affluent areas, etc.). We sought to sample schools from both the intervention and control groups. For the BPMA school sample, we also aimed to include some schools new to mixed attainment and others with an established practice. For the BPS trial, we sought to represent schools with varied numbers of set levels (ranging from four to 11 for different subjects). We also interviewed English and maths teachers in these schools to help contextualise students' experiences of setting or mixed attainment grouping and provide another dimension to the analysis of grouping approaches in secondary schools.

A total of 245 students took part in the qualitative research, via 86 focus groups and 27 individual interviews. This included ten group and 27 individual interviews conducted in the pilot study.[12] The main phase of the BPMA trial consisted of 15 focus groups with 58 students (27 boys and 31 girls) aged 11/12 (Year 7). The main phase of the BPS trial consisted of 31 focus groups with 118 students (56 boys and 62 girls) aged 12/13 (Year 8) taught in sets.[13] The majority of students were interviewed with peers at similar attainment levels so as to aid our understanding of some of the more nuanced experiences of attainment grouping by different groups of learners. This also helped to create a 'safe' space for students to articulate their feelings and experiences, which we recognised could be difficult in the presence of those in other sets or at different attainment levels (Boaler, 1997). Including the pilot stage, the sample of the BPMA trial included 36 high prior attainers, 31 middle prior attainers, and 21 low prior attainers.[14] The sample for the BPS main trial[15] included 38 top set, 40 middle set, and 40 lower set students. Students came from a broad range of ethnic and socio-economic backgrounds. The school and student pseudonyms used in this book were assigned by the research team.

Focus groups lasted between 40 and 60 minutes. The topic areas differed somewhat by trial. Students in the BPS schools were asked about: experiences of school and maths/English; self-perception as a learner; perceived reasons for setting; views about setting; feelings about being in their set; views of students in different (top, middle, bottom) sets about setting; perceived impact of setting on learner identities; experiences of and views on teaching in different sets; and experiences of grouping practices in primary school. In addition to experiences of school and maths/English, as well as self-perception as a learner, topics covered with students in the BPMA schools included: perceived reasons for mixed attainment grouping; impact of mixed attainment on students (including those at different attainment

TABLE 3.1 Description of schools in the sample

	Project phase	Trial	Condition	Ofsted category	% FSM	School type	Location
School A	Pilot	BPMA	n/a	Good	29.8	Academy – converter	Suburban, Midlands
School B	Pilot	BPS	n/a	Good	32.5	Local Authority school	Inner city, London
School C	Pilot	BPS	n/a	Outstanding	24.7	Local Authority school	Inner city, London
School D	Pilot	BPS	n/a	Outstanding	8.7	Academy – converter	Suburban, Greater London
School E	Pilot	BPMA	n/a	Outstanding	9.8	Academy – converter	Suburban, Surrey
School F	Pilot	BPMA	n/a	Outstanding	58.5	Local Authority school	Inner city, London
School G	Pilot	BPMA	n/a	Good	50.2	Local Authority school	Inner city, London
School L	Main	BPMA	Control	Outstanding	59.6	Academy sponsor led	Inner city, London
School M	Main	BPMA	Intervention	Good	18.3	Academy –converter	Semi-rural, East of England
School N	Main	BPMA	Intervention	Good	19.2	Local Authority school	Urban, North of England
School O	Main	BPMA	Intervention	Good	43.5	Academy sponsor led	Urban, Midlands
School P	Main	BPS	Control	Outstanding	5	Academy – converter	Urban, Midlands
School Q	Main	BPS	Intervention	Good	16	Academy sponsor led	Urban, South Coast
School R	Main	BPS	Intervention	Good	12	Academy – converter	Urban, North West England
School S	Main	BPS	Control	Good	21	Local Authority school	Suburban, Greater London
School T	Main	BPS	Intervention	Requires improvement	24	Academy – converter	Urban, North of England
School U	Main	BPS	Control	Requires improvement	28	Academy – converter	Semi-rural, South East England
School V	Main	BPS	Control	Good	21	Local Authority school	Suburban, Greater London
School W	Main	BPS	Control	Good	7	Academy – converter	Semi-rural, Midlands
School X	Main	BPS	Intervention	Good	17	Local Authority school	Suburban, Greater London
School Y	Main	BPS	Intervention	Outstanding	22	Academy – converter	Suburban, Greater London

level); experiences of being/learning in mixed classes; perceptions of mixed attainment teaching; experiences of and views on grouping practices in primary school; views on setting; and perceived impact on students in different sets.

In addition to students, we interviewed 56 teachers, including two in a pilot BPMA school. In the BPMA trial, eight English and 12 maths teachers took part in 18 interviews (four teachers were interviewed in pairs). In the BPS trial, 15 English and 19 maths teachers took part in 34 interviews. These interviews generally lasted between 30 and 40 minutes. The questions were adapted to suit the trial. The main topic areas included: rationale for mixed attainment grouping (or setting) and for other types of grouping across different year groups and subjects; experiences of, and views on, mixed attainment; experiences of, and views on, setting; perceived impact of setting on students' learner identities; approaches to differentiation in mixed attainment classes or approaches to teaching different sets. Additionally, teachers in the intervention group were asked about their experiences with the relevant trial.

All interviews were digitally audio recorded, transcribed, and anonymised prior to analysis. The data was then organised using the NVivo software package. Interviews and focus groups were thematically coded by a member of our research team as per an agreed coding scheme, covering key interview questions and areas of interest. Two additional researchers validated the coding on a sub-sample of interviews. Any discrepancies were discussed and resolved in time for the successive in-depth analysis by separate researchers, who sought to identify specific patterns within participants' interviews relating to key research questions – as exemplified by the different chapters in the book. To help us systematically examine patterns in the coded data, a classification grid was produced for each individual interviewee. For example, students were categorised by prior attainment, set level, gender, socio-economic status, and ethnicity; while BPS teachers were classified by the subjects and set level they taught.

Data were also subjected to theoretically informed analysis drawing primarily on the sociological literature that helped to conceptualise the social construction of educational inequality. To tease out the relationship between self-confidence and attainment grouping (Chapter 4), we drew on the sociological constructs of self-fulfilling prophecy (Merton, 1948) and labelling (Lemert, 1951; Becker, 1963). These perspectives suggest that the application of a label to an individual or group precipitates social actions and behaviours which result in the original label (prophecy) coming true (self-fulfilling). To explore students' constructions of attainment grouping (Chapters 4 and 5), we drew on psycho-social theory (Hallway & Jefferson, 2000); specifically psycho-social theoretical application of object relations, theoretical concepts of defendedness and projection (Klein, 1952, 1963). Additionally, we suggested that social reproduction theories are helpful in understanding how attainment grouping shapes disadvantaged students' perceptions about their own status and 'ability'. We also argued however that the attainment structures act upon all students via certain discourses that are mobilised inside schools (Chapter 5). For instance, we drew on Foucauldian analysis of discourse (Foucault, 1980; Parker, 1990) to understand the nature of discourses young people draw on to justify setting, such as meritocracy and conceptions of a 'natural order' (Francis et al., 2017). New Public Management (Dunn & Miller, 2007) accountability pressures are also key to our interpretation of teacher views on grouping practices in Chapters 6, 7, and 8, although in the analysis of these interviews we wanted to be primarily 'grounded' in themes that have emerged from the data.

Ethical considerations

There was considerable uncertainty in this study about the relative effectiveness of our 'best practice' versus traditional approaches to grouping students for learning. Therefore, we feel that the issues some raise in relation to the ethics of randomisation in trials (i.e. the perception of 'denying' some participants access to a beneficial programme) are not significant for this study (Connolly et al., 2007). Besides, all students in the control group were exposed to regular grouping practices, as considered appropriate by the educational professionals in their schools. As discussed earlier, both interventions were based on decades of research, were piloted in the run-in study that engaged teachers and thus had a promise of determining the superior approach to grouping students, and with the intention to improve students' outcomes and equity. Efforts were made to ensure the study was scientifically promising, with safeguards being put in place to address various otherwise potential threats to validity, including: conducting statistical power analysis to determine a sample size and intended analysis; ensuring random allocation; and appointing an independent evaluator.

Detailed information materials were developed by the research team and reviewed and approved by the university research ethics committee to ensure that the nature of the research study was communicated clearly to potential participants. At the recruitment stage, the study protocol was explained to every headteacher and/or heads of relevant departments and their consent was obtained to run the trial. In the circumstances where the intervention is delivered by teachers to the whole school or class as part of the normal timetable, it is considered good practice to allow participants to opt out from the evaluation of the programme, including any tests, surveys, or interviews (Connolly et al., 2007). To this end, a month before data collection started, all parents of Year 7 students in 139 participating schools were sent information about the study and given an opportunity to ask additional questions or opt out their children. As a result, 68 children were withdrawn from the study. Additionally, full consent was required from all teachers and students taking part in surveys and research interviews.

The consideration of the ethics of data collection with young people was of particular importance. Although we initially asked proxies (parents and teachers) to give consent for children to participate in research, we also made an effort to ensure that the participation of students in surveys and interviews was sufficiently informed and voluntary. A consent paragraph was included in online surveys, giving students information on, amongst others: voluntary participation;

risks; confidentiality/anonymity; and the right to withdraw. At the start of the interviews, and before signing consent forms with students, researchers explained in simple language the purpose of research and confidentiality issues, including how the data are anonymised and used in reporting. Being particularly mindful of the feelings of students in low sets, we wanted to reassure students that they did not have to take part in interviews or answer any questions they did not want to answer, and, furthermore, that they could stop taking part at any time. Only two students declined to take part in a focus group after our introductions and another student chose to withdraw later in the process. All three withdrawals were bottom set students for whom the topic was evidently more uncomfortable and emotionally charged than for those in higher sets. Overall, we felt that the focus group environment introduced an element of collaboration and reduced power imbalance between young people and researchers, giving students more control of the discussion, a chance to listen and react to each other's views or to refrain from answering particular questions.

The differing values of the individual researchers on the project team can of course influence to some extent differing collection, analysis, and interpretation of the data. To mitigate against this, a set of methodological standards and principles put in place ensured that we could attain an agreed-upon trustworthy portrayal of the issues under consideration. To enhance the credibility of the qualitative data collection, all members of the research team followed the same interview proto-col. The interview data was fully transcribed and coded using an agreed coding scheme. As outlined earlier, a consensus was sought on analytical approaches. Working on a mixed methods research, we benefitted from being able to call upon the knowledge of experienced colleagues in various methodological tradi-tions to verify our conclusions.

Limitations of the study

By far the most significant challenge we faced over the duration of this study was the attrition of the schools, a common issue in educational RCT studies in England (Dawson et al., 2018) and elsewhere. In an attempt to reduce attrition in the con-trol group, monetary incentive was offered so that schools would be less likely to 'drop out', and be more amenable to visits from the research team. This strategy helped to keep the control schools involved, but the main limitation was that the large proportion of intervention schools ceased for various reasons to deliver the BPS intervention in the second year of the trial. Despite signing memoran-dum of understanding documents prior to signing up, schools in the intervention group found that the time commitment expected and the amount of data required were problematic, and participation over two academic years meant that the staff changes made it harder for schools' continued participation.

Thus, the evaluation of the trial suggested that it is difficult to make conclusions about the effectiveness of the BPS intervention with respect to students' outcomes due to the extent of missing follow-up data. Additionally, our mixed methods research has identified potential explanations for a lack of effect between BPS intervention and 'business as usual' attainment grouping as including: a) low fidelity in applying the practices required, due to schools' environmental and cultural circumstances; and b) the impact of setting on students' general self-confidence in learning. For example, we have found that better qualified teachers and senior teachers continue to be more frequently placed with high sets (see Chapter 6), that practical issues such as timetabling impede optimal and accurate set allocation practice (see Chapter 7); and that a self-fulfilling prophecy impacts students in the intervention as well as control schools (see Chapter 4).

The scale of the BPMA intervention was originally small which meant that outcome measures could not be extrapolated. Furthermore, issues with compliance resulted in reduced differences between the intervention and control groups. The majority of schools in the control group were also practising mixed attainment grouping, and there was non-compliance with mixed attainment grouping in the intervention group in some schools, who returned to setting in the second year of the intervention. However, we learnt much from this trial and we demonstrated the feasibility of applying this approach to mixed attainment grouping (see Chapter 8).

Chapter summary

This chapter outlined the design and methodology of the large-scale study from which data discussed in following chapters is drawn. It set out the key principles of the two educational interventions which were evaluated using randomised controlled trials: one large-scale intervention investigating setting across 126 schools, and a small-scale feasibility trial investigating mixed attainment across 13 schools. It also provided some detail regarding the main datasets that we analyse in subsequent chapters, namely the surveys conducted with 12,997 young people aged 11/12 and 9,501 young people aged 12/13 and close to 1,000 of their teachers, as well as the interviews with 245 students and 56 teachers. Some of the approaches adopted in analysing the data, as well as ethical considerations, were discussed and this chapter concluded with a reflection on the limitations of the study.

Notes

1 The ratio of randomisation for the BPS trial was 1:1. The randomisation was carried out by the evaluators of the project – the National Foundation for Educational Research (see Roy et al., 2018b).

2 Four regional workshops were provided across the two-year intervention, with the expectation that teachers from each participating department (English and/or maths) would attend each workshop and then cascade their learning to colleagues. The four workshops were delivered by the project team after the school day via twilight sessions in six regional hubs across England. The sessions, as discussed in Chapter 7, were geared towards supporting teachers with implementing 'Best Practice in Setting' principles, both structural and pedagogical. The first session took place in July 2015, immediately after randomisation

and before the start of the trial. This session gave an overview of the intervention, reminding teachers of each of the stipulations and their basis in the research literature. Teachers were encouraged to reflect on the practices in their schools and consider what actions would be needed in order to make sure that the stipulations were met. The second session took place in autumn 2015, before the half-term break. This session addressed the need for high expectations for all students regardless of prior attainment, and the conceptualisation of 'ability' as flexible and improvable through effort. The research literature was shared with teachers, who then participated in activities that encouraged reflection on their expectations of students from different backgrounds and how to encourage students to consider their ability as flexible. The third session, in Spring 2016, addressed the entitlement of all students to a rich curriculum. In response to requests from teachers, we also added additional material on differentiation, as some teachers had been finding the broad range of prior attainment in their classes (as a result of the stipulation to have three or four set levels) challenging. The final session, in September 2016, was designed as an opportunity to go back over the intervention with teachers and check in with their progress.

3   The ratio of randomisation for the BPMA trial was 2:1 in order to have a sufficiently large intervention group (see Roy et al., 2018a).

4   Four full days workshops and two twilights were held in two regional hubs. The sessions were geared towards supporting teachers with applying Best Practice in Mixed Attainment teaching principles in the classroom, including flexible within-class grouping, high expectations of all students, and effective differentiation. The project team has also produced high quality print materials for the professional development programme (Taylor et al., 2015).

5   One key area of negotiation with teachers was the use of 'nurture groups' (discussed in Chapter 8). Our expectation had been that all students within a year group would be included in mixed attainment classes, but some schools wanted to provide separately for the very lowest-attaining students. However, we decided to allow schools to use nurture groups in our trial in order to support recruitment to it, while recognising that this is a potential limitation of our approach (Taylor et al., 2017).

6   See GL Assessment website for further information on their progress test series: www. gl-assessment.co.uk/products/progress-test-series/.

7   These measures were obtained for all participants from the National Pupil Database (NPD), which contains data matched and linked using pupil names, dates of birth, and other personal and school characteristics, to pupils' attainment and exam results over a lifetime school attendance in England. See www.gov.uk/government/collections/national-pupil-database.

8   Of the students in BPS trial who completed the baseline survey and provided their demographic data, there were 51.9% boys, 48.1% girls; 73.8% White, 8.8% Asian, 5.9% Black, 11.6% mixed or other; 25% free school meals (FSM) eligible students. Of the students in BPMA trial, there were 50.4% boys, 49.9% girls; 84.6% White, 3.2% Asian, 3% Black, 9.1% mixed or other; 24.1% free school meals (FSM) eligible students.

9   Of the students in BPS trial who completed the final survey and provided their demographic data, there were 50.7% boys; 49% girls; 60% White, 5.2% Asian, 5.5% Black, 5.2% other (24.5% of students did not provide their ethnicity); 23.5% free school meals (FSM) eligible students. Of the students in BPMA trial, there were 51% boys, 49% girls; 79.5% White, 2.2% Asian, 4.8% Black, 2.7% other (10.7% did not provide their ethnicity); 22.2% free school meals (FSM) eligible students.

10 Of 7,296 students who completed surveys at both points in time, 6,540 students were from 64 BPS schools (28 intervention and 36 control) and 756 students were from seven BPMA schools (six intervention and one control).

11 The items were drawn or adapted from several existing instruments: SDQII (Marsh, 1990); TIMSS questions (IEA, 2011) and PISA questions (OECD, 2012); an earlier UK-based study on attainment grouping (Ireson & Hallam, 2001). Many items were created by the project team drawing on existing sociological literature.

12 Although we used both methods in the pilot phase, the decision was made to interview students in groups in the main phase of the study. We found that group environments provided security, reduced power imbalance and offered a more relaxed atmosphere where students did not have to supply lengthy verbal accounts but, reacting to each other's perspectives, could more fully articulate their own implicit views. We draw in this book on data collected in both phases.

13 Although two participating schools taught English in mixed attainment groups rather than sets.

14 No attainment data was available for one participant. Our definitions of students' attainment levels were based on their Key Stage 2 (KS2) test results attained on completion of primary school: low attaining – below level 4 in the KS2 tests; middle attaining – at level 4 in the KS2 tests; high attaining – at level 5 or above in the KS2 tests.

15 Although in the main phase of the BPS study we asked teachers to put together groups of students who were consistently in top, middle, and bottom English and maths sets, this was not the case in the pilot study, where primarily maths set was used to form focus groups.

References

Ball, S. J. (1981). *Beachside comprehensive: a case-study of secondary schooling.* Cambridge: Cambridge University Press.

Becker, H. (1963). *Outsiders.* New York: Free Press.

Boaler, J. (1997). When even the winners are losers: evaluating the experiences of top set students. *Journal of Curriculum Studies, 29*(2), 165–182.

Boaler, J., Wiliam, D., & Brown, M. (2000). Students' experiences of ability grouping-disaffection, polarisation and the construction of failure. *British Educational Research Journal, 26*(5), 631–648.

Bosworth, R. (2013). What sort of school sorts students? *International Journal of Quantitative Research in Education, 1*(1), 20–38.

Connolly, P. (2009). The challenges and prospects for educational effectiveness research. *Effective Education, 1*(1), 1–12.

Connolly, P., Biggart, A., Miller, S., O'Hare, L., & Thurston, A. (2007). *Using randomised controlled trials in education.* London: Sage.

Croll, P. & Moses, D. (1985). *One in five.* London: Routledge & Kegan Paul.

Dawson, A., Yeomans, E., & Brown, E. R. (2018). Methodological challenges in education RCTs: reflections from England's Education Endowment Foundation. *Educational Research, 60*(3), 292–310.

Delisle, J. (2015). Differentiation doesn't work. *Education Week.* Retrieved from www.edweek.org/ew/articles/2015/01/07/differentiation-doesnt-work.html.

Dixon, A., Drummond, M. J., Hart, S., & McIntyre, D. (2002). Developing teaching free from ability labelling: back where we started? *FORUM: for Promoting 3–19 Comprehensive Education, 44*(1), 8–12.

Dunn, W. N. & Miller, D. Y. (2007). A critique of the new public management and the neo-Weberian state: advancing a critical theory of administrative reform. *Public Organization Review, 7*(4), 345–358.

Dunne, M., Humphreys, S., Dyson, A., Sebba, J., Gallannaugh, F., & Muijs, D. (2011). The teaching and learning of pupils in low-attainment sets. *Curriculum Journal, 22*(4), 485–513.

Dunne, M., Humphreys, S., Sebba, J., Dyson, A., Gallannaugh, F., & Muijs, D. (2007). *Effective teaching and learning for pupils in low attaining groups.* London: DfES Publications.

Education Endowment Foundation. (2018). *Sutton Trust-EEF teaching and learning toolkit.* London: Education Endowment Foundation.

Flores, J. (1999). *Tracking middle school students for instruction: a study of homogeneous and hetero-geneous grouping.* MA thesis. California State University, San Marcos.

Foucault, M. (1980). *Power/knowledge: selected interviews and other writings, 1972–1977.* New York: Pantheon.

Francis, B., Archer, L., Hodgen, J., Pepper, D., Taylor, B., & Travers, M-C. (2017). Exploring the relative lack of impact of research on 'ability grouping' in England: a discourse analytic account. *Cambridge Journal of Education, 47*(1), 1–17.

Gazeley, L. & Dunne, M. (2007). Researching class in the classroom: addressing the social class attainment gap in initial teacher education. *Journal of Education for Teaching, 33*(4), 409–424.

Gillborn, D. & Youdell, D. (1999). *Rationing education: policy, practice, reform, and equity.* Buckingham: Open University Press.

Hacker, R., Rowe, M., & Evans, R. (1991). The influences of ability groupings for secondary science lessons upon classroom processes. Part 1: Homogeneous groupings, Science Education Notes. *School Science Review, 73*, 125–129.

Hallam, S. & Ireson, J. (2005). Secondary school teachers' pedagogic practices when teaching mixed and structured ability classes. *Research Papers in Education, 20*(1), 3–24.

Hallway, W. & Jefferson, T. (2000). *Doing qualitative research differently.* London: Sage.

Hamilton, L. & O'Hara, P. (2011). The tyranny of setting (ability grouping): challenges to inclusion in Scottish primary schools. *Teaching and Teacher Education, 27*(4), 712–721.

Hart, S. (Ed.) (1996). *Differentiation and the secondary curriculum: debates and dilemmas.* London: Routledge.

Hodgen, J. & Webb, M. (2008). Questioning, dialogue and feedback. In S. Swaffield (Ed.), *Unlocking assessment* (pp. 73–89). Oxford: Routledge.

IEA. (2011). *TIMSS 2011 student questionnaire.* Boston, MA: IEA.

Ireson, J. & Hallam, S. (2001). *Ability grouping in education.* London: Paul Chapman.

Ireson, J., Hallam, S., & Hurley, C. (2005). What are the effects of ability grouping on GCSE attainment? *British Educational Research Journal, 31*(4), 443–458.

Jackson, B. (1964). *Streaming: an education system in miniature.* London: Routledge and Kegan Paul.

Kelly, S. (2004). Are teachers tracked? On what basis and with what consequences. *Social Psychology of Education, 7*(1), 55–72.

Klein, M. (1952). *Developments in psycho-analysis.* London: Hogarth Press.

Klein, M. (1963). *Our adult world and other essays.* London: Heinemann.

Kutnick, P., Sebba, J., Blatchford, P., Galton, M., Thorp, J., MacIntyre, H., & Berdondini, L. (2005). *The effects of pupil grouping: literature review.* London: Department for Education and Skills.

Lemert, M. E. (1951). *Social pathology.* New York: McGraw-Hill.

Lou, Y., Abrami, P. C., Spence, J. C., Poulsen, C., Chambers, B., & d'Apollonia, S. (1996). Within-class grouping: a meta-analysis. *Review of Educational Research, 66*(4), 423–458.

Macqueen, S. (2012). Academic outcomes from between-class achievement grouping: the Australian primary context. *The Australian Educational Researcher, 39*(1), 59–73.

Marsh, H. W. (1990). *Self description questionnaire II manual: self-description questionnaire II.* Sydney: University of Western Sydney, Macarthur.

Merton, R. K. (1948). The self-fulfilling prophecy. *The Antioch Review, 8*(2), 193–210.

Moller, S. & Stearns, E. (2012). Tracking success: high school curricula and labor market outcomes by race and gender. *Urban Education, 47*(6), 1025–1054.

Muijs, D. & Dunne, M. (2010). Setting by ability – or is it? A quantitative study of determinants of set placement in English secondary schools. *Educational Research*, *52*(4), 391–407.

OECD. (2012). *PISA 2012 student questionnaire*. Paris: OECD Publishing.

OFSTED. (2013). *The report of her Majesty's chief inspector of education, children's services and skills 2012/13: Schools*. Manchester: Ofsted Publications.

Page, R. (1989). The lower-track curriculum at a 'heavenly' high school: 'Cycles of prejudice'. *Journal of Curriculum Studies*, *21*(3), 197–221.

Papay, J. & Kraft, M. (2015). Productivity returns to experience in the teacher labor market: methodological challenges and new evidence on long-term career improvement. *Journal of Public Economics*, *130*, 105–119.

Parker, I. (1990). Discourse: definitions and contradictions. *Philosophical Psychology*, *3*(2–3), 187–204.

Roy, P., Styles, B., Walker, M., Bradshaw, S., Nelson, J., & Kettlewell, K. (2018a). *Best Practice in Grouping Students Intervention B: mixed attainment grouping. Pilot report and executive summary*. London: Education Endowment Foundation.

Roy, P., Styles, B., Walker, M., Morrison, J., Nelson, J., & Kettlewell, K. (2018b). *Best Practice in Grouping Students Intervention A: best practice in setting. Evaluation report and executive summary*. London: Education Endowment Foundation.

Slavin, R. E. (1987). Ability grouping and student achievement in elementary schools: a best-evidence synthesis. *Review of Educational Research*, *57*(3), 293–336.

Slavin, R. E. (1996). Research on cooperative learning and achievement: what we know, what we need to know. *Contemporary Educational Psychology*, *21*(1), 43–69.

Sukhnandan, L. & Lee, B. (1998). *Streaming, setting and grouping by ability: a review of the literature*. Slough: NFER.

Taylor, B., Francis, B., Archer, L., Hodgen, J., Pepper, D., Tereshchenko, A., & Travers, M-C. (2017). Factors deterring schools from mixed attainment teaching practice. *Pedagogy, Culture and Society*, *25*(3), 327–345.

Taylor, B., Travers, M-C., Francis, B., Hodgen, J., & Sumner, C. (2015). *Best Practice in Mixed-Attainment Grouping*. London: King's College London/EEF.

Tomlinson, C. A. (1995). Deciding to differentiate instruction in middle school: one school's journey. *Gifted Child Quarterly*, *39*(2), 77–87.

Willis, G. B. (2005). *Cognitive interviewing: a tool for improving questionnaire design*. London: Sage.

4

THE IMPACT OF ATTAINMENT GROUPING ON PUPIL OUTCOMES

Attainment and self-confidence

The focus of this chapter is squarely on the impact of different grouping practices on *pupil outcomes*. We discussed in Chapter 2 how the wider research on grouping by attainment is primarily focused on attainment outcomes, but has also considered other impacts and outcomes on pupils. These include self-confidence and self-concept. Given we have already analysed the existing research literature on attainment outcomes in Chapter 2, this chapter will attend especially to elaborating the prior literature and our own findings on the impact of attainment grouping on self-confidence. We begin however by looking at explanations for the established trends precipitated by attainment grouping on pupil attainment outcomes.

Attainment grouping and attainment outcomes: exploring explanations for the patterns

In Chapter 2 we outlined the findings from the extensive literature on the impact of attainment grouping on educational attainment outcomes. We highlighted the number of studies and meta-analyses, and some of the complexity at stake, including occasionally contradictory findings. Our summary is that *overall* these practices are not of significant benefit to attainment, with a negative impact for low attainment groups.

Our own study, outlined in Chapter 3, does not contribute to debates on the comparative impacts of setting v mixed attainment practice, because it was designed as two different RCTs (one looking at setting, and statistically powered; the other looking at mixed attainment practice, and designed as a non-statistically powered pilot study). Instead, the study enabled the assessment of: i) impact or otherwise of an evidence-informed intervention seeking to improve equity in setting, on pupil attainment, in comparison to the control group of schools practising 'business as usual' tracking. And, ii) indicative findings on the impact of an intervention seeking to establish good practice in mixed attainment pedagogy, compared with mixed attainment practice in a control group. The latter RCT was not statistically powered, rendering outcome findings indicative; and moreover we feel that the intervention was insufficiently distinctive from some of the practice in the control group (also mixed attainment) to draw meaningful conclusions. In relation to the 'Best Practice in Setting' study, the independent evaluation showed no impact of the intervention on attainment outcomes (Roy et al., 2018). This result indicates that in spite of best efforts to improve equity in setting practices, 'Best practice in setting' does not improve outcomes (e.g. for low attainers) because either a) the act of placing pupils in 'labelled' groups undermines all else, or b) detrimental practices associated with setting are too hard to change. Our longitudinal study did, however, enable us to demonstrate that attainment of bottom set pupils gets comparatively worse over time (over a two year period), whereas for top groups their attainment improves over two years. This clearly demonstrates the inequitable impacts of setting on different pupil groups, and the impact for social inequality given the social composition of high and low attainment sets.

So what are the detrimental practices associated with setting? The wealth of studies on attainment grouping has evidenced a diverse range of differential practices that potentially explain the poorer progress and outcomes for pupils in low attainment groups. Our review of the literature distilled seven different explanations (Francis et al., 2017a), and we used the evidence here to directly inform the design of our intervention, which sought to remediate the tendencies identified, as we explained in Chapter 3. The seven explanations are as follows:

- **Misallocation to groups**. Research shows that allocation is frequently biased, with pupils from working class and certain minority ethnic backgrounds more likely to be allocated to a low attainment group even after controlling for prior attainment.
- **Lack of fluidity of groups**. Research suggests that in spite of teacher perceptions that there is meritocratic movement between sets, in practice this occurs rarely. Once a pupil is placed in a set or stream they are likely to stay there, irrespective of performance.
- **Quality of teaching for different groups**. Some studies have found that better qualified, and/or longer serving teachers are more likely to be placed with high sets.
- **Teacher expectations of pupils**. It is suggested that teacher expectations of pupils are influenced by their set placement, with an impact on pedagogy provided and opportunities afforded.
- **Pedagogy, curriculum, and assessment applied to different groups**. Somewhat relatedly, it has been found that pupils in low sets tend to be offered a narrower curriculum, with less opportunity for independent learning. They are also frequently subject to 'capped' and/or tiered exam paths according to their set placement.

- **Pupil perception and experiences of 'ability' grouping, and impact on their learner identities**. Perhaps unsurprisingly given the above bullet points, set placement has been shown to impact pupils' experience of school and their self-perception.
- These different factors working together to cause a **self-fulfilling prophecy**.

The latter two bullet points relate to *pupils'* perceptions. Having briefly considered the various other explanations for differences in pupils' attainment outcomes – all of which will be developed further later on in the book – we will attend in the rest of this chapter to pupil perceptions and experiences of attainment grouping, focusing particularly on the impact on their self-confidence.

The impact of attainment grouping on self-confidence

The concept of self-fulfilling prophecy was originally developed by Merton (1948), and sociologists have built on his ideas, drawing in the sociological concept of labelling (Becker, 1963; Lemert, 1951). These theories suggest that the application of a label to an individual or group precipitates social actions and behaviours as other individuals, groups, and organisations interpret the labelled individual/group and their actions *according to the label* – and this in turn results in the original label (prophecy) coming true (self-fulfilling). If we apply these concepts to attainment grouping, we might assume that designation to a group ascribed as either 'low ability' or 'high ability' – a very direct label – would precipitate understandings on the part of the individual student and others (parents, teachers, peers etc.) that their academic capability accords with this designated label. This in turn would be predicted to have consequences for the pupils' self-perception, expectations, and related engagement or otherwise, and their subsequent behaviours in relation to learning; and consequences for the perceptions and expectations, and subsequent interactions, applied to them by teachers, peers, and so on (Jackson, 1964). Hence, potentially resulting in the prophecy of 'high' or 'low attainer' being fulfilled. In Chapter 7 we shall discuss how teacher and organisational expectations of pupils are impacted by these labels too: the low expectations that are precipitated by the label 'low attainer' for those in low attainment groups, often result in particular pedagogic and curriculum offers and exam qualification routes (see, e.g. Dunne et al., 2007; Ireson & Hallam, 2001; Ireson et al., 2005; Rubie-Davies, 2007). But also generated are particular behaviours, perceptions, and dis/associations in the young people concerned as they respond to having been labelled 'low ability' or 'high ability'. This includes pupils' self-perception of themselves as learners.

Research on the impact of attainment grouping on self-confidence

Various prior research has demonstrated that self-perception impacts young people's educational outcomes, and that these self-perceptions can be related to attainment grouping. For example, Linchevski and Kutscher (1998) showed that young people with similar prior attainment levels performed better when placed in higher attainment classes than in lower attainment classes. Of course given other points made in this book about inequalities in quality of pedagogy and/or curriculum offers targeted at different attainment groups, self-perception is not the only potential explanation for such unequal outcomes. But it seems likely that the pupils' internalisation of labelling according to placement in attainment groups also impacted performance.

Carol Dweck's (2008) work on 'mindset' also highlights the importance of student self-perception for learning, and the detrimental implication of messages that 'ability' is fixed. Dweck argues that a 'growth mindset' sees learning as integrally challenging, and blocks and difficulties as challenges to be overcome by determination and diligence. This fosters application and resilience, productive for progress and learning outcomes. Whereas in contrast, a 'fixed mindset' sees progress in learning as expressive of inherent 'ability', with difficulties understood as indicative of natural ability or otherwise. This attitude instils a fatalistic belief that if learning doesn't come smoothly it isn't worth bothering, which is detrimental to progress and outcomes. Clearly, this proposition speaks to the concept of self-fulfilling prophecy. Dweck's well-developed experimental research and interventions to support growth mindset have been widely evaluated (Blackwell et al., 2007; Claro et al., 2016; Paunesku et al., 2015; Yeager et al., 2013), and there have been some promising evaluations of interventions (Rienzo et al., 2015).

So, pupil self-perception in relation to their capacity in different areas of the school curriculum, or more generally (e.g. as 'bright', 'quick', 'dull', 'slow', 'good at maths', 'rubbish at French', and so forth), has interested researchers. Such indicators are indicative of well-being, as well as potentially having knock-on relationships with attainment, liking for school, and so on. Nevertheless, researchers have approached this topic from different disciplinary lenses, applying different concepts as a consequence. International research on this topic includes attention to the constructs of self-confidence, self-concept, self-efficacy, and self-esteem. These constructs are all somewhat distinct, but are not always clearly distinguished. Sociological work tends to explore notions of self-confidence and esteem. For example, researching in the UK and focusing on self-confidence, Brown et al. (2008) found that lack of self-confidence was among reasons that pupils were deterred from pursuing maths at post-16. Self-confidence and self-esteem have also been extensively analysed in relation to gender and learning (see e.g. Elwood, 1995; Booher-Jennings, 2008). Researching in Flanders and analysing self-esteem in relation to attainment grouping (tracking), Houtte et al. (2012) found that students on 'academic track' have significantly higher self-esteem than students on 'vocational track'. They also found differences between students varied depending on school type, leading Houtte et al. (2012) to hypothesise that in schools that contain both vocational and academic tracks, students on academic track may compare themselves with the vocational track students, resulting in a higher awareness of status differences and consequently higher self-esteem.

Meanwhile, psychologists have frequently applied the construct of self-concept. Ireson and Hallam (2009) explored pupils' academic self-concept in relation to attainment grouping, and found that self-concept was correlated with attainment grouping across the three subject areas they investigated, with those in the top attainment groups having higher self-concept than those in low attainment groups. However, in this study they found this relationship to be subject-specific: the correlation with respective attainment groups did not extend to *general* self-concept. This latter finding contrasted with those from an earlier study they had carried out, which had found that students in schools using 'moderate levels of setting' had higher general self-concept; and that setting in English tended to lower the self-concepts of the higher attaining pupils and to raise the self-concepts of lower attaining pupils (Ireson & Hallam, 2001). Such complexity and contradiction have also emerged in research on this topic in other (inter)national contexts. For example, researching in Singapore, and focusing on streaming in school, Liem et al. (2015) found that pupil academic self-concept differed negligibly between streams; whereas Liu et al. (2005) found that streaming appeared to have a negative impact for the academic self-concept of lower 'ability' stream students in Singapore (albeit they also found this relationship reduced over a three-year period). Belfi et al.'s (2012) literature review on the topic concluded that 'ability' grouping is beneficial for the academic self-concept of lower attaining students; whereas Kulik and Kulik's (1982) meta-analysis found no relationship between tracking and self-concept. So the research on self-concept presents quite a mixed picture.

However, Marsh's (1984) work adds an additional dimension with some possible explanatory power in regard to this inconsistency in research findings on the topic of self-concept and attainment grouping. Marsh argues that self-concept is by nature relativistic, depending on some frame of reference; and that therefore attainment grouping is likely to have 'substantial effects on self-concepts within different ability groupings' (1984; p. 799): in other words, a pupil's academic self-concept will be influenced by their views of their capability in relation to others, and this in turn will be influenced by attainment grouping, including by who else is in the particular attainment group. To this end, Marsh (1984) suggests that students may have higher self-concept if they compare themselves favourably to the peers in their group; what he refers to as the 'big-fish–little-pond effect'. Marsh et al. (2008) later showed that equally 'able' students have lower academic self-concept when attending schools where average attainment levels are high, than when attending schools where pupil attainment is low. This 'big-fish–little-pond' proposition has generated much interest among self-concept researchers (see, e.g. Chmielewski et al., 2013; Preckel et al., 2010; Suk Wai Wong & Watkins, 2001), and Marsh's findings have some synergy with the sociological findings of Houtte et al. (2012) (see above). This is clearly a complex set of propositions, and the different 'layering' of impacts of labelling and/or peer comparison for students within a school system (for example, attending a school with a 'good' or 'bad' reputation [Reay & Lucey, 2001], or vocational/academic school [Houtte et al, 2012]; position within a hierarchy of streams and sets within a school; and comparison with other students within the given attainment group), are difficult to disaggregate or control for in research.

To summarise: prior to our research, a variety of distinct constructs around pupil self-perception have been applied in relation to attainment grouping within the existing body of research, and this research has produced a range of findings with few consistent trends. However, tentative trends from the findings have been that attainment grouping tends to have *some* impact on pupil self-perception, and that relationality (i.e. to what pupils are comparing themselves) has a bearing on this. It is notable that the existing research has tended to have a quantitative focus: as such it has not attended closely to pupils' articulated experiences in explaining these patterns, or indeed engaged thoroughly with these experiences and their implication for pupil well-being.

Our study adopts the inclusive construct of self-confidence, in approaching this topic of the impact of attainment grouping on pupils' self-perception and well-being. Seeking to contribute to this ongoing debate, and to include analysis of the views of pupils, we drew on our large-scale survey data to analyse whether young people's self-confidence in their educational capabilities differs depending on the attainment set in which they are placed. In light of the literature discussed above, we wanted to explore both i) whether or not set level relates to self-confidence *in relation to the curriculum subjects concerned*, and ii) whether or not set level relates to self-confidence *in learning more generally*. We used our qualitative data to explore the experiences reported by students and which underpin the quantitative trends identified, drawing on these accounts to better understand both the nature of these views and experiences, and how they inform the patterns in the quantitative data. We have applied psycho-social theory (Hollway & Jefferson, 2000; see elaboration in Chapter 3) to explore pupils' perceptions of attainment grouping.

The quantitative data reported in this chapter is based on the responses of students in 86 schools participating in the 'Best Practice in Setting' study (i.e. those experiencing setting). As we explained in Chapter 3, the first questionnaires were administered in autumn 2015, soon after those pupils being set had arrived at secondary school and had been placed in attainment groups. We then conducted a further survey round when these same pupils had reached the end of Year 8, to explore the impact of two years of experience of this grouping on their self-confidence, and school and subject. We focused on three self-confidence indicators: self-confidence in English, self-confidence in maths, and general self-confidence in learning (for details of the items used for each, see Francis et al., 2017b).

Self-confidence and perceived set level in English and maths

To provide an initial feel for the nature and extent of the relationship between set allocation and self-confidence, descriptive statistics from one of the items ('I am not very good at English/maths') are summarised in Table 4.1. As can be seen, for both subjects, there is a clear relationship between set allocation and self-confidence in that subject. Those in the bottom sets, for example, are about three times more likely to agree with the statement compared to those in the top sets. Nevertheless,

TABLE 4.1 Pupils' self-assessment of their ability in maths and English

Statement	Allocated Set in Maths or English	Agree or Strongly Agree		Undecided		Disagree or Strongly Disagree	
'I am not very	Top Set	329	10.5%	239	24.1%	2,574	81.9%
good at maths'	Middle Set	1,292	24.1%	892	16.6%	3,180	59.3%
(n=9,773)	Bottom Set	436	34.4%	237	18.7%	594	46.9%
'I am not very	Top Set	210	13.7%	176	11.5%	1,146	74.8%
good at English'	Middle Set	736	27.6%	481	18.0%	1,452	54.4%
(n=4,922)	Bottom Set	242	33.6%	147	20.4%	332	46.1%

Source: Francis et al., 2017b

nearly half of those in the bottom sets in both subjects, tend to disagree with this statement. So this illuminates the way in which overall trends in our findings mask a great deal of complexity, and specifically that we should remember that in spite of the trend, not *all* students in bottom sets lack self-confidence (or, in the case of top sets, that these students all have high self-confidence).

This relationship was more formally analysed using multi-level models, which were used to calculate the adjusted mean scores in self-confidence (see Francis et al., 2017b for full details). The adjusted mean scores in self-confidence in maths and English by perceived set allocation (i.e. as reported by pupils) are summarised in Table 4.2. It can be seen that there is a clear relationship, with levels of self-confidence in the subjects increasing as students perceive themselves to be in higher sets. The relationship appears to be slightly stronger in maths, with the mean scores for those in the top sets being a little over two thirds of a standard deviation higher than those in the bottom (Hedges' $g = 0.71$; 95% CI: 0.64, 0.78), whereas it is half a standard deviation in English ($g = 0.51$; 95% CI: 0.41, 0.61). It is also notable that the gap is larger between those in the top and middle sets compared to those in the middle and bottom sets. This pattern is also illustrated in Figure 4.1, showing the higher level of self-confidence for pupils in top sets for the subjects concerned, in relation to their peers in other sets.

TABLE 4.2 Adjusted mean scores in self-confidence in maths and English by perceived set allocation in those subjects in school[*]

Sets	Maths			English		
	Mean	SD	N	Mean	SD	N
Top Sets	28.40	4.72	2,930	28.23	5.29	1,350
Middle Sets	25.58	5.62	4,559	26.08	5.80	2,055
Bottom Sets	24.84	5.81	1,067	25.41	6.02	543

[*] Adjusted mean scores calculated using three-level multi-level models and controlling for gender, family occupational background, ethnicity, and total number of sets in each school.

Source: Francis et al., 2017b

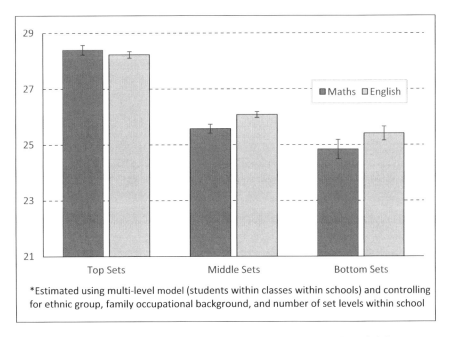

*Estimated using multi-level model (students within classes within schools) and controlling for ethnic group, family occupational background, and number of set levels within school

FIGURE 4.1 Adjusted mean scores for self-confidence in maths and English by perceived set allocation

General self-confidence in learning by perceived set level in English and maths

Given the findings from previous research summarised earlier, we were also interested in examining whether this relationship between self-confidence and perceived set level was largely restricted to self-confidence in the particular curriculum subject in which pupils were set, or whether it was also reflected in the pupils more general self-confidence in relation to learning. After all, it might be argued that, if setting is based on prior attainment at a given subject, it is unsurprising that higher achieving pupils are more confident in that subject than are lower achieving ones. Whereas, if there were a link between set level in particular subjects and *general self-confidence in learning*, this would comprise a greater indictment of a negative influence of setting. To answer this question, the above analysis was repeated applying this broader measure of general self-confidence in learning. We found that there is indeed also a clear relationship between perceived set allocation and general levels of self-confidence, and that this relationship is very similar for set level at English and maths.

This new finding demonstrates that the impact of setting on self-confidence extends beyond the subjects in which setting applies, to pupils' self-confidence in learning more generally. Again, the size of the gap in mean scores from top to bottom sets is slightly larger for maths compared to English. In contrast to the findings

TABLE 4.3 Adjusted mean scores in general self-confidence by perceived set allocation in maths and English in school*

Sets	Maths Sets			English Sets		
	Mean	SD	N	Mean	SD	N
Top Sets	26.17	3.24	2,988	26.15	3.34	1,354
Middle Sets	25.20	3.71	4,682	25.22	3.70	2,069
Bottom Sets	24.18	4.19	1,096	24.45	3.93	542

* Adjusted mean scores calculated using three-level multi-level models and controlling for gender, family occupational background, ethnicity, and total number of sets in each school.

Source: Francis et al., 2017b

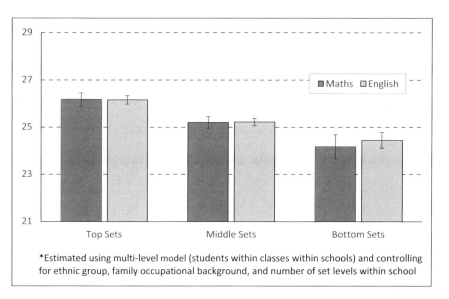

*Estimated using multi-level model (students within classes within schools) and controlling for ethnic group, family occupational background, and number of set levels within school

FIGURE 4.2 Adjusted mean scores for general self-confidence by perceived set allocation

on set level and self-confidence in particular subjects (maths and English), the gaps between top, middle, and bottom, appear to be broadly similar.

What is even more striking is our soon-to-be detailed findings (Francis et al., forthcoming) that self-confidence of those pupils in low attainment groups *decreases over time*, in comparison to those in high attainment groups whose confidence *increases* over time. Our longitudinal analysis shows that when compared with two years previously, there was a general trend that pupils had higher self-confidence in the subject area of maths or English if they were placed in the top set and a significantly lower self-confidence when placed in the bottom set in maths, when compared with an average student in the middle set. Figure 4.3 provides an exemplar of our broader findings here.

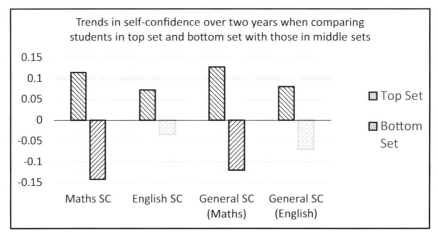

* Statistically significant results in bold.

FIGURE 4.3 Overview of the effect sizes for the three level models comparing post-test mean gains in self-confidence by set level, controlling for number of sets in school, family occupation, ethnicity and gender

This comprises a further important indication of causality of the impact of attainment group placement on self-confidence (as it is hard to conceive any other explanation for this growing divergence in self-confidence over time between set levels). And indeed, we argue that this provides evidence of a snowball effect for self-fulfilling prophecy: the prophecy not just being fulfilled, but actually concentrated as it is continually reinforced over time.

So to summarise here, we can see that a clear relationship exists between self-confidence and set level, both in the subject areas in which setting occurs, and in the case of learning more broadly. This strongly supports the hypothesis that the labelling process associated with set allocation precipitates a self-fulfilling prophecy. For those pupils allocated to high attainment sets, this allocation and the label 'high attainer' provoke positive associations with the subject concerned and promote their self-confidence; whereas for those in lower sets the reverse is the case.

Pupils' views: student perceptions about attainment grouping and self-confidence

Many pupils articulated an awareness of the labelling element implicit in the act of setting. As Fred (Sets 1 English and maths, White-British, middle class, School Z) observes, 'We can try to hide it, but it is blatantly saying, "You are less intelligent than this person". So, I think some people definitely feel a bit miffed about that.'

Likewise, pupils highlighted the impact of the label in precipitating self-fulfilling prophecy in those concerned:

> Yes, some people think if they're in a lower set they're not good at anything.
> *(Kenneth, Set 1 English, Set 2 maths, African heritage,*
> *middle SES, School C)*

> Well, it does sound really disheartening and really disappointing if you're put into a lower group when maybe in your old school you were in a higher group and it makes you upset and a lot less excited to do the work, and stuff. If you're in the top group, you'd be like, 'Yeah! I want to do this work, it will be hard and fun'. But then when you're in the lower groups, you're like, 'I'm in the lower group. It will be rubbish and boring because I'm stupid' or whatever.
> *(Henry, mixed attainment class, White British, middle SES, School E)*

It was also notable that this labelling was not seen as indicating *present attainment*, but rather, a pupil's fixed ability. For example, James (Set 2 English, Set 4 maths, White British, low SES, School B) explains that, 'It affects us because it makes you feel either you are cleverer or have better abilities, or not very good abilities . . . or not very good, basically', and confesses that 'I think like that sometimes'.

As James' quote illustrates, an ingredient in this perceived self-fulfilling prophecy is the impact on self-confidence precipitated by the label. In the following extract from a mixed attainment class focus group (School E), the pupils make this point explicitly:

Alice: [. . .] if you're in the same attainment group then if you're all low level but you know there's a higher group than you, then you might feel less confident, like you're not doing as well as you should.

Iris: [. . .] I think it can knock their confidence [..]. So if there was a way that they could stop people from knowing which was top and bottom, then it would be easier, because then they wouldn't know whether they were moving up or down and they could still feel confident.

Hilda: Definitely.

Camilla: Definitely.

Henry: Yes.

Camilla: Because it can really lower your self-esteem. If you think you're a lot better than you are and then you're put in the bottom group for something and you'd be like . . . it might upset you, it might make you feel angry and it would definitely affect the way you thought of school.

The group's further discussion powerfully evokes other potential debilitating effects of placement in a low attainment group:

Chris: Especially if all your friends in the higher group and then you're in the lower group and they're all talking about, 'What did you get on this test?' and you did it on a different test.

Camilla:	And you didn't do very well.
Chris:	Yes, you didn't do that well, or something, you feel a bit left out.
Camilla:	You might feel a bit 'Special'. A bit disabled, a bit Special Needs, stuff like that.
Hilda:	Because last year I was, well all the way through my primary school, I was always in the bottom set for spelling, I've never really, since then, I've never really, if my mum goes, 'You need to practise your spelling' I always feel I never want to practise it because I always think that I'm always going to get it wrong and I'm never going to get it right because I'm really bad at spelling and I'll always be really bad at spelling. I don't know, in some ways it would make you want to try harder to get into the higher set but, for me, I don't want to try because it would just be . . . I'd feel like –
Chris:	Humiliation.
Hilda:	– then I'll get it wrong and I'd be really humiliated myself if I get it wrong. So I don't really know, but that's how I feel about it.

As we have discussed elsewhere (Francis et al., 2017b), this transcript extract contains various emotionally laden and difficult themes. One of these is the alienation, or 'Othering' (cf. de Beauvoir, 1953) of pupils in low attainment groups. This occurs both practically and symbolically. The practical segregationist consequences of setting on pupil social relations is illustrated by Chris' point about the taking of different tests, and the socially excluding effects of such delineations ('you feel a bit left out'). But this also symbolically marks pupils as different, with impact on self-esteem illustrated by Chris' remarks on consequently feeling one is not doing 'that well' and feeling 'a bit Special'. This latter is a reference to Special Educational Needs,[1] and the allusion highlights several things. Firstly, that 'Special Educational Needs' is another manifestation of labelling operating in schools, also used as a proxy for 'ability' (as in Chris' remark), in spite of the wide range of conditions that the designation Special Educational Needs can include (for example, from high performing autism to ADHD, and so on). And disturbingly, how this label continues to be denigrated in spite of the ostensible 'inclusion' of young people with these additional needs within state education (Blatchford & Webster, 2018; Dytham, 2016; Webster & Blatchford, 2017). Chris' allusion to feeling 'a bit Special', then, illuminates the abject status of the 'low ability group' in school, with the implication for peer relationships and individual psyches. The social and psychological consequences of academic 'failure' are reinforced by Chris and Hilda's use of the word 'humiliation' to articulate shame and impotence. And, Hilda's frank vocalisation of her difficulties with spelling provide a moving illustration of self-fulfilling prophecy in action.

These issues of peer dynamics were also reflected in the frequent concerns expressed by young people about the stigmatisation of being associated with a low attainment group. The importance of respect – both self-respect and respect from peers – has been demonstrated in prior research (Archer et al., 2007); and emerged frequently in our interviews with young people. For example, Salima (Bangladeshi, low SES, School F) observes that,

> in my primary school I didn't like my maths class, because the people that were in the higher group, Miss, she treated them with more respect and stuff. The people in the lower group, she thought they needed a lot of help and stuff. She didn't really treat us like the way she treated the higher tables and stuff.

Tanvi (mixed attainment class, South Asian, SES unknown, School F) asserts that if placed in a low attainment group, 'You'd be like, "There's so many people in the high levels, and I'm just stuck here. I feel the odd one out, and I wish I was a high level, because then, my parents would be proud of me, as well."' Again, his suggestion that parents would be proud of placement in a 'high level' implies the converse for a low group, illustrating the burden of stigma that these pupils must bear. In a similar vein, Riya (mixed attainment groups, Indian, higher SES, School F) reports her prior experiences of having been placed in a low attainment group in primary school:

> So, yeah, it feels kind of weird. It's like the teachers don't like you because they think that you're dumb, and then the other people are smarter than you. [Salima: Yeah] And, it makes you feel a bit weird. That's why I wasn't really confident when I was in primary, because when I was in here I was in the low group, but then later I tend[ed] to be in the highest one. But, I was not really confident because I would be scared if someone laughed at me if I said something wrong.

Riya's point about teacher perceptions and their impact is also picked up by Rani, in the same focus group, who shared the experience of placement in a low attainment group during primary school, and claims that 'the teachers treat you like two-year-olds'. This perceived infantilisation of pupils in low attainment groups was a running theme in the pupil data. We discuss this point in relation to *teacher* perceptions (and implications for pedagogical provision) in more depth in Chapter 6. However, the overarching point is that Riya's words again illustrate the impact of attainment grouping on self-perception and self-confidence – according to Riya, with lasting effects, even now that she has been moved into higher groups. We also found that this reported infantilisation of pupils in low sets was attested, and even adopted by, other pupils. For example, top-set pupil Fred (White British, high SES, School Z) and Brian (White and Asian mixed heritage, high SES, School E) reflect on the experiences of low group pupils:

Fred: I'd imagine they felt quite a lot less confident about themselves, yes, but then in a way I think they're congratulated a lot more for what they do, regardless of what it is, than we are. So, I think that probably cancels each other out and so it comes around a bit neutral, really.

I: That's interesting.

Brian: I think . . . yes, you are . . . if you say rewarded, I'd say patronised a lot more for what you achieve. It's like . . . let's say Set Four was a baby, and then Set One was a fully grown person. You'd see a baby walking and you're like, 'Oh, congratulations', like, 'Wow. How are you doing that?' You see a fully grown person walking and you don't bat an eyelid.

Here Fred postulates that low-set pupils receive meaningless praise; and Brian affirms Fred's view with an exemplar that revealingly uses the analogy of a baby. In this way, a set of disparaging assumptions are projected on to low-set pupils, who are positioned as inane objects of patronage.

Elsewhere we apply psycho-social theory (Hollway & Jefferson, 2000) to this and other interview extracts (Francis et al., 2017b), arguing that this example may be read as one of projection (see Klein, 1952, 1963), wherein vulnerabilities are split off from/by top-set pupils and projected on to low-set pupils, who are pathologised and Othered. Diane Reay (2015) has additionally argued that within psycho-social relations in educational environments, affective transactions become 'sedimented' in classed habitus. She argues that:

> The learning that comes through inhabiting pathologised spaces within the field often results in a predilection for shame, fear, anxiety, or even righteous indignation, while the internalisation of social inequalities in the privileged can result in dispositions of superiority, entitlement, disdain but also a predilection for guilt, ambivalence and discomfort.
>
> *(p. 12)*

Arguably precisely such affective phenomena underpin Fred and Brian's articulations, which reflect superiority, some disdain, and certainly 'Othering' of low attainment group pupils. Fred and Brian's (middle) class status, in comparison with lower attainment group pupils (whom as we have explained *tend* to be working class pupils and/or those from disadvantaged backgrounds) exemplifies the way social class inequality can interweave such constructions of difference. For some other pupils this resulted rather in guilt and discomfort: looking back at her primary school experience, Alexis (mixed attainment class, White European, middle SES, School E) explains, 'Because my friend, she is really good at maths, but she was put in the bottom group, and I think that ruined her confidence in maths so I felt really sorry for her. But I couldn't do anything of course. [..] I'm just a student.'

In summary, our findings provided much evidence to support Anaya's (mixed attainment groups, Indian, middle SES, School F) assertion that 'Sets ruin your self-esteem'. However, of course the reverse was the case for many pupils in higher groups. At the other end of the spectrum of experience, setting could be seen to have a positive, reinforcing impact on the self-confidence and authenticity of those in high attainment groups. For example, Robin (Sets 1 English and maths,

White and Black Caribbean, low SES, School C) explains that he likes being in the top set, and that it makes him feel 'Confident because I know I have good work'. Boaler (1997) has found that many pupils, especially girls, dislike the pressure they experience from being placed in high groups, and/or to experience impostor syndrome. However, we did not record such articulations in our interviews.

Nevertheless, we did find evidence that the implications of attainment grouping for distinctions in social status within the school environment impacted in turn on social relations and (dis)harmony between pupils. The high self-esteem and/or perceived complacency of higher attainment group pupils, combined with the lower confidence and resentment from some of those in lower sets, appeared on occasion to provoke a 'them and us' mentality. This extract from a maths Set 2 focus group at School B is illustrative:

Adam: Yeah, in Set 1 they think they're so smart because they're in a high set.
Janne: No.
Adam: 'Oh, I'm better than you because I'm in the higher set'.
Tavi: They do that a lot, because there are some people in Set 1 for English, that they think just because they're intelligent they don't need to learn anything.
Janne: Yes.
Tavi: So they start being silly instead of starting to do their work.
Adam: You never know. They could go down.
Tavi: Yeah, they could. One of them has already been at our level.
Adam: Who?
Tavi: Tyrell.
Adam: From what?
Tavi: From Set 1.

This extract may be read as an example of splitting and projection as a means of psychological defence. Insecurities of being in a lower set are split off by projecting snobbery and complacency to those in the top set, and this middle set group construct themselves as wisely knowing, and morally superior, in comparison to their top-set peers. However, in relation to the argument we are making on social relations, it is worth reflecting how our 'comprehensive' schools are fostering social divisions via attainment grouping. And that, given the longstanding evidence we rehearsed in Chapter 2 concerning the socio-economic (and ethnic and gendered) composition of different attainment groups, these social divisions also have a strongly classed dimension.

More positive constructions of attainment grouping

It is important to record at this point that not all young people presented placement in a low attainment group as harmful to self-confidence. Two pupils within our sample even constructed it as beneficial to self-confidence:

I think it would affect what they think about themselves but I think in a good way. Because the high attainers, like the people who get the higher grades, they'd feel good about themselves because obviously they've gotten the higher grades. People who haven't gotten as much of a high grade, they probably would build up their confidence, build up their determination, and try and try until they get to the higher stage. All around . . . good about themselves.

(Kashvi, mixed attainment class, South Asian,
high SES, School F)

Like, obviously there's a difference between thriving in the bottom set and then moving up a set but really struggling there, and sometimes you wish there was a middle set in between two sets. So I think it can be harsh on people's confidence if they're, kind of, they often find they see someone else doing really, really well in something that they thought everyone struggled with. [. . .] I think the fact that they've even put us in sets is actually kind in a way, that they've done that.

(Monica, Sets 1 English and maths, White British,
unknown SES, School D)

Here attainment grouping is presented as protective to those in low attainment groups, who might be intimidated or daunted by higher attainers if working with them in a mixed attainment class. It is worth noting that these pupils articulating this possibility were themselves in high sets; the view was not expressed by any lower set pupils in our sample. On the other hand, the hypotheses of Herb Marsh (1984) regarding relational perceptions of attainment (in this case, 'little fish, big pond') do lend the proposition some credibility.

While these two represented isolated cases, a few more pupils pointed out that setting affects individual pupils differently. For example, Janet (Sets 2 and 3, Black African heritage, unknown SES, School C) reflects of her own set placement, 'it doesn't affect me, how I think about myself. I'm still confident even though I'm not in the top set'. We discuss pupils' opinions on attainment grouping further in the next chapter.

Discussion/conclusion

So, our study has provided clear evidence of negative impact of setting for the self-confidence of pupils in low attainment groups (and the positive impact on the self-confidence of those placed in high attainment groups).

We have established significant relationships between set level and pupil self-confidence – for both of the key curriculum subjects of maths and English, *and* for general self-confidence in learning. The clarity of these patterns established across an unusually large sample of Year 7 pupils helps to clarify prior debates in the literature about the impact or otherwise of setting on self-confidence and self-concept. And our findings concerning the impact on general self-confidence in learning are especially significant because they suggest that setting has broader implications for learning beyond the specific subjects in which setting takes place. In this sense, it is also especially salient that our longitudinal analysis (Francis et al., forthcoming) shows that the differences in self-confidence between set levels is exacerbated over time, with low-set pupils' self-confidence worsening (significantly so in the maths group, for maths and general self-confidence), and those in high sets self-confidence significantly growing across the board. We have presented this as self-fulfilling prophecy in action, highlighting the snowball effect of this phenomenon. However, we would also reiterate the point for social in/justice from this evidence: that those pupils who most need help and support (low attainers – disproportionately representing those from socially disadvantaged backgrounds) are being further disadvantaged by the impact of placement in low attainment groups; while those high attainers already thriving (and disproportionately representing more affluent pupils) are being helped. This is deeply concerning from educational improvement and social justice perspectives.

Meanwhile, a further contribution is the voice of pupils from our qualitative data, often missing from large-scale quantitative and meta-analytic studies. Year 7 pupils are aware of the labelling effects of setting, and indeed many of them volunteered accounts of self-fulfilling prophecy precipitated. We have also attempted to tease out some of the psycho-social implications of attainment grouping, and in this chapter and the next we present some material wherein pupils speak of the pain and shame of their ascribed set group (see also Marks, 2016, for findings in primary schools. And the next chapter looks more closely at implications for social status, and impact on social hierarchies and relations in school). The findings concerning infantilisation and denigration of low attainment groups need to be taken especially seriously by educators. There are serious implications for pupils' confidence (as our quantitative data shows), with knock-on effects for pupils' feelings about school, which could have long-term implications for educational associations and outcomes. But also, implications for social relations within school and the mutual respect that so many schools are trying hard to foster. Here it is important to also reiterate the concern that Special Educational Needs – conflated by some pupils with low attainment – remains a denigrated label.[2] The impact of labelling on low attainers, and those designated 'SEN', requires urgent attention.

To conclude, our findings provide strong evidence that the impact of labelling on pupil self-confidence is one explanation for the poorer progress of those in low attainment groups, and contrasts to those in high attainment groups. Implications for equality of opportunity and social in/justice are clear. Schools need to reflect to ensure that a range of important different ends – student outcomes, well-being, community, and progress – are balanced so far as possible, and that practices adopted are justified by research evidence. This reflection is needed to ensure that those pupils most in need of support to improve are not being further held back by grouping practices.

Notes

1 'Special Educational Needs' is the official label used in the British education system to refer to those learners designated as having learning problems or disabilities.
2 See Norwich and Kelly (2004) and Monchy et al. (2004) for findings on bullying of young people with SEN in mainstream schools.

References

Archer, L., Hollingworth, S. & Halsall, A. (2007) 'University's not for me — I'm a Nike person': urban, working-class young people's negotiations of style, identity and educational engagement, *Sociology*, *41*(2), 219–237.

Becker, H. S. (1963). *Outsiders*. New York: Free Press.

Belfi, B., Goos, M., De Fraine, B., & Van Damme, J. (2012). The effect of class composition by gender and ability on secondary school students' school well-being and academic self-concept: a literature review. *Educational Research Review*, *7*(1), 62–74.

Blackwell, L. S., Trzesniewski, K. H., & Dweck, C. S. (2007). Implicit theories of intelligence predict achievement across an adolescent transition: a longitudinal study and an intervention. *Child Development*, *78*(1), 246–263.

Blatchford, P. & Webster, R. (2018). Classroom contexts for learning at primary and secondary school: class size, groupings, interactions and special educational needs. *British Educational Research Journal*, *44*(4), 681–703.

Boaler, J. (1997). When even the winners are losers: evaluating the experiences of 'top set' students. *Journal of Curriculum Studies*, *29*(2), 165–182.

Booher-Jennings, J. (2008). Learning to label: socialisation, gender, and the hidden curriculum of high-stakes testing. *British Journal of Sociology of Education*, *29*(2), 149–160.

Brown, M., Brown, P., & Bibby, T. (2008). 'I would rather die': reasons given by 16-year-olds for not continuing their study of mathematics. *Research in Mathematics Education*, *10*(1), 3–18.

Chmielewski, A. K., Dumont, H., & Trautwein, U. (2013). Tracking effects depend on tracking type: an international comparison of students' mathematics self-concept. *American Educational Research Journal*, *50*(5), 925–957.

Claro, S., Paunesku, D., & Dweck, C. S. (2016). Growth mindset tempers the effects of poverty on academic achievement. *Proceedings of the National Academy of Sciences*, *113*(31), 8664–8668.

de Beauvoir, S. (1953). *The second sex*. London: Jonathan Cape.

Dunne, M., Humphreys, S., Sebba, J., Dyson, A., Gallannaugh, F., & Muijs, D. (2007). *Effective teaching and learning for pupils in low attaining groups*. London: DCSF.

Dweck, C. S. (2008). *Mindset: how you can fulfil your potential*. New York: Random House.

Dytham, S. (2016). *Relational popularity and social status in secondary school*. Unpublished PhD thesis, University of Warwick.

Elwood, J. (1995). Undermining gender stereotypes: examination and coursework performance in the UK at 16. *Assessment in Education: Principles, Policy & Practice*, *2*(3), 283–303.

Francis, B., Archer, L., Hodgen, J., Pepper, D., Taylor, B., & Travers, M-C. (2017a). Exploring the relative lack of impact of research on 'ability grouping' in England: a discourse analytic account. *Cambridge Journal of Education*, *47*(1), 1–17.

Francis, B., Connolly, P., Archer, L., Hodgen, J., Mazenod, A., Pepper, D., Sloan, S., Taylor, B., Tereshchenko, A., & Travers, M-C. (2017b). Attainment grouping as self-fulfilling prophecy? A mixed methods exploration of self confidence and set level among year 7 students. *International Journal of Educational Research*, *86*, 96–108.

Francis, B. Craig, N., Hodgen, J., Taylor, B., Tereshchenko, A., Connolly, P. & Archer, L. (forthcoming). The impact of tracking by attainment on pupil self-confidence over time: demonstrating the accumulative impact of self-fulfilling prophecy. *British Journal of Sociology of Education*.

Hollway, W. & Jefferson, T. (2000). *Doing qualitative research differently*. London: Sage.

Houtte, M. V., Demanet, J., & Stevens, P. A. J. (2012). Self-esteem of academic and vocational students: does within-school tracking sharpen the difference? *Acta Sociologica*, *55*(1), 73–89.

Ireson, J. & Hallam, S. (2001). *Ability grouping in education*. London: Paul Chapman.

Ireson, J. & Hallam, S. (2009). Academic self-concepts in adolescence: relations with achievement and ability grouping in schools. *Learning and Instruction*, *19*(3), 201–213.

Ireson, J., Hallam, S., & Hurley, C. (2005). What are the effects of ability grouping on GCSE attainment? *British Educational Research Journal*, *31*(4), 443–458.

Jackson, B. (1964). *Streaming: an education system in miniature*. London: Routledge and Kegan Paul.

Klein, M. (1952). *Developments in psycho-analysis*. London: Hogarth Press.

Klein, M. (1963). *Our adult world and other essays*. London: Heinemann.

Kulik, C.-L. C. & Kulik, J. A. (1982). Effects of ability grouping on secondary school students: a meta-analysis of evaluation findings. *American Educational Research Journal*, *19*(3), 415–428.

Lemert, E. M. (1951). *Social pathology*. New York: McGraw-Hill.

Liem, G. A. D., McInerney, D. M., & Yeung, A. S. (2015). Academic self-concepts in ability streams: considering domain specificity and same-stream peers. *The Journal of Experimental Education*, *83*(1), 83–109.

Linchevski, L. & Kutscher, B. (1998). Tell me with whom you're learning, and I'll tell you how much you've learned: mixed-ability versus same-ability grouping in mathematics. *Journal for Research in Mathematics Education*, *29*(5), 533–554.

Liu, W. C., Wang, C. K. J., & Parkins, E. J. (2005). A longitudinal study of students' academic self-concept in a streamed setting: the Singapore context. *British Journal of Educational Psychology*, *75*(4), 567–586.

Marks, R. 2016. *Ability Grouping in Primary Schools*. London: Critical Publishing.

Marsh, H. W. (1984). Self-concept, social comparison, and ability grouping: a reply to Kulik and Kulik. *American Educational Research Journal*, *21*(4), 799–806.

Marsh, H. W., Seaton, M., Trautwein, U., Lüdtke, O., Hau, K. T., O'Mara, A. J., & Craven, R. G. (2008). The big-fish–little-pond-effect stands up to critical scrutiny: implications for theory, methodology, and future research. *Educational Psychology Review*, *20*(3), 319–350.

Merton, R. K. (1948). The self-fulfilling prophecy. *The Antioch Review*, *8*(2), 193–210.

Monchy, M. d., Pijl, S. J., & Zandberg, T. (2004). Discrepancies in judging social inclusion and bullying of pupils with behaviour problems. *European Journal of Special Needs Education*, *19*(3), 317–330.

Norwich, B. & Kelly, N. (2004). Pupils' views on inclusion: moderate learning difficulties and bullying in mainstream and special schools. *British Educational Research Journal*, *30*(1), 43–65.

Paunesku, D., Walton, G. M., Romero, C., Smith, E. N., Yeager, D. S., & Dweck, C. S. (2015). Mind-set interventions are a scalable treatment for academic underachievement. *Psychological Science*, *26*(6), 784–793.

Preckel, F., Götz, T., & Frenzel, A. (2010). Ability grouping of gifted students: effects on academic self-concept and boredom. *British Journal of Educational Psychology*, *80*(3), 451–472.

Reay, D. (2015). Habitus and the psychosocial: Bourdieu with feelings. *Cambridge Journal of Education*, *45*(1), 9–23.

Reay, D. & Lucey, H. (2001). *'Wanting the best': school 'choice' in different class contexts*. ESRC Transitions Project Paper 5. London: King's College London.

Rienzo, C., Rolfe, H., & Wilkinson, D. (2015). *Changing mindsets: evaluation report and executive summary*. London: Education Endowment Foundation.

Roy, P., Styles, B., Walker, M., Morrison, J., Nelson, J., & Kettlewell, K. (2018). *Best Practice in Grouping Students Intervention A: Best Practice in Setting evaluation report and executive summary*. London: Education Endowment Foundation.

Rubie-Davies, C. M. (2007). Classroom interactions: exploring the practices of high- and low-expectation teachers. *British Journal of Educational Psychology*, *77*(2), 289–306.

Suk Wai Wong, M. & Watkins, D. (2001). Self-esteem and ability grouping: a Hong Kong investigation of the big fish little pond effect. *Educational Psychology*, *21*(1), 79–87.

Webster, R. & Blatchford, P. (2017). *The Special Educational Needs in Secondary Education (SENSE) study final report: a study of the teaching and support experienced by pupils with statements and education, health and care plans in mainstream and special schools*. London: UCL Institute of Education/Nuffield Foundation.

Yeager, D. S., Paunesku, D., Walton, G. M., & Dweck, C. S. (2013). How can we instill productive mindsets at scale? A review of the evidence and an initial R&D agenda. Retrieved from: https://web.stanford.edu/~gwalton/home/Welcome_files/YeagerPauneskuWaltonDweck%20-%20White%20House%20R%26D%20agenda%20-%205-9-13.pdf.

5

PUPILS' EXPERIENCES OF DIFFERENT GROUPING PRACTICES

This chapter explores set allocation and misallocation practices, and young people's perceptions of attainment grouping and of mixed attainment practice. It argues that young people's perceptions are entangled with the wider discourses around 'ability' and meritocracy, and constrained by the prevailing ideology of 'ability' hierarchy that supports the structure of attainment grouping in schools. We begin the chapter by outlining evidence related to the reproduction of gendered, classed, and racialised patterns of inequality through attainment grouping. We then focus on pupils' perceptions of setting practice. We explore the reasons for various positive and negative views on setting in greater depth via analysis of interview data from pupils. Lastly, we analyse the attitudes of pupils of different attainment levels to mixed attainment practice, focusing on their explanations for their preferences or aversion to mixed attainment classes.

Gendered, classed, and racialised patterns within attainment grouping

How young people are allocated to sets in practice was one of main questions in this research study. We found that nearly a third of pupils (31%) in our 'business as usual' control group of schools in the Best Practice in Setting (BPS) trial were 'misallocated' to attainment sets in maths, compared to what would have been predicted by using Key Stage 2 results (Connolly et al., forthcoming). Our analysis of the baseline school-reported set levels for maths and English (see Archer et al., 2018) revealed that, in those schools that used setting, there were significant differences in the composition of sets by pupil gender, ethnicity, social class, and free school meals (FSM) status. For instance, boys were more likely to find themselves in bottom sets for English than girls (boys comprised 60% of pupils in bottom sets for English, compared with 40% of girls). Conversely, significantly more boys than girls were in the top set for mathematics (56% of boys, and 44% of girls). Hence these patterns reflect longstanding gender stereotypes (see Francis & Skelton, 2008; Riegle-Crumb & Humphries, 2012). Looking at data in terms of classed patterns, less privileged pupils from low socio-economic status households and those eligible for FSM were significantly more likely to be in middle and lower sets for both English and mathematics. Again, this reflects trends long-established in existing literature (e.g. Jackson, 1964; Ball, 1981; Muijs & Dunne, 2010). There were also differences in ethnicity, with White pupils being significantly more likely to be in top sets for English (81%) and mathematics (77%), whereas Black and mixed-ethnicity children (and Asian pupils in the case of English) were more likely to be in lower sets for both subjects.

Moreover, we showed that these patterns did not simply reflect inequalities in prior attainment. Our additional analysis of pupils that had been misallocated compared to their Key Stage 2 attainment found that Black pupils were 2.54 times more likely to be misallocated to lower sets for maths than White pupils (Connolly et al., forthcoming). Asian heritage pupils were also slightly more likely to be misallocated to a lower set than their White counterparts. Gender patterns were also evident, with girls more likely to be misallocated to lower sets for maths, and boys for English. These deeply disturbing findings suggest that patterns in set placement reflecting unequal starting points are also compounded by bias.

So, we can see that setting reflects and illuminates inequitable social and educational trends. We have therefore argued that setting could be viewed as an educational technology that both reflects and reproduces the interests of dominant social groups, by reproducing relations of privilege (see Archer et al., 2018). The distribution of pupils across sets reflects interactions of gendered, classed, and racialised power relations that are produced by (and in turn perpetuate) a number of dominant social hierarchies and cultural assumptions. These include: the gendered nature of subjects (namely the association of mathematics with masculinity and English with femininity); the classed nature of 'ability' (the concentration of middle-class pupils in top sets and working-class pupils in lower sets); and the cultural dominance of 'whiteness' (White pupils being more likely to be directed to top sets, Black pupils to low sets).

The raced, classed, and gendered institutional cultures, discourses and practices are interconnected with young people's learner identities, social relations, and actions (Francis, 2000; Gillborn & Youdell, 2000; Archer, 2003; Youdell, 2006; Richards, 2017). Attainment grouping, research has suggested, helps to configure young people's naturalisation of ideas around 'ability' and 'merit' within and beyond schools, with working-class pupils being most affected by school messages about their 'ability' identity (Abraham, 1995; Hamilton, 2002). The widespread exposure to hierarchical notions of 'ability' also shape young people's experiences in mixed attainment classes. Disadvantaged pupils were found to rationalise unequal treatment in the mixed attainment context by differences in academic 'ability' and 'behaviour' among learners (Gillborn & Youdell, 2000).

And, despite liking mixed attainment mathematics, 'average' pupils were found to implicitly prioritise the potential needs of the high attainers, expressing concerns about whether 'excellence' [sic] students were stretched enough in mixed attainment classes (Walls, 2009, p. 192). Studies in the US on de-tracking threw light on the complex interplay of cultural and political issues within these spaces, mediated by racial and socio-economic tensions, as well as constructions of academic competence amongst students and teachers in the classroom (Rubin, 2003, 2008; Bixby, 2006; Modica, 2015). For example, Rubin's (2003) ethnography has demonstrated that daily events and interactions in a de-tracked classroom reinforced minority students' prior negative understandings about their social and academic possibilities. Another study argued that when low tracks get dismantled 'without altering prevailing hierarchies in schools' even higher-attaining students from minority ethnic backgrounds feel unwelcome in culturally isolating high-track classes where they sense lack of respect (Yonezawa et al., 2002, p. 40).

While classed, gendered, and raced identities were mostly implicit in our qualitative research with young people, we felt that young people's position in the 'ability' hierarchy of schools cross-cut social identities. When asked about views on setting and mixed attainment practice pupils commonly evoked discourses of 'ability' and 'merit' in relation to their experiences and senses of themselves and others as learners. We suggest that measurement, categorisation and differentiation practices in school and associated discourses around 'ability' provide a useful framework for examining young people's attitudes to grouping practices. We therefore adopt an 'attainment' perspective in the rest of the chapter. Prior research has also repeatedly indicated that learners of different attainment levels could have different views on and experiences of grouping practices (Hallam & Ireson, 2006). We begin by outlining the views of the pupils in the surveys.

Attainment patterns in perceptions of setting: what surveys tell us

One part of our surveys asked pupils taught in sets and in mixed attainment classes to tell us about their views on setting. This 'perceptions-of-setting' component contained 17 statements, to which participants were asked to respond on a five-point scale from strongly disagree to strongly agree.[1] The means of the 'perceptions-of-setting' variable shown in Tables 5.1 and 5.2 reveal that, on

TABLE 5.1 Means of perceptions of setting, by type of grouping in maths

	Sets	*Mixed*	*Overall difference*
	M	*M*	*Sig. (p)*
Year 7	3.66	3.55	<.001
Year 8	3.41	3.37	.005

TABLE 5.2 Means of perceptions of setting, by type of grouping in English

	Sets	Mixed	Overall difference
	M	M	Sig. (p)
Year 7	3.67	3.56	<.001
Year 8	3.42	3.38	.013

average, pupils in sets reported more positive perceptions of setting than pupils who were taught in mixed attainment classes. Moreover, there is a slight, but statistically significant, drop in means in Year 8, suggesting that both cohorts of pupils developed more negative perceptions of setting over two years in secondary school, including a sharper drop for those in sets.

Looking closely at the means of pupils taught in sets, Table 5.3 suggests that there are overall differences between the perceptions of setting among pupils in highest, middle, and lowest sets. These differences in attitudes are statistically significant, both among pupils in maths and English sets in Year 7 and Year 8. Consistent with the above finding, over time pupils in all sets become less positive about setting.[2] Pupils in the bottom set have the lowest mean score on the scale, indicating that they hold the least positive perceptions of setting (see also Archer et al., 2018).

We found more similarities among pupils in mixed attainment classes than among pupils taught in sets. The differences in mean scores on the 'perceptions-of-setting' attitudinal scale were small, and notably non-significant among pupils taught in mixed attainment classes in Year 7. However, in line with other research (Kutscher & Linchevski, 2000; Hallam & Ireson, 2006) and our modelling of baseline data (see Archer et al., 2018), we also found that pupils of low prior attainment become more negative about setting than other attainment groups after two years in mixed attainment classes. Our analysis of the young people's interviews later in the chapter suggests that these low-attaining pupils' greater negativity towards setting indicates enjoyment of mixed attainment grouping.

TABLE 5.3 Means of pupil perceptions of setting, by set level

	[1] Highest set	[2] Middle sets	[3] Lowest set	Overall difference	Paired differences		
					[1–2]	[1–3]	[2–3]
	M	M	M	Sig. (p)	Sig. (p)	Sig. (p)	Sig. (p)
Year 7: maths	3.71	3.64	3.56	<.001	<.001	<.001	.006
Year 8: maths	3.47	3.40	3.31	<.001	<.001	<.001	<.001
Year 7: English	3.71	3.65	3.63	.004	.005	.176	1.000
Year 8: English	3.46	3.40	3.33	<.001	.003	.002	.180

Young people's 'negative' views of setting: who and why

The qualitative data largely supported the quantitative analysis in that more pupils from lower sets tended to say that they did not like being in these sets and would prefer to 'move up' (see also Hallam & Ireson, 2007). When asked how they felt about being in the lower sets, Bobby, James, and Lydia were typical in their replies:

> Dumb, just not as smart as them [friends in higher sets].
>
> *(Bobby, Set 5 maths, Set 3 English, Irish,*
> *middle SES, School P)*

> Because I'm in Set 4 I feel a bit embarrassed about that because other people are in the higher sets.
>
> *(James, Set 4 maths, Set 2 English, White British,*
> *low SES, School B)*

> Bad. I feel like I can do better.
>
> *(Lydia, Set 4 English, Set 2 maths, White Other,*
> *low SES, School C)*

These comments about feeling 'embarrassed' and 'bad' convey a notion of stigma in which low sets are associated with inferiority. These feelings were summed up powerfully by Nissa (Set 5 maths, Set 2 English, White and African, higher SES, School C), who said 'I almost died' on finding out that he had been allocated to the bottom maths set. He further explains:

> For maths I'm in the bottom set and it was hard for me to tell my mum because I thought she'd be disappointed. But because in English I'm in Set 2 my mum is proud of me, like really proud, and I was proud saying it.

Perhaps not surprisingly, Nissa argued in his interview that set placement affects the way that students think about their abilities, and whether they enjoy school. Likewise, Hakeem's (Sets 3 English and maths, African, low SES, School S) words evoke embarrassed frustration, hierarchisation, and the equation of being in a low set with being 'dumb':

> [W]hen we did our end of year assessments, Set 1 and Set 2 got different papers which were a lot harder than ours, but then Set 3, Set 4, Set 5, and Set 6 would, like, get the same paper which will make us feel dumb because, like, someone's smart but like they've got to do the dumb, lower paper, because of their set.

Indeed, various of the pupils' interviews exemplified shame and anxiety experienced in inhabiting the 'pathologised space' (Reay, 2015) of the bottom set. Unsurprisingly, pupils, particularly those closest to the bottom set, expressed their relief that they had (for now) avoided or escaped being allocated to the most-disparaged grouping:

> Well, I used to be in Set 5, then I moved up to Set 4, so I'm happy now, because I've moved up. Set 4 is one of the better classes to be in.
>
> *(Levon, Set 4 maths, Set 2 English, White and*
> *Black Caribbean, middle SES, School C)*

> Yeah, I don't mind. It's better than being in Set 5.
>
> *(Emily, Set 4 maths, Set 1 English, White Other,*
> *low SES, School C)*

As we have argued elsewhere (Archer et al., 2018), these articulations from pupils reflect the 'hidden injuries' (Sennett & Cobb, 1972/1993) of labelling and social hierarchisation – such as the 'embarrassment' and recognition of being ascribed 'the lowest' through allocation to the bottom set – that are experienced by pupils who have to inhabit such positions of inferiority. Such experiences ought not to be considered lightly by educators.

Young people at the top of the setting hierarchy displayed awareness of the negative impact the practice of attainment grouping had on some pupils:

> They think they've been put in that set because they think they're not as good as some other people. So that could harm in what they think about themselves and coming to school.
>
> *(Brad, Sets 1 English and maths, White British,*
> *low SES, School W)*

> I think they might like feel a bit deflated, like they might wake up and they might not want to go to school because they might be in the bottom set and they just like don't want to go.
>
> *(Elsa, Sets 1 English and maths, White British,*
> *middle SES, School P)*

> Because if you're in a lower set you might think that you're never going to make it to the top set and it might affect what your achievements are.
>
> *(Nafisa, Sets 1 English and maths, Pakistani,*
> *higher SES, School T)*

However, for many of these pupils the practice seemed justifiable on the basis of 'natural' talent, ability, and meritocracy (see Archer et al., 2018). The concerns of top set pupils, such as remarks about teachers' excessively high expectations across the whole range of subjects, are nothing like the concerns of those who find themselves in lower sets. In some schools our research participants complained about set bullying. In the following extract, pupils who were in Set 3 (out of 5) for maths in School X speak eloquently about the impact of setting on differentiation and polarisation culture within school – the concept developed and documented in earlier sociological studies conducted in the UK (Hargreaves, 1967; Lacey, 1970; Ball, 1981).

Sauba:	I feel like some people, well, a lot of people, I think everybody, they feel like, when they look at their thing and they think, 'Oh, I'm in Set 5,' they get upset. And it's embarrassing to walk into, like, a Set 5 class, or a Set 4 class.
Raad:	Yeah, they tease you.
Sauba:	Yeah.
Interviewer:	Do they?
All:	Yeah.
Interviewer:	Have you seen that happen?
All:	Yeah.
Interviewer:	What sort of things happen?
Sauba:	It's like, 'Shut up, you're dumb, you're in Set 5. I'm smarter than you,' just that, you know. And I think that can bring down people's self-esteem.
Afraima:	And they just brag about what they've got, like, high marks and stuff like that, and we're just like, 'Hello?'

Furthermore, some narratives point to hierarchies of social and academic status within lower ranges of attainment grouping too, supporting prior findings by Ball (1981) and Gillborn and Youdell (2000):

> When your friends are waiting for you they say, 'What set are you in?' They can say like, 'Set 4' but that's better than being in Set 5.
> *(Nissa, Set 5 maths, Set 2 English, White and African,*
> *higher SES, School C)*

In this discussion of the impact of attainment grouping on pupil social relations and status in school, it is important to bear in mind that time is experienced differently by children to adults: one of us has discussed elsewhere how days and years at school stretch out for young people (their school days being literally most of their lifetime at this point), who have no choice but to attend (Francis, 2000). Consequently, within this intense and encompassing world of school, the importance of social relations and status within school for pupils' daily lives and perceptions of self cannot be understated. Status with peers, and self-pride, are vital defences for thriving within an often highly hierarchised and challenging social world of school peer relations, and our analysis shows how they may be damaged or bolstered by attainment grouping, depending on high/low group allocation.

The pupils in lower sets were the most likely to raise questions about the legitimacy of set allocation, notably complaining that their efforts and improvements in attainment did not translate into set movement. As we shall discuss in Chapter 7, the majority of teachers in our study were sceptical about the benefits of set movement. Yet, several pupils complained in despair that they could not understand why they 'never seem to move on' despite doing 'my best'. For example:

> [I]t makes me think, 'Why can't I be taught with everyone else who's in the top group?' And then I try my best and I do try my best. Even though it's my best and I get put low – not low – but in a different group than the high group, so it feels like if that's my best and this is all I can do, what can I do?
>
> *(Martina, Sets 3 English and maths, mixed heritage, low SES, School D)*

As we discuss later in the chapter, young people accept that set allocation is a process dominated by the decisions of teachers, but believe that hard work should be rewarded. Therefore, some, like the boys below, seriously question why their improved attainment does not translate into moving up a set:

> I actually don't like it [setting] because sometimes they can, like, mix you up and they might think you've done bad when you actually didn't do bad. And last year they put me in the wrong set, yeah, and the teacher that I had, she always complained about me but I always kept on doing good stuff and she never said anything. So now after I had this test, just because a person got higher than me I can't move up.
>
> *(Mukthar, Set 6 English, Set 3 maths, Bangladeshi, low SES, School S)*

> And then some teachers would say you might be moving up, but in the end, you don't move up.
>
> *(Hakeem, Sets 3 English and maths, African, low SES, School S)*

The pupils' confusion hints at how discourses and organisational patterns within school can work to hide the operation of power, or practices that perpetuate a range of inequalities, making it difficult to question and challenge the 'fairness' of particular practices.

Young people's 'positive' views of setting

It is important to note that, as the quantitative data reported at the beginning of this chapter shows, some young people had mostly positive attitudes to setting. Their explanations are discussed below in light of the wider discourses around 'positive' aspects of attainment grouping.

'It's just the right level for me'

We have previously discussed (see Archer et al., 2018) that higher-set pupils often felt deserving of their place and conversely, they tended to believe that pupils in lower sets were also deserving of their position. For instance, in the following quote Tylor reproduces a popular view (see Francis et al., 2017a) that practice of segregation by 'ability' caters for assumed 'natural' differences between the pupils:

> [. . .] maybe, you have some more intelligent people and that is just what has happened. [. . .] That's how you develop and stuff.
>
> *(Tylor, Sets 1 English and maths, White British,*
> *middle SES School R)*

This comment is congruent with the internalisation and reproduction of what Archer et al. (2018) refer to as a 'cultural arbitrary', in which pupil educational outcomes are seen as the product of 'natural' talent and 'ability'. The implication of this would be that the practice of setting is not, in itself, unfair, and does not play a role in producing differential outcomes. It appears from young people's reflections below that they believe that setting is in place to enable all pupils, and particularly those who 'don't have much learning abilities', to work on the 'appropriate' level:

> Children that don't have as much learning abilities, yeah, they could be put down into lower groups so that as they go on they can move up, so that they don't get hard work that they can't do and they don't understand.
>
> *(Robin, Sets 1 English and maths, White and Black*
> *Caribbean, middle SES, School C)*

> But I think that's good. I think obviously it has to upset you being in some, but I think it's all for, kind of . . . it's good for you because you don't want to be being stretched more than you can be stretched.
>
> *(Monica, Sets 1 English and maths, White British,*
> *unknown SES, School D)*

In a similar vein, although evidently disappointed about being recently moved down to Set 2, Makeen (African, middle SES, School S) tries to negotiate a positive learner identity for herself, citing an improved understanding and a slower pace of work as beneficial for her learning:

Interviewer: How do you feel in Set 2?

Makeen: Erm, I don't feel so bad that I am down because it's actually the right pace for me and I think it's more beneficial so I feel like I understand it much more since then.

Interviewer
[to Zainub]: How do you feel in Set 1, now that you've moved up?

Zainub: Yes, I feel quite proud that I moved up but like when people move down, like Makeen, I don't think it's a bad thing. People might think it's a bad thing like to move down but I don't think that. I think it's, like, just to fit you, so, yes.

Zainub's (Sets 1 English and maths, Pakistani, middle SES) sympathetic remark that it is not 'a bad thing' to move down because 'it's just to fit you' illustrates the awkward moral management all pupils have to involve themselves in to construct setting in justifiable terms in alignment with the dominant school order.

But what about the views of learners in the low sets? We found that approximately half of the pupils in lower sets said they were broadly satisfied with their set placement and offered various reasons to rationalise their placement. These pupils strongly identify with 'levels' attained at standardised tests at the end of primary school, supporting prior research findings on the 'regulatory' function of such assessment on learners, whereby they come to view themselves and their peers 'in terms of the levels to which [their] performance in the SATs is ascribed' (Reay & Wiliam, 1999, p. 346).

Interviewer: Bottom as well. How do you like being in that set?
Poppy: I quite like it because it's like I mostly understand it because it's like my level, so I don't mind it.

(Set 3 English, Set 5 maths, White British, low SES, School P)

Interviewer: Would you prefer to be in another set?
Janet: No, because I think my school knows best for me and they don't want to give me anything that's too hard for my abilities.

(Set 4 English, Set 3 maths, African, unknown SES, School C)

We found that even those pupils who described their work in low sets as 'easy' were cautious (e.g. 'I don't really know what other sets are like' – Bobby, Irish, middle SES, School P) or even anxious about moving to a higher set (e.g. 'out of my comfort' – Helen, White British, middle SES, School U). Bobby's and Helen's self-doubt resonates with teachers' constructions of students in low attainment groups as dependent learners who benefit from specific pedagogic approaches, including a slower pace of delivery, repetition, and rehearsal, more one-to-one time with the teacher and the like (Dunne et al., 2011; McGillicuddy & Devine, 2018; Mazenod et al., 2019). These discourses and practices, explored further in Chapter 6, shape some pupils' views that setting is designed to 'protect' low-set pupils from 'feel[ing] bad' (Ella, Sets 3 English and maths, White British, low SES, School Q). Furthermore, the discourses which position low-set learners as dependent, slow, and unconfident have justified segregation by attainment for some pupils in low attainment groups. These pupils also sometimes showed appreciation of pedagogical approaches associated with bottom sets, such as small class sizes, and those that often have been seen in academic literature as unhelpfully reflective of low expectations. For example, Luke (Set 5 maths, Set 3 English, White British, higher SES, School P) explains, 'I like that they don't pressure you because you're slightly lower and they like help you if you need help'.

We have also found pupils in lower sets using a range of methods for seeking defence from Othering and deficit positioning (Klein, 1952, 1963; Lucey & Reay, 2002), including 'moral defence' (see Celani, 2010), internalisation, and/or more ambivalent responses (see Francis et al., 2017b for elaboration). For example, Kevin (Set 4 maths, White Other, low SES, School C) appears to have internalised his set level, explaining:

> I've heard people, they like freak out about being moved down a set and then they even get jealous if people get moved up a set. It's like, 'Don't worry about it. Just get used to it'.

Kevin's fatalistic approach may defend against the vulnerable, engaged approach Kevin projects onto others. However, his apparently nonchalant and resigned 'embrace' of his low group status potentially has negative consequences for his ambitions and his learning, besides raising questions about the psychic implications of this approach. It is notable that Kevin (and the other pupils quoted in this chapter) is *only in Year 7* – the start of his secondary schooling. Yet his psychological defence precipitates him into already 'opting out' of hopes and engagement with his own education. Significantly also, Kevin is a White working class boy – member of a group about which British educationalists frequently express concern due to their comparative underachievement (and 'lower aspiration') (see e.g. Páll Sveinsson, 2009 for discussion; Reay, 2002). White working class boys are among the key groups over-represented in low attainment groups. Given the masculine propensity to opt out of competitions that can't be won (see Francis, 2000 for discussion of this phenomenon in the classroom; Jackson, 2002), Kevin's case highlights a strong hypothesis that attainment grouping may contribute to working class boys' well-recorded disengagement with schooling, impacting in turn their educational attainment. Research is needed to explore this hypothesis more closely.

Individualised responsibility, and meritocracy

Pupils frequently presented the hierarchy of setting as a meritocracy, underpinned by a 'natural' order, but wherein if you were 'good enough' you would move up. For example, Tavi (Set 1 English, Set 2 maths, unknown ethnicity, low SES, School B) points out below that teachers commonly employ this discourse to motivate pupils.

Interviewer:	And what about the low sets, Set number 3 or Set number 4 for that?
Adam:	They try and achieve higher.
Tavi:	They try and achieve higher.
Adam:	They work harder.
Tavi:	They need to try to do . . . the teacher says that when you go to Set 3 or Set 2 it doesn't actually matter. You'll be learning the same thing, but in an easier way. But if you try even harder than the teacher's explaining to you, you might have a chance to go on to a level higher.

Other pupils across the schools also construct movement between sets as a real possibility, like these learners from lower sets:

> If you're in a lower set, you're going to have to get easier work, so that you can understand it, so you can work up to a higher set.
>
> *(Janet, Set 4 English, Set 3 maths, African, unknown SES, School C)*

> I mean, if the teachers think that you are not as advancing as well as others, then they should put you down. But they should say not to worry about it, and once they get more used to it, they are going to be moved back up.
>
> *(Kevin, Set 4 maths, White Other, low SES, School B)*

> Just because you're in Set 5 maybe next week you probably might move up to Set 4 or something like that. So it doesn't mean that you always stay in Set 5 or the low set. You'll still be able to do what you normally do in Set 5 but I just think sometimes some people put themselves down a bit thinking 'oh, I'm going to stay in Set 5 forever'. So it will probably take, like, a month for me to move up to Set 4.
>
> *(Naomi, Set 5 maths, Caribbean, middle SES, School X)*

Hence pupils were optimistic about set movement. Relatedly, some participants constructed lower sets as motivational rather than harmful for learner self-confidence (see Chapter 4). Malik, a higher set pupil, and Mansoora, a low-set pupil, both argue that being in low sets could be viewed as a positive challenge:

> If you're in a lower set it's basically kind of like a challenge so you want to get to the higher set.
>
> *(Malik, Set 1 English, Set 2 maths, African, middle SES, School C)*

> Yes, it, kind of, pressures students, like, into thinking that they're not doing well so then they challenge themselves and, like, revise more and learn more so then they could get up to the higher set.
>
> *(Mansoora, Set 5 maths, mixed/multiple ethnicity, middle SES, School X)*

As we discuss elsewhere (Francis et al., 2017b), such views illustrate a faith in meritocracy and work ethic: set designation is seen as reflecting merit and rewarding excellence, and placement in a lower set is envisaged to incentivise hard work and 'determination' to move upwards. Again, note the assumption that was prevalent in these articulations that students will *want* to move up, and the implications for self-perception among those students that don't/can't. However, pupils' faith in fair meritocratic reward for hard work is unfortunately not borne out by research. As we explained in Chapter 2, the evidence shows that actually, once pupils are placed in a set or stream they are likely to stay there irrespective of performance – and in Chapter 7 we explain some of the practical explanations for this lack of fluidity. In this light, pupils' articulations of faith in meritocratic fairness are lent pathos. The discourse of meritocracy transfers responsibility for success or failure on individual learners, and inculcates a naive faith in the redemption of 'moving up'. In Foucauldian terms, this can be seen as an exemplification of governmentality, whereby individual subjects (in this case, pupils) actively interpolate the discourses that regulate them and 'buy in' to these processes of self-governance that then require no coercion (Foucault, 1980; Rose, 1999).

Mixed attainment grouping as experienced by learners at low, middle, and high prior attainment

In this section we attend to the perceptions of pupils experiencing mixed attainment teaching, with a focus on the respective views of those with different levels of prior attainment. Prior studies indicate that students could have different experiences according to their attainment levels. For example, Kutscher and Linchevski (2000) found that low- and middle-attaining pupils preferred learning mathematics in mixed groups, while results were more variable for those with high prior attainment. There is further evidence that less confident learners dislike the competitive and stressful environment of top sets (Boaler, 1997), while studies with 'gifted and talented' students have found a stronger preference for homogeneously grouped classes (Shields, 2002; Adams-Byers et al., 2004). Likewise, in Hallam and Ireson's (2006) large-scale survey, a greater proportion of pupils in bottom sets for all curriculum subjects expressed preference for mixed attainment classes compared to those in middle and top sets.

Our content analysis of pupil interviews and focus groups about their views and experiences of mixed attainment revealed a mixed picture, where nonetheless more pupils were consistently positive than negative about mixed attainment grouping (see Tereshchenko et al., 2018). We now turn to consider the reasons that each group of pupils offered, as well as the key differences found between pupils of different prior attainment levels.

High-attaining pupils: between equity and individualism

We found that half (18 out of 35) the high-attaining pupils spoke positively about their mixed attainment classes, and a further nine pupils discussed both positive and negative aspects of mixed attainment grouping. A significant proportion of pupils who expressed positive views drew on equity discourses that emphasised the ability of this grouping system to support fairness and equality of opportunity. The majority of the pupils believed that mixed attainment promoted the academic inclusion of peers at lower attainment levels through access to the curriculum content, and perhaps to the pedagogy, that in the setting system would be 'deemed beyond the "bottom" stream' (Abraham, 1995, p. 15).

> [L]ess able at maths, they get taught the same thing as people who are more able and so they're not like left behind.
>
> *(Lara, White British, higher SES, School K)*

> [I]f there's like a class of lower achieving students [. . .] they wouldn't have that much like ability to share with the other students, whereas if you're a higher student, you can easily share ideas with them.
>
> *(Gary, White British, higher SES, School M)*

Many respondents with high prior attainment valued the social inclusivity of mixed attainment grouping. Chris (White British, higher SES, School E) found the diversity of mixed classes interesting: 'I do quite like the mixed groups because you get to see what other people are thinking'. In some ways, being in mixed attainment classes shaped these pupils' support of the education system where, to quote Abraham (2008), the 'needs' of at least some higher attainers are related to 'helping others' as opposed to just 'striving ahead' (p. 861). Offering help to others was also framed as a benefit to their own learning, not just to the learning of those at low attainment level – the view that coheres with research on the positive effects of cooperative learning on highest attainers and those offering explanations (Slavin, 1996). For example, Muna (South Asian, higher SES, School F) thought that 'if you're helping another person maybe you learn something new'. Likewise, Evelyn (White British, higher SES, School N) argued, 'if the higher level students are helping the lower level, they might learn some more by helping them as well'.

High-attaining pupils from other schools also described how the inclusive mixed attainment pedagogy could fill potential gaps in their knowledge and deepen their understanding:

> [T]hen while they're teaching sort of the lower level, the higher levels can maybe listen to things that they've missed out on when they've been away or something.
>
> *(Evelyn, White British, higher SES, School N)*

> [S]ay you're quite good and you forget about the easy stuff, you learn from the ones that aren't as good because they just keep going through the easy stuff.
>
> *(Simon, White British, low SES, School K)*

Yet, despite recognising that mixed attainment supported equity, many high-attaining pupils were also academically competitive and adopted a meritocratic view of education – that equality of opportunity implies maximising the potential of individual pupils in accordance with their merit (i.e. 'abilities').

The high-attaining pupils who expressed negative views of the mixed attainment grouping tended to describe their lessons as being 'easy', 'boring', 'a bit dull', 'slow', and 'not challenging enough'. The quote below captures such sentiments:

> Then the bright kids, it's quite hard for them because when we have the easy stuff, it bores them quite easily because they can just do it and then they're sitting there because they've done it and there's not much for them to do because they find it so easy.
>
> *(Camilla, White British, higher SES, School E)*

On the one hand, as further discussed in Chapter 8, these concerns relate to a recognised challenge of meeting the varied 'needs' of pupils within mixed attainment classes (Hart, 1992). Some previous work described a lack of appropriate change in the teaching approaches and content of the lessons in schools which adopted all attainment teaching (cf. Ball, 1981), where, as Rubin (2008) found, higher attainers could be 'bored' with 'stuff that I kind of already knew' (p. 687), and even lower attainers felt their 'classes were easy, so I didn't have a challenge' (p. 665). However, given that we do not have evidence of such uninspiring pedagogy in our study schools, it might be that the views and learner identities of the high-attaining pupils in our sample have been influenced earlier by attainment structures and cultures in primary schools. We found that many pupils had experienced attainment grouping prior to arrival at secondary school, and Yonezawa et al. (2002) maintain that 'students who are labelled gifted in elementary school develop a habitus of entitlement' (p. 52).

Several high-attaining pupils in our study used the language of 'behaviour', rather than 'ability', to justify their desire to be kept apart from 'distracting students' who 'mess around' and, supposedly, 'just don't really enjoy the subject' (Felicity, White British, higher SES, School K). The majority of the young people however described mixed attainment grouping as limiting their individual academic progress, thus reproducing the 'common sense' view supported by most politicians, teachers, and parents that pupils are best engaged in learning on their level of 'ability' (see Francis et al., 2017a for discussion).

Furthermore, high-attaining pupils have been previously described as operating according to the pragmatic code of 'making the grade' (Becker et al., 1968, quoted in Bixby, 2006, p. 119). The following quote exemplifies their instrumental focus on certification, alongside recognition that mixed attainment is good for pupils at lower level of attainment:

> I think it benefits the lower-ish people because they feel encouraged to do better but the higher people, they might not feel pushed enough to get better grades.
>
> *(Alice, South Asian, higher SES, School A)*

These views by the pupils highlight the need to recognise the challenge of implementing mixed attainment in a context infused by individualistic interests, investments, and desires, and resistance from those who perceive benefit from the separation by 'ability' within the comprehensive system (see, for example, Oakes et al., 1997; Reay et al., 2011; Burris, 2014). Indeed, Loveless (2009) found that suburban schools serving students from higher socio-economic backgrounds were least likely to respond to the US policy recommendations on de-tracking. It is possible, however, that effectively differentiated teaching in heterogeneous classes (discussed in Chapter 8) could contribute to resolving the tensions between the higher-attaining pupils individualistic orientations and their support for the learning and social benefits, and egalitarian principles of mixed attainment grouping related to reduction of inequality.

Low-attaining pupils: between 'empowered' and 'positioned' learner identities

It was notable that a great majority of low prior attainers enjoyed learning in mixed attainment classes. Sixteen out of 21 of these pupils strongly appreciated mixed attainment grouping for its inclusive and collaborative environment. Many articulated a strong awareness of a range of opportunities available to them due to the conditions in mixed attainment classrooms. For example, Mabel (White British, middle SES, School M) appreciated access to a less stratified curriculum – a chance she would not have had in the bottom set to learn about 'what the good people are doing' and thus being able to realise 'what you are good at'. Likewise, being exposed to 'what [others] are doing' helped Rania (South Asian, middle SES, School F) 'see things that I am able to do'. Debbie (White British, low SES, School O) noted that, where attainment grouping segregates pupils socially as well as by attainment, mixed attainment grouping facilitated the ability to 'talk [things] through and make friends and then that could, like, help with your work'. Although Debbie's classmate Colm (White British, low SES, School O) initially had doubts about whether he belonged in mixed classes, being 'really nervous' about sitting 'next to the smart people', he later changed his perception of his learning capacity and came to believe that being taught in a mixed attainment class would open up his opportunities beyond the school, including 'a better job', 'a nice family' and 'a nice house'. By contrast, in Ireson and Hallam's (2001) study of setting, the better long-term prospects such as 'good jobs' and 'lots of money' were associated among low-set pupils with top sets, while students in lower sets were described as 'left for unemployment' (p. 98).

That young people are aware of how mixed attainment grouping facilitates opportunities to learn and get help from peers has been previously identified in literature (Hallam & Ireson, 2007). In the maths classroom where pupils worked in homogeneous groups, lower prior attainers reportedly accomplished very little on their own without the input of more competent peers or teachers (Kutscher & Linchevski, 2000). Collaborative work in mixed attainment maths classes, on the other hand, allowed learners who were regarded as weaker 'to shine in some areas' (Boaler et al., 2000, p. 645). Most of our interviews reflected these issues:

> I think it's better because since there's different abilities, you can help some people and some other people can help you in return. So then you get extra help for like if you're in one of the lowers with loads of people who aren't very good at maths and there's only like one teacher then you can't get other students to help you.
>
> *(Adele, School N, White British, middle SES)*

It is notable, given that low-attaining pupils are often constructed as benefitting from receiving help in mixed attainment classes, that Adele highlights the ability to help others as a benefit for all pupils, including low prior attainers. We found that while many higher attainers expressed preferences for individual learning at faster pace (see also Adams-Byers et al., 2004; Boaler, 1997), the learner identities of the lower prior attainers in mixed attainment classes were constituted by their preference for collaboration and shared responsibility for the learning of others. Asked about why they preferred mixed attainment classes, a number of our participants revealed the importance they attached to learning together as a community for mutual benefit:

> Because, like, as Furud said, it's 32 brains and from one brain everybody can learn and say if somebody got something wrong, other brains can help them and then they work on their own.
>
> *(Hichem, Arab, low SES, School L)*

> The fact that everybody around me is helpful and they can give you advice on the things you don't understand, and I can help other people gain more knowledge.
>
> *(Rania, Bangladeshi, middle SES, School F)*

The above comments speak to Hart et al.'s (2004) findings on the impact of teaching based on the principles of trust, co-agency, and community on young people's learner identities within classrooms free from ability labelling. They argue that such classrooms produce 'empowered learners' who take active responsibility for supporting one another's progress.

Nevertheless, a small number of respondents with low prior attainment expressed a dislike of mixed attainment practice. The following reason given by one of our study participants could appear to confirm the existing belief among the proponents of setting that low-attaining pupils would be intimidated and disheartened by challenging work and the faster pace of the mixed attainment lessons (see Hallam & Ireson, 2005; Mazenod et al., 2019; Rosenbaum, 1999).

> I'd prefer it if we were all the same level classes because then there's some people that have the same levels as me, not just all higher and it will be easier, I think.
>
> *(Lauren, White British, low SES, School K)*

Such views could be read in light of the self-fulfilling prophecy literature discussed in Chapter 4. Indeed, young people's 'levelled' aspirations and expectations, and their learner identities may be affected by the inferior position in the 'ability' hierarchy of the school (Boaler, 2008; Hart et al., 2004; Yonezawa et al., 2002). As the majority of our participants had had some experience of 'ability' grouping in primary school, it could be that they adopted what the system had already been communicating to them about their identities as learners (see Marks, 2016; Scherer, 2016; Walls, 2009), resulting in some of the pupils doubting their capacity to succeed in a more demanding mixed attainment environment. However, it is also plausible that some pupils that struggle with significant areas of academic work may feel intimidated by working with peers who appear never to.

It is noteworthy that low-attaining pupils with ambivalent views of mixed attainment grouping centred their criticism on a lack of attention to differentiation for pupils' individual needs that is considered 'pivotal to a fair system where all children are able to succeed' (Hart, 1992, cited in Taylor et al., 2015, p. 26).

> Sometimes it's really hard because the teachers think that we all understand it because there is higher people who do understand it and then they just move along.
>
> *(Haley, White British, middle SES, School N)*

> Because it's not really fair on the people who think like they can't do it, but then the teacher's like paying more attention to the people that have done it and just like, 'Oh yes, you've done really well'. When you like put your hand up and say, 'I don't really understand any of this', and they're just like, 'You'll get the hang of it'.
>
> *(Kayla, Irish, higher SES, School N)*

These pupils seem to agree with some of the negative remarks by the higher-attaining peers related to the practical implications of mixed attainment teaching. They also highlight the need to ensure special provision for struggling learners in mixed attainment classes to maximise their chances for academic success (Burris et al., 2008).

Middle-attaining pupils: comparison, competition, and status

Interestingly, our group of middle-attaining pupils seemed to be more ambivalent about mixed attainment than pupils of other attainment levels, with 12 pupils conveying positive views, 13 negative views and four mixed views. As we demonstrate next, their views were infused by the concerns regarding their status in the academic hierarchies of the school.

The pupils at middle attainment who held positive views of mixed attainment grouping focused on benefits for their own learning, in contrast with the pupils at high attainment level, who saw the benefits of mixed attainment primarily for low-attaining classmates. Asked about what she thought of mixed attainment grouping at her school, Shazana (South Asian, higher SES, School F) reflected,

> I think it's a really good idea because we can teach each other, rather than being at the same level and knowing the same things and not knowing the same things, so if I don't get something I will ask somebody who does.

Like most pupils with low prior attainment, the middle attainers thought that working with other pupils facilitated their progress. It was good to learn in a mixed class because 'you need other's help', said Maryam (Arab, low SES, School L).

Other participants noted that getting help or hearing from other pupils made them 'learn more from their answers' (Claire, White British, middle SES, School A), 'see what they agree with' and 'always [learn] something new' (Mehdi, White British, higher SES, School L).

We also found that this group of middle-attaining pupils appreciated 'equal work' (Vanita, South Asian, higher SES, School F). Their opposition to separation by attainment, described by one boy as 'favouritism towards the intelligent' (Josh, White British, middle SES, School O), might be explained by the worries middle attainers previously revealed in relation to their 'precarious' position in the 'ability' hierarchy of the schools – that 'they might indeed be assigned to the lower tracks in the following year' and, as a result, 'feel inferior' (Kutscher & Linchevski, 2000). Furthermore, several pupils made critical allusion to the limits imposed by attainment grouping on young people's learning and future opportunities:

> I just think that it's better for the school to like put different people together because it's not just about intelligent and lower because the lower people might have high dreams.
>
> *(Cara, White British, middle SES, School O)*

> I don't think it's fair to like split people because of their ability because then some people won't learn the things that they need to learn to get to university and go pass their GCSEs and A Levels.
>
> *(Kian, Black, low SES, School K)*

The issue of 'status' (e.g. feeling clever and respected – Hallam and Ireson (2006)) is implicit in the concerns of the pupils cited above. Anxieties around losing their 'status' within the 'ability' hierarchy shaped the negative views of mixed attainment among the other group of middle-attaining participants. The following allusion to the quick work pace of 'clever people' is significant for understanding the concerns of this group of pupils about their position in the academic 'race':

> It's like some stuff I know pretty well. It's just the other kids that don't know it. But sometimes I don't know the stuff, and then there's tons of clever people like racing ahead of me.
>
> *(Lee, White and Asian, higher SES, School E)*

Comparing themselves with high-attaining peers and assessing their 'ability' as inferior, those dissatisfied middle-attaining pupils felt 'frustrated', 'discouraged', and 'embarrassed' due to 'struggling' with the work they perceived as being 'hard' and, therefore, above their 'ability' level:

> Because certain people could be struggling and sometimes in certain lessons, I'm not the smartest person in the lesson, so they are giving out hard work and I don't understand it and they can't expect you to do it if it's mixed.
>
> *(Mary, White British, middle SES, School A)*

> I feel like I am, kind of, struggling on the work and everyone else gets it and stuff like that so I, kind of, feel a bit more discouraged if everyone else gets it and I don't and I also feel quite frustrated if that happens.
>
> *(Edie, White British, higher SES, School N)*

One key factor that seemed to contribute to the distress of middle-attaining pupils was the use of peer tutoring where high attainers were always placed in the role of the helper by teachers who are often pressured to provide challenge for 'the most able' (Ofsted, 2015). This left some pupils feeling 'babied' and even 'humiliated':

> [P]eople that have finished, they go round helping everyone else. I kind of find it a bit humiliating because I'm just sitting there and everyone knows that I haven't finished and everyone else has.
>
> *(Hilda, White British, middle SES, School E)*

These experiences suggest that the well-intentioned strategies adopted by teachers to cater for the needs of both high- and lower-attaining pupils can lower self-confidence, highlight differences, and even promote labelling and antagonism towards high attainers. For instance, high-attaining pupils were described as 'show-offs' by middle-attaining peers at School K. As Roberts (2016) argues, a less problematic solution to utilising the strengths of pupils of different attainment is to find ways to place 'the more capable peer' in role as 'a co-collaborator in the learning process', rather than 'a teacher of those less capable' (p. 44).

Finally, a small number of participants bemoaned the presence of low-attaining pupils in their classes. These pupils openly distanced themselves from low-attaining peers whom they described as being 'at different stages', 'hard to cooperate' with, 'asking loads of questions', 'stopping the whole class from doing their work', and the like. Suzanna (White and Black African, low SES, School A) voiced a typical view:

> I don't like working with people who are mixed abilities because say people who aren't as high a level as us, they could be just asking loads of questions, 'I don't understand', and stopping the whole class from doing their work when you just want to get it done and go home.

These views are similar to the discourses of competitive individualism by high-attaining pupils. However, a notably larger portion of high attainers in our sample were more cooperative than these middle attainers and open to the idea of providing assistance to pupils of low prior attainment. This further highlights the point that the necessity of pupils to navigate and assert their place in the learnt 'ability' hierarchy of the school might take priority over values of fairness and social responsibility.

Chapter summary

This chapter started by presenting data on the unequal distribution of learners across sets by gender, social class, and ethnic background, and patterns of mis/allocation. Then we considered the attitudes of young people to setting in surveys, concluding that overall pupils in sets have more positive attitudes than pupils in mixed attainment classes. While pupils in low sets predictably displayed most negative attitudes to setting, we also highlighted our novel finding that pupils in all sets become significantly more negative about setting over two years in secondary school. We also discussed the negative implications of attainment grouping for social identities of pupils with respect to stigmatisation of being in a low set, and the negative impact of attainment grouping within peer social hierarchies. Yet, we have shown in this chapter that the setting practice seemed justifiable for many high- and low-set pupils on the basis of 'natural' talent, 'ability', and meritocracy. They believed that set placement directly reflects merit, and that those in lower groups who excel will be rewarded by moving up, while those in higher groups who make less progress will be moved down accordingly. As we observe above, evidence suggests that in fact practice in schools frequently does not reflect these assumptions (see Flores, 1999; Dunne et al., 2007; Dunne et al., 2011; Hallam & Ireson, 2005). Indeed, set placement based exclusively on prior attainment, and rigorous periodic set movement (again based exclusively on prior attainment) are two of the requirements demanded within our BPS intervention. Often schools have found these measures hard to implement in practice for a variety of reasons (see Chapter 7).

With respect to young people's experiences of mixed attainment grouping, and in line with other research, we found that this approach to pupil grouping was especially appreciated by those at low prior attainment. However, our analysis somewhat challenges prior research findings on the proportions of higher attainers that do not support mixed attainment, and suggests a more nuanced picture in which many high and middle attainers also appreciate aspects of mixed attainment grouping. While in 'setted' schools pupils in top sets tend to prefer setting (Hallam & Ireson, 2006), we highlighted many high-attaining pupils' commitment to communitarianism and social justice that they felt underpinned mixed attainment practice. The middle attainers who spoke positively about mixed attainment also felt the practice indicated that their school was committed to equity. However, our analysis also highlighted that a small number of low-attaining pupils appeared to doubt their ability to succeed in heterogeneous classes, while some higher-attaining pupils expressed entitlement to preferential treatment. The negative views of pupils also suggest that it is important to distinguish between mixed attainment *grouping* and mixed attainment *teaching*. It appears that some of the complaints relate to the teaching approaches where mixed attainment lessons are designed for the 'average' pupil. Thus, some lower-attaining pupils may feel 'left behind', while higher-attaining pupils may feel 'a bit held back'. We discuss the implications of these findings in relation to teachers' views on the challenges and promises of mixed attainment practice in Chapter 8.

Notes

1 A composite variable was created from these items for comparison of pupils' mean attitudes to setting across and within the two trials, as well as over time. Young people's perceptions were scored (on the scale 1–5) so that higher mean scores reflect agreeing with positive aspects of setting and disagreeing with negative aspects of setting.

2 Further nuances in the attitudes of different sub-groups of pupils were identified by paired-group statistical tests. While pupils in different mathematics sets held significantly different views on setting, both in Year 7 and Year 8, the picture is not consistent across English sets. The means of pupils in the middle and lowest English sets did not differ significantly in Year 7 and in Year 8, suggesting that both groups held broadly similar views on setting. However, it is notable that pupils in the highest English set expressed significantly more positive attitudes towards setting than their peers in middle English sets, both in Year 7 and Year 8. Again, we can see that setting becomes less popular for all pupil sub-groups by the end of Year 8.

References

Abraham, J. (1995). *Divide and school: gender and class dynamics in comprehensive education.* London: The Falmer Press.

Abraham, J. (2008). Pupils' perceptions of setting and beyond – a response to Hallam and Ireson. *British Educational Research Journal, 34*(6), 855–863.

Adams-Byers, J., Whitsell, S. S., & Moon, S. M. (2004). Gifted students' perceptions of the academic and social/emotional effects of homogeneous and heterogeneous grouping. *Gifted Child Quarterly, 48*(1), 7–20.

Archer, L. (2003). *Race, masculinity and schooling: Muslim boys and education.* Maidenhead: Open University Press.

Archer, L., Francis, B., Miller, S., Taylor, B., Tereshchenko, A., Mazenod, A., Pepper, D., & Travers, M-C. (2018). The symbolic violence of setting: a Bourdieusian analysis of mixed methods data on secondary students' views about setting. *British Educational Research Journal, 44*(1), 119–140.

Ball, S. J. (1981). *Beachside comprehensive: a case-study of secondary schooling.* Cambridge: Cambridge University Press.

Bixby, J. (2006). Authority in detracked high school classrooms: tensions among individualism, equity, and legitimacy. In J. L. Pace & A. Hemmings (Eds.), *Classroom authority: theory, research, and practice* (pp. 113–134). Mahwah, NJ: Erlbaum.

Boaler, J. (1997). When even the winners are losers: evaluating the experiences of 'top set' students. *Journal of Curriculum Studies, 29*(2), 165–182.

Boaler, J. (2008). Promoting 'relational equity' and high mathematics achievement through an innovative mixed-ability approach. *British Educational Research Journal, 34*(2), 167–194.

Boaler, J., Wiliam, D., & Brown, M. (2000). Students' experiences of ability grouping-disaffection, polarisation and the construction of failure. *British Educational Research Journal, 26*(5), 631–648.

Burris, C. 2014. *On the same track: how schools can join the twenty-first-century struggle against resegregation.* Boston: Beacon Press.

Burris, C. C., Willey, E., Welner, K., & Murphy, J. (2008). Accountability, rigor, and detracking: achievement effects of embracing a challenging curriculum as a universal good for all students. *Teachers College Record, 110*(3), 571–607.

Celani, D. (2010). *Fairbairn's object relations theory in the clinical setting.* New York: Columbia University Press.

Connolly, P., Taylor, B., Francis, B., Archer, L., Hodgen, J., Mazenod, A., & Tereshchenko, A. (forthcoming, accepted). The misallocation of students to academic sets in maths: a study of secondary schools in England. *British Educational Research Journal.*

Dunne, M., Humphreys, S., Sebba, J., Dyson, A., Gallannaugh, F., & Muijs, D. (2007). *Effective teaching and learning for pupils in low attaining groups.* London: DfES Publications.

Dunne, M., Humphreys, S., Dyson, A., Sebba, J., Gallannaugh, F., & Muijs, D. (2011). The teaching and learning of pupils in low-attainment sets. *Curriculum Journal, 22*(4), 485–513.

Foucault, M. (1980). *Power/knowledge: selected interviews and other writings, 1972–1977.* New York: Pantheon.

Flores, J. (1999). *Tracking middle school students for instruction: a study of homogeneous and heterogeneous grouping.* MA thesis. California State University, San Marcos.

Francis, B. (2000). *Boys, girls, and achievement: addressing the classroom issues.* London: RoutledgeFalmer.

Francis, B., Archer, L., Hodgen, J., Pepper, D., Taylor, B., & Travers, M-C. (2017a). Exploring the relative lack of impact of research on 'ability grouping' in England: a discourse analytic account. *Cambridge Journal of Education, 47*(1), 1–17.

Francis, B., Connolly, P., Archer, L., Hodgen, J., Mazenod, A., Pepper, D., Sloan, S., Taylor, B., Tereshchenko, A., & Travers, M-C. (2017b). Attainment grouping as self-fulfilling prophecy? A mixed methods exploration of self confidence and set level among Year 7 students. *International Journal of Educational Research, 86*, 96–108.

Francis, B. & Skelton, C. (2008). *Reassessing gender and achievement: questioning contemporary key debates.* Abingdon: Routledge.

Gillborn, D. & Youdell, D. (2000). *Rationing education: policy, practice, reform, and equity.* Buckingham: Open University Press.

Hallam, S. & Ireson, J. (2005). Secondary school teachers' pedagogic practices when teaching mixed and structured ability classes. *Research Papers in Education, 20*(1), 3–24.

Hallam, S. & Ireson, J. (2006). Secondary school pupils' preferences for different types of structured grouping practices. *British Educational Research Journal, 32*(4), 583–599.

Hallam, S. & Ireson, J. (2007). Secondary school pupils' satisfaction with their ability grouping placements. *British Educational Research Journal, 33*(1), 27–45.

Hamilton, L. (2002). Constructing pupil identity: personhood and ability. *British Educational Research Journal, 28*(4), 591–602.

Hargreaves, D. H. (1967). *Social relations in a secondary school.* London: Routledge & Kegan Paul.

Hart, S. (1992). Differentiation. Part of the problem or part of the solution? *Curriculum Journal, 3*(2), 131–142.

Hart, S., Dixon, A., Drummond, M. J., & McIntyre, D. (2004). *Learning without limits.* Maidenhead: Open University Press.

Ireson, J. & Hallam, S. (2001). *Ability grouping in education.* London: Paul Chapman.

Jackson, B. (1964). *Streaming: an education system in miniature.* London: Routledge and Kegan Paul.

Jackson, C. (2002). 'Laddishness' as a self-worth protection strategy. *Gender and Education, 14*(1), 37–50.

Klein, M. (1952). *Developments in psycho-analysis.* London: Hogarth Press.

Klein, M. (1963). *Our adult world and other essays.* London: Heinemann.

Kutscher, B. & Linchevski, L. (2000). *Moving between mixed-ability and same-ability settings: impact on learners.* Paper presented at PME24. Hiroshima, Japan.

Lacey, C. (1970). *Hightown grammar: the school as a social system.* Manchester: Manchester University Press.

Loveless, T. (2009). *Tracking and detracking: high achievers in Massachusetts middle schools.* Washington, DC: Thomas B. Fordham Institute.

Lucey, H. & Reay, D. (2002). A market in waste: psychic and structural dimensions of school-choice policy in the UK and children's narratives on 'demonized' schools. *Discourse: Studies in the Cultural Politics of Education, 23*(3), 253–266.

Marks, R. (2016). *Ability-grouping in primary schools: case studies and critical debates.* Northwich: Critical Publishing.

Mazenod, A., Francis, B., Archer, L., Hodgen, J., Taylor, B., Tereshchenko, A., & Pepper, D. (2019). Nurturing learning or encouraging dependency? Teacher constructions of students in lower attainment groups in English secondary schools. *Cambridge Journal of Education, 49*(1), 53–68.

McGillicuddy, D. & Devine, D. (2018). 'Turned off' or 'ready to fly' – ability grouping as an act of symbolic violence in primary school. *Teaching and Teacher Education, 70,* 88–99.

Modica, M. (2015). 'My skin color stops me from leading': tracking, identity, and student dynamics in a racially mixed school. *International Journal of Multicultural Education, 17*(3), 76–90.

Muijs, D. & Dunne, M. (2010). Setting by ability – or is it? A quantitative study of determinants of set placement in English secondary schools. *Educational Research, 52*(4), 391–407.

Oakes, Jenny, Amy Stuart Wells, Makeba Jones, and Amanda Datnow. (1997). Detracking: the social construction of ability, cultural politics, and resistance to reform. *Teachers College Record, 98*(3), 482–510.

OFSTED. (2015). *The most able students: an update on progress since June 2013.* Manchester: Ofsted Publications.

Páll Sveinsson, K. (Ed.) (2009). *Who cares about the white working class?* London: Runnymede Trust.

Reay, D. (2002). Shaun's story: troubling discourses of white working-class masculinities. *Gender and Education, 14*(3), 221–234.

Reay, D. (2015). Habitus and the psychosocial: Bourdieu with feelings. *Cambridge Journal of Education, 45*(1), 9–23.

Reay, D. & Wiliam, D. (1999). 'I'll be a nothing': structure, agency and the construction of identity through assessment. *British Educational Research Journal, 25*(3), 343–354.

Richards, B. N. (2017). Tracking and racialization in schools: the experiences of second-generation West Indians in New York City. *Sociology of Race and Ethnicity, 3*(1), 126–140.

Riegle-Crumb, C. & Humphries, M. (2012). Exploring bias in math teachers' perceptions of students' ability by gender and race/ethnicity. *Gender & Society, 26*(2), 290–322.

Roberts, J. (2016). The 'more capable peer': approaches to collaborative learning in a mixed-ability classroom. *Changing English, 23*(1), 42–51.

Rose, N. (1999). *Governing the soul: the shaping of the private self.* London: Free Association Books.

Rosenbaum, J. E. (1999). If tracking is bad, is detracking better? *American Educator, 47*(4), 24–29.

Rubin, B. C. (2003). Unpacking detracking: when progressive pedagogy meets students' social worlds. *American Educational Research Journal, 40*(2), 539–573.

Rubin, B. C. (2008). Detracking in context: how local constructions of ability complicate equity-geared reform. *Teachers College Record, 110*(3), 646–699.

Scherer, L. (2016). 'I am not clever, they are cleverer than us': children reading in the primary school. *British Journal of Sociology of Education, 37*(3), 389–407.

Sennett, R. & Cobb, J. (1972/1993). *The hidden injuries of class*. New York: W.W Norton & Co.

Shields, C. M. (2002). A comparison study of student attitudes and perceptions in homogeneous and heterogeneous classrooms. *Roeper Review*, *24*(3), 115–119.

Slavin, R. E. (1996). Research on cooperative learning and achievement: what we know, what we need to know. *Contemporary Educational Psychology*, *21*(1), 43–69.

Taylor, B., Travers, M-C., Francis, B., Hodgen, J., & Sumner, C. (2015). *Best Practice in Mixed-Attainment Grouping*. London: King's College London/EEF.

Tereshchenko, A., Francis, B., Archer, L., Hodgen, J., Mazenod, A., Taylor, B., Pepper, D., & Travers, M-C. (2018). Learners' attitudes to mixed-attainment grouping: examining the views of students of high, middle and low attainment. *Research Papers in Education*, 1–20.

Walls, F. (2009). *Mathematical subjects: children talk about their mathematics lives*. Dordrecht: Springer.

Yonezawa, S., Wells, A. S., & Serna, I. (2002). Choosing tracks: 'freedom of choice' in detracking schools. *American Educational Research Journal*, *39*(1), 37–67.

Youdell, D. (2006). *Impossible bodies, impossible selves: exclusions and student subjectivities*. Dordrecht: Springer.

6

THE IMPACT OF ATTAINMENT GROUPING ON PEDAGOGY AND PRACTICE

In this chapter we explore what is known about the challenging issues of teacher quality, teacher expectations, and quality of pedagogy, in relation to different attainment groups. We draw on the prior literature and findings from our surveys, interviews, and focus groups to shed light on the hypotheses from the literature suggesting that low sets and streams tend to be offered poorer quality teachers and teaching, stemming from low expectations and labelling of pupils, as well as different structural dis/incentives within the school system.

'Quality' of teachers and set allocation

In any school it is likely that there will be some variability in the effectiveness of the teachers who work there (Husbands & Pearce, 2012) and research suggests that quality of teaching has the strongest impact on pupil outcomes (Coe et al., 2014; Hattie, 2012). The impact of a good teacher is particularly profound on pupils from disadvantaged backgrounds (Ainscow et al., 2012; Sutton Trust, 2011) and those with low prior attainment (Black & Wiliam, 1998). School leaders must therefore decide how to allocate teachers, inflected by awareness of which classes will be taught by teachers known to be effective, and which will be taught by those who are less so. A range of factors may be taken into account, including the characteristics of the different classes, the qualities and aptitudes of the teachers, and indeed teacher preferences. Where attainment grouping is used, it is likely that perceptions of different sets will play a part. Indeed, Jackson (1964) found that headteachers allocated teachers to the attractive higher streams as a reward for experience and seniority. Gillborn and Youdell (2000) found that leaders triaged provision in order to maximise GCSE results, with resources focused on pupils with the potential to achieve at least five C grades at GCSE.

Prior research finds that pupils in lower-attaining sets are more likely to be taught by teachers considered to be of lower 'quality' and receive lower quality instruction (Ireson & Hallam, 2001; Oakes, 1985; Slavin, 1990). Good and Marshall (1984) found that teachers of lower sets were less well-prepared. Students in low-attaining sets are also less likely to be taught by a subject specialist (Kelly, 2004), and more likely to have changes in teacher within a school year (Boaler et al., 2000) or be taught by a novice teacher (Papay & Kraft, 2014). Measuring the 'quality' of teachers and teaching is of course controversial and not straightforward. Slavin (1990) points out the difficulty of identifying lower quality instruction: for example, is covering curriculum content at a slower pace poor quality instruction or appropriate differentiation for struggling learners? However, there are some indicators such as the level and type of qualification a teacher holds, level of curriculum subject expertise, and length or type of teaching experience, all of which have been used with some validity. In particular, length of experience shows some association with effectiveness (Rockoff et al., 2011). Evidence around qualification levels is mixed, but there is some evidence that teachers with strong subject knowledge are more effective (Coe et al., 2014) and that US teachers with higher licensure test scores are more effective (Clotfelter et al., 2006), with both findings receiving some support from a further research study by Boyd et al. (2008).

We have found some evidence to support these prior claims about distribution of teachers to set groups from our study. We explored the relationship between 'teacher quality' and set level taught by teachers in our control group, and compared the characteristics of teachers allocated to the lowest set with teachers allocated to higher sets. For some measures, such as seniority within the school, length of experience, or teacher qualification level there was no obvious pattern. However, we did find a clearer trend when we looked at the relationship between teachers' *subject* qualification and the set level taught. Teachers allocated to the lowest set were less likely to have a degree-level qualification in their subject (English or mathematics), but were more likely to have just a GCSE or A Level qualification (see Table 6.1). Combined with our finding that pupils from disadvantaged backgrounds were more likely to be allocated to the lowest sets, this is an example of a socially unjust practice.

TABLE 6.1 Highest qualification in subject taught

Teacher qualification level	Highest and middle sets	Lowest sets
Undergraduate or higher degree	99 (65%)	17 (46%)
A Level or equivalent	45 (29%)	15 (41%)
GCSE or equivalent	9 (6%)	5 (14%)
Total	153 (100%)	37 (100%)

Source: Francis et al., 2019

TABLE 6.2 Highest qualification in subject taught, teachers of lowest sets

Teacher qualification level	Intervention group	Control group
Undergraduate or higher degree	24 (62%)	17 (46%)
A Level or equivalent	10 (26%)	15 (41%)
GCSE or equivalent	5 (13%)	5 (14%)
Total	39 (100%)	37 (100%)

Source: Francis et al., 2019

We were also interested in whether this socially unjust practice could be changed through our intervention. Comparing the teachers allocated to lowest sets in our intervention and control groups, we found that there was some supporting evidence for this. While the proportion of teachers with just a GCSE in the subject taught was similar in both groups, more low set teachers in the intervention group had at least an undergraduate degree (see Table 6.2). This lends some evidence that an intervention to improve equity in setting practice – here teacher allocation – can improve equity in allocation.

While in focus groups we did not ask pupils directly about the quality of teaching they received, we did ask whether they felt that pupils in different sets received 'different teachers' or 'different types of teaching'. The majority of pupils said they did not feel there was a difference between groups (perhaps unsurprising, given the vague question), however, a few pupils did feel that there was a difference between sets and offered their views on what made teaching distinctive for different groups.

Some pupils felt that different quality teachers were assigned to different sets:

> Some teachers say that Set 1 teachers are, like, the smarter teachers, that they have better teachers; and Set 5, they give to those teachers that don't really understand.
>
> *(Sauba, set 3, Black African, low SES, School X)*

> Because, like, I'm not trying to be rude but like when you're in the higher set you get, like, better teachers than the lower set or the middle set, you just get teachers in the middle.
>
> *(Asima, set 3, Black African, low SES, School S)*

The injustice of such perceived practice was articulated by Joaquin (Set 3, White Other, low SES, School X) who complains that this inequitable allocation 'shouldn't happen because we all need good teachers to learn'.

However, these views were only expressed by a small number of pupils, and pupil accounts also confirmed that it was possible for schools to take different approaches to teacher assignment. There were examples of teachers being allocated to both lowest and highest sets. And at School R, which was taking part in the intervention, a pupil from a middle set noted that the lowest set was taught by the Head of Maths:

Like, I think they're at, like, the lower set, because if she's the leader of maths, she probably knows a bit more than the other teachers. And that is going to help them get better, if you know what I mean.

(Leroy, Set 2 maths, Set 3 English, White/Black African mixed,
low SES, School R)

Leroy's words hint at both the symbolic and pedagogical impact that such placements which channel resource to the low sets may have.

However, there was far greater strength of feeling from pupils about the quality of *teaching* they received depending on set level, and we turn to this issue next.

Quality of teaching, and setting

Our survey included questions about quality of teaching for low attainment groups. As shown in Table 6.3, nearly two-thirds (64%) of pupils provided positive answers, agreeing[1] that 'low achievers are given good quality teaching', and even more (70%) disagreeing that 'low achievers are given poor quality teaching.' However, in both cases, pupils in the lowest mathematics sets (those most likely to have first-hand experience of the quality of teaching provided to low achievers) were somewhat more critical of the quality of teaching for low achievers. 17% of low-set pupils said that 'low achievers are given poor quality

TABLE 6.3 Pupil attitudes to quality of teaching, by maths set level

Low achievers are given good quality teaching

	Strongly disagree	Slightly disagree	Neither agree/disagree	Slightly agree	Strongly agree	Total
Highest set	116	128	750	692	1417	3103
	3.7%	4.1%	24.2%	22.3%	45.7%	100%
Middle set	284	277	1292	1142	1896	4891
	5.8%	5.7%	26.4%	23.3%	38.8%	100%
Lowest set	87	79	268	269	471	1174
	7.4%	6.7%	22.8%	22.9%	40.1%	100%
Total	487	484	2310	2103	3784	9168
	5.3%	5.3%	25.2%	22.9%	41.3%	100%

Low achievers are given poor quality teaching

	Strongly disagree	Slightly disagree	Neither agree/disagree	Slightly agree	Strongly agree	Total
Highest set	1905	437	541	120	105	3108
	61.3%	14.1%	17.4%	3.9%	3.4%	100%
Middle set	2664	665	987	325	265	4906
	54.3%	13.6%	20.1%	6.6%	5.4%	100%
Lowest set	566	154	260	89	104	1173
	48.3%	13.1%	22.2%	7.6%	8.9%	100%
Total	5135	1256	1788	534	474	9187
	55.9%	13.7%	19.5%	5.8%	5.2%	100%

teaching' (compared with 11% overall), and 14% disagreed that 'low achievers are given good quality teaching' (compared with 11% overall). It is encouraging to find that more than two-thirds of pupils regard the quality of teaching for low-achieving pupils positively (including a majority of low-set pupils), but notable that low attainers are a little more sceptical.

Teacher expectations and related pedagogy

It was striking that pupils in different sets consider the teaching to be of a very different type or quality when they are being taught by the same teacher. If applying the indicators of 'quality' commonly used by researchers (level qualification and so on), a teacher is of course the same 'quality' regardless of set level. However, research suggests that teachers differ in the expectations that they have of different sets, resulting in variation in pace and quality of *pedagogy* (Ireson et al., 2005; Mazenod et al., 2019; Murphy & Hallinger, 1989).

Gamoran (1992) outlines a number of ways in which the experience of teacher expectation and pedagogy varies between sets. He notes that the pace of presentation and the complexity of subject material is greater in higher sets, that the climate is more 'academic' and that teachers of higher sets may be more 'skilful'. Both Rosenbaum (1976) and Oakes (1990) identify a relationship between the set taught and the amount of time and enthusiasm given to lesson preparation, with lower set lessons receiving less investment; however in Hallam and Ireson's (2005) study teachers reported that they did not spend more time preparing for high-attaining sets.

The research literature typically characterises the work provided to higher sets as fast-paced and challenging, while pupils in lower sets experience lessons that are slow in pace and cover a restricted curriculum both in terms of breadth and depth (Boaler et al., 2000; Ireson et al., 2005). A number of researchers observe that pupils in higher sets are encouraged to be more autonomous in their learning, with greater opportunities for problem-solving, while those in lower sets are given repetitive tasks aimed at reinforcement and recall (Hallam & Ireson, 2005; Kelly, 2004; Oakes, 1985). Gamoran (1992) notes that higher sets are usually entered for more challenging courses with more demanding curricula, a finding echoed by Gillborn and Youdell (2000). Hallinan (1994) found that high-attaining tracks received more instructional time. Another point of difference is the amount of homework set, with higher sets found to receive more (Ireson & Hallam, 2001).

Our own research found much more evidence of variation in expectations and pedagogy than we found of variation in teacher quality. One of the strongest trends to emerge from the pupil interview data was the view that teachers of high sets were more strict than those of the lower sets. This was very commonly articulated by pupils, notably across all levels of attainment. The following examples from our data are indicative:

> When you go to higher sets, the teachers are strict.
>
> *(Ahmed, Set 2, Bangladeshi, low SES, School T)*

In the higher sets, you get stricter teachers, but in the lower sets you get more, like, laidback teachers that just explain it more.

(Andrea, Set 1, White British, low SES, School U)

When you are in a higher set teachers become strict and they just give comments out, even if you do like a small thing. In the lower set, they try more to help you instead of just giving comments out or start[ing] shouting at you.

(Mikaal, Set 5, Pakistani, middle SES, School T)

Yeah, I think as you get lower down in sets the teachers get nicer. Then the higher up, they get more strict.

(Lyle, Set 4, White British, low SES, School U)

With a very small number of exceptions, pupils across our sample – including from different schools and across the full range of prior attainment – shared this view that teachers of high sets were more exacting in their expectations of pupils. What is also significant is that, while not all pupils appreciated 'strictness', these high expectations of behaviour and learning were regarded as *an investment in pupils*, and pupils inferred that where discipline standards were lower, this signified a lack of care:

Ahmed: In higher sets . . . you know when you go to higher sets, the teachers are more strict, but in lower sets they're not that strict.

Nafisa: They don't really care.
Students perceived teachers' disciplinary and academic expectations to be closely linked.

In set six, I don't know, but I probably think that, like, they probably get it a little bit easy because they don't understand as much, then set one they are pushed to the limit.

(Mandy, Set 3, White British, low SES, School U)

I remember my old teacher when I was in set four used to be a bit more laid back so it wouldn't be. I mean we'd still be working loads but it wouldn't be as challenging at times and then now I've gone into set three it is different.

(Connor, Set 3, White British, low SES, School W)

And in addition to distinct expectations of behaviour and application, students also considered that teachers provided very different work for them in different sets. In response to our survey, 87% of pupils reported that they slightly or strongly agreed that 'top sets are given more challenging work', with patterns of agreement fairly similar across set levels (Table 6.4).

These differing expectations were evident in the very different pedagogical approaches frequently reported by pupils. High sets were seen to experience more independent learning, and faster paced, more demanding work. Brad (Set 1, White

TABLE 6.4 'Top sets are given more challenging work' by maths set level

	Strongly disagree	Slightly disagree	Neither agree/disagree	Slightly agree	Strongly agree	Total
Highest set	32	45	180	758	2087	3102
	1.0%	1.5%	5.8%	24.4%	67.3%	100%
Middle set	95	117	490	1335	2887	4924
	1.9%	2.4%	10.0%	27.1%	58.6%	100%
Lowest set	32	26	143	282	697	1180
	2.7%	2.2%	12.1%	23.9%	59.1%	100%
Total	159	188	813	2375	5671	9206
	1.7%	2.0%	8.8%	25.8%	61.6%	100%

British, low SES, School W) observes, 'I think as well that with the higher sets, you're more, like, trusted to do stuff, like go on the learn pads and it's more different ways of learning suited to you'. And Luke (Set 5 maths, Set 3 English, White British, high SES, School P) concurs, 'If you're in the top sets they let you like get on with it'. Whereas low sets were seen to be slower paced and scaffolded: Anah (Set 1 maths, mixed attainment English, Arab, low SES, School V) cites a teacher that tends to teach 'the lower sets because he's quite slow paced and he likes to do it step by step'; and Aaliyah (Sets 1 maths and English, African, low SES, School V) reports her friend's experience that their lower set teacher is 'really slower paced', in contrast to a high set teacher who is 'very strict and wants you to do as best as you can in your lessons'.

Students were very much aware of the different expectations and pedagogies employed by teachers of different sets. For example Ella (Set 3, White British, low SES, School Q) recognised that although everyone addresses the same topics it was still the case that 'some lessons are harder', identifying that teachers would extend a question such as 'what does the phrase mean?' as used with lower sets, to 'what does the phrase mean and why have they used it?' for higher sets. Similarly, Sabrina (Set 4, Other White, low SES, School U) observed that 'instead of doing really hard stuff', the lowest set 'would probably write, like, a story board or draw a story board'.

As observed at the beginning of this chapter, it is difficult to distinguish between expectations and pedagogy that are appropriately differentiated to be supportive for low groups, and the low expectations and impoverished pedagogy identified by researchers as associated with low sets (Ireson & Hallam, 2001). Advocates for setting argue that homogeneous grouping enables teachers to target curriculum and pedagogy more appropriately to the pupils in each group than is possible in a mixed attainment group (Rubin, 2006). In other words, differentiation of provision between sets is integral to the rationale for setting. However, this requires that expectations, pedagogy, and potentially even curriculum may be different for each set group and it is no longer possible to argue that the offer is 'equal' for all pupils.

Furthermore, as we shall see, pupils in low attaining sets report that they are dissatisfied with the offer they receive, which suggests that adaptation for different sets may not be entirely successful. We shall return to this point in Chapter 9.

Some pupils identified that teachers tended to infantilise pupils in low sets, for example observing with frustration that 'the teacher can kind of feel like a mum when you're a baby' (Jackie, Set 2, White British, low SES, School Q) and that 'they talk slow' and 'sometimes like they're helping you even if you want to do it by yourself' (Bobby, Set 5 maths, Set 3 English, White British, middle SES, School P). Charlene (Set 3 maths, Set 2 English, White British, low SES, School S) speculated that pupils in low sets were taught 'easier methods' and that 'the teacher might talk, like, babyish to them to make sure they understand'. These uncomfortable examples illustrate how pupils experience the pedagogy in low sets as patronising. In some cases, pupils in lower sets felt that they were capable of much more than teachers were asking of them, with Helen (Set 5, White British, middle SES, School U) observing that when the teacher asked her class to 'carry on' with the task they were doing, 'but we've already done it, the stuff we are carrying on'. Indeed, some pupils also voiced the concern that the teaching they were receiving in low sets was insufficient to help them learn the knowledge they needed. Graham (lowest set, White British, low SES, School W) recognised that his teacher tried to make the learning 'more fun' but complained that 'we need to do the learning as well because when it comes to actually doing a test, we don't get it'. Elsewhere (Mazenod et al., 2019) we discuss the implications of such findings more extensively, arguing that 'nurturing' pedagogies may impede pupils' learning via insufficiently challenging curriculum and by inculcating dependent learning habits in students – as well as frequently being resented as patronising by pupils, as articulated above. None of this is conducive to educational engagement.

Hence, while pupils did not, in the main, comment on variation in *teacher* quality between sets, we have seen that there was strength of feeling that expectations of behaviour and work ethic were very different in the higher and lower sets. Moreover, pupils complained that the pedagogy and approach of teachers in the lower sets was deficient in failing to provide the richness of experience and subject content accumulated by higher set pupils, and in making pupils feel babied by their teachers.

Teachers' views on setting and pedagogy

We have heard in detail pupils' views of their teachers' expectations and pedagogy for different sets. Now we turn to hear the teachers' views. In our teacher survey we asked a number of questions about their expectations and classroom practices. A summary of their responses can be found in Table 6.5 (maths teachers) and Table 6.6 (English teachers). Teachers do not appear to share pupils' beliefs that they are stricter with higher-attaining pupils: teachers' responses to the statements 'I am stricter with high-attaining students' and 'I am stricter with low-attaining students' are broadly similar, with 'neither agree nor disagree' being the most popular response for mathematics and English teachers for both statements. For both statements, maths and English teachers were more likely to say they disagreed than agreed, suggesting that teachers tend to believe they are equally strict with high and low attaining pupils. In fact, in the teacher interviews the word 'strict' was barely used and where teachers did use it, they were mainly referring to how 'strict' (i.e. rigid or rigorous) the approach to setting was. One exception was Larry, a maths teacher from School Q, who used the word 'strict' to report something a pupil had said (see below). It is possible that there are differences in how 'strictness' is understood by pupils and by teachers, and that teachers' survey responses indicate a feeling that they have equally high *expectations* of high and low attaining pupils when it comes to classroom standards, while pupils perceive differences in the standards articulated and/or *achieved* in different classrooms. Furthermore, teachers were more likely to agree that they expected to spend more time keeping low-attaining pupils on task (55% of maths teachers and 57% of English teachers), suggesting that even though they expected the same 'strictness' or standards in high and low attaining groups, low-attaining pupils' behaviour was more likely to be time-consuming to address.

TABLE 6.5 Maths teachers' expectations and classroom practices (n=373)

	Strongly disagree	Slightly disagree	Neither agree/ disagree	Slightly agree	Strongly agree	Missing
Teachers should expect students with high prior attainment to exceed national targets	11 2.9%	34 9.1%	61 16.4%	138 37.0%	97 26.0%	32 8.6%
Colleagues have high expectations of all students regardless of prior attainment	5 1.3%	40 10.7%	44 11.8%	120 32.2%	131 35.1%	33 8.8%
I expect high-attaining students to cover topics in more depth	5 1.3%	8 2.1%	23 6.2%	118 33.6%	186 49.9%	33 8.8%
I expect high-attaining students to cover more topics	11 2.9%	30 8.0%	39 10.5%	117 31.4%	143 38.3%	33 8.8%
I expect more independent work from high-attaining students	12 3.2%	30 8.0%	41 11.0%	128 34.3%	129 34.6%	33 8.8%
I expect more analytical thought from high-attaining students	5 1.3%	10 2.7%	23 6.2%	142 38.1%	160 42.9%	33 8.8%
I expect high-attaining students to work at a faster rate	4 1.1%	21 5.6%	42 11.3%	124 33.2%	149 39.9%	33 8.8%
I encourage more discussion between high-attaining students	21 5.6%	72 19.3%	93 24.9%	99 26.5%	53 14.2%	35 9.4%
I use extension activities to stretch high-attaining students	1 0.3%	4 1.1%	17 4.6%	115 30.8%	203 54.4%	33 88.%
I spend more time preparing for high-attaining students	67 18.0%	113 30.3%	114 30.6%	30 8.0%	16 4.3%	33 8.8%
I provide more feedback on high-attaining students' work	74 19.8%	106 28.4%	104 27.9%	33 8.8%	20 5.4%	36 9.7%

	Strongly disagree	Slightly disagree	Neither agree/disagree	Slightly agree	Strongly agree	Missing
I am stricter with high-attaining students	86 / 23.1%	68 / 18.2%	136 / 36.5%	40 / 10.7%	10 / 2.7%	33 / 8.8%
Some activities I do not expect low-attaining students to do	15 / 4.0%	47 / 12.6%	43 / 11.5%	156 / 41.8%	79 / 21.2%	33 / 8.8%
I expect to spend more time keeping low-attaining students on task	18 / 4.8%	55 / 14.7%	61 / 16.4%	147 / 39.4%	58 / 15.5%	34 / 9.1%
I provide more practical activities for low-attaining students	19 / 5.1%	70 / 18.8%	91 / 24.4%	126 / 37.1%	34 / 9.1%	33 / 8.8%
I provide more detailed feedback on low-attaining students' work	49 / 13.1%	92 / 24.7%	121 / 32.4%	44 / 11.8%	32 / 8.6%	35 / 9.4%
I do more repetition and rehearsal with low-attaining students	11 / 2.9%	34 / 9.1%	43 / 11.5%	171 / 45.8%	81 / 21.7%	33 / 8.8%
I spend more time preparing for low-attaining students	30 / 8.0%	68 / 18.2%	109 / 29.2%	82 / 22.3%	49 / 13.1%	34 / 9.1%
I set more structured work for low-attaining students	8 / 2.1%	23 / 6.2%	53 / 14.2%	184 / 49.3%	72 / 19.3%	33 / 8.8%
I am stricter with low-attaining students	85 / 22.8%	84 / 22.5%	120 / 32.2%	38 / 10.2%	13 / 3.5%	33 / 8.8%

TABLE 6.6 English teachers' expectations and classroom practices (n=185)

	Strongly disagree	Slightly disagree	Neither agree/disagree	Slightly agree	Strongly agree	Missing
Teachers should expect students with high prior attainment to exceed national targets	8 / 4.3%	19 / 10.3%	35 / 18.9%	64 / 34.6%	35 / 18.9%	24 / 13.0%
Colleagues have high expectations of all students regardless of prior attainment	2 / 1.1%	12 / 6.5%	20 / 10.8%	57 / 30.8%	67 / 36.2%	27 / 14.6%
I expect high-attaining students to cover topics in more depth	2 / 1.1%	7 / 3.8%	9 / 4.9%	64 / 34.6%	76 / 41.1%	27 / 14.6%
I expect high-attaining students to cover more topics	11 / 5.9%	38 / 20.5%	34 / 18.4%	41 / 22.2%	34 / 18.4%	27 / 14.6%
I expect more independent work from high-attaining students	6 / 3.2%	8 / 4.3%	18 / 9.7%	59 / 31.9%	67 / 36.2%	27 / 14.6%
I expect more analytical thought from high-attaining students	4 / 2.2%	13 / 7.0%	11 / 5.9%	55 / 29.7%	75 / 40.5%	27 / 14.6%
I expect high-attaining students to work at a faster rate	2 / 1.1%	19 / 10.3%	21 / 11.4%	67 / 36.2%	49 / 26.5%	27 / 14.6%
I encourage more discussion between high-attaining students	15 / 8.1%	39 / 21.1%	30 / 16.2%	43 / 23.2%	29 / 15.7%	29 / 15.7%

(continued)

TABLE 6.6 (continued)

	Strongly disagree	Slightly disagree	Neither agree/ disagree	Slightly agree	Strongly agree	Missing
I use extension activities to stretch high-attaining students	3 1.6%	2 1.1%	4 2.2%	72 38.9%	75 40.5%	29 15.7%
I spend more time preparing for high-attaining students	28 15.1%	57 30.8%	45 24.3%	23 12.4%	3 1.6%	29 15.7%
I provide more feedback on high-attaining students' work	36 19.5%	44 23.8%	43 23.2%	23 12.4%	9 4.9%	30 16.2%
I am stricter with high-attaining students	36 19.5%	52 28.1%	52 28.1%	14 7.6%	3 1.6%	28 15.1%
Some activities I do not expect low-attaining students to do	21 11.4%	41 22.2%	19 10.3%	56 30.3%	21 11.4%	27 14.6%
I expect to spend more time keeping low-attaining students on task	4 2.2%	22 11.9%	26 14.1%	78 42.2%	27 14.6%	28 15.1%
I provide more practical activities for low-attaining students	8 4.3%	28 15.1%	40 21.6%	66 35.7%	14 7.6%	29 15.7%
I provide more detailed feedback on low-attaining students' work	30 16.2%	43 23.2%	48 25.9%	22 11.9%	12 6.5%	30 16.2%
I do more repetition and rehearsal with low-attaining students	4 2.2%	14 7.6%	21 11.4%	82 44.3%	35 18.9%	29 15.7%
I spend more time preparing for low-attaining students	15 8.1%	29 15.7%	37 20.0%	49 26.5%	26 14.1%	29 15.7%
I set more structured work for low-attaining students	2 1.1%	8 4.3%	10 5.4%	81 43.8%	54 29.2%	30 16.2%
I am stricter with low-attaining students	36 19.5%	34 18.4%	53 28.6%	21 11.4%	13 7.0%	28 15.1%

Behaviour was also addressed in some of the teacher interviews (though fewer than one might perhaps expect). Some teachers indicated equitable expectations and practices across sets: Charleen (English, School W) asserts that 'all sets, they will be expected to behave that certain way. And there's not really any allowances'. However, others expressed trends that are commonly articulated in the research literature and anecdotally. For example, Hayley (mathematics, School R) identifies the 'best-behaved classes are your higher ability ones', suggesting a difference in pupil behaviour and in demands on teachers between set levels. She argues that it 'would be unfair' to allocate only high or low attaining classes to a teacher, because of the different implications for workload: 'it does, actually, take a lot more, in the lesson, with a bottom ability, than it does with a top'. Likewise, Janet (English, School S) explicitly distinguishes between the behaviour in Set 6 and Set 2:

Janet:	behaviour [in Set 6] can be a struggle [. . .]
Interviewer:	Okay. Behaviour would not be a challenge in Set 2?
Janet:	No.

Teachers' views were much clearer in relation to expectations of learning according to set groups, however. In our survey with teachers, over two-thirds of maths teachers agreed that they expected higher-attaining pupils to cover more topics, work in greater depth and at a faster pace, and show greater independence and analytical thought. English teacher responses were patterned slightly differently, which may reflect subject disciplinary distinctions in exam curricula and culture. As with maths teachers, over two-thirds of English teachers agreed that they expected high-attaining pupils to work in greater depth and show greater independence and analytical thought. However, fewer English teachers reported that they expected a faster rate of work from high-attaining pupils (63%) or for higher-attaining pupils to cover more topics (41%). The latter finding is likely to be as a result of English GCSE not having 'tiered' examinations, in contrast to the 'foundation' and 'higher' tiers for mathematics GCSE. Students who are expected to achieve the highest grades in English GCSE do not need to study additional content, while pupils aiming for the highest grades in mathematics GCSE must cover more topics for the higher paper than lower attaining pupils will study for the foundation paper. Similar responses were given to the statement 'Some activities I do not expect low-attaining students to do', with 63% of mathematics teachers and 42% of English teachers agreeing with this statement. The parallel with covering different topics can be seen clearly with the proportions of teachers who slightly or strongly disagreed with this statement: maths teachers were much less likely to disagree (17%) than were English teachers (34%), likely reflecting the different curriculum requirements. However, even taking this into account, both maths and English teachers are less likely to expect low-attaining pupils to complete the same number/type of tasks as their high-attaining schoolmates.

Implicit in teachers' responses to these questions is a difference in curriculum offer to higher and lower attaining pupils.

These findings are echoed in the teacher interviews. Candice (mathematics, School V) describes the difference between a lesson taught to a high group and a low group:

> Generally, I think, the content would probably be different, so the level of work that I would teach would be a higher level for a top set as opposed to a bottom set. Probably the pace would be faster.

A similar view is offered by Ajda (mathematics, School X), who initially says 'the content would be pretty much the same' for higher and lower groups, but that 'perhaps due to time you'd cover less of it [in lower groups]', implying a difference in pace between groups. And Chloe (English, School R) describes the difference between teaching *Romeo and Juliet* to top and bottom set Year 8: 'You're teaching, obviously, exactly the same content but the pace and the delivery is totally different'. Chloe goes on to explain that she had taught different content to the two groups, 'trying to challenge the top set to include GCSE and A Level terminology', while it 'took [the bottom set] a lot longer' to be able to rise to the challenge of using some GCSE terminology. Chloe clearly tried to stretch both her groups and considered herself to have high expectations (represented by teaching material from higher year groups to Key Stage 3 pupils), but expectations were at different levels and took different amounts of time to realise. She summarises the situation thus, 'that becomes a little bit tricky in terms of how much you can deliver, and the pace at which you can deliver it, really'.

Estrella (mathematics, School Y) explains that she feels there are few differences between how she teaches different streams (School Y transpired to be setting within three streamed bands): 'as much as possible I give them the curriculum in the same way, I teach them in the same way'. However, she went on to concede that the 'kind of work' she gives has different levels of challenge for the different streams, 'the approach only for [the top stream] will be in-depth whereas in [the middle and lower streams] will probably be not really in-depth and challenging them with out of the box problems shall we say'. This distinction reveals an interesting conundrum: Estrella feels that she is teaching the same curriculum at the same pace, yet it still seems that the curriculum opportunities are different for different streams. For this teacher there seems to be a dilemma around not wanting to provide different curricula (equality of offer for all students) and finding an explanation that justifies the difference.

By way of contrast, Sanjiv (English, School S) embraces the differentiation setting offers, explaining that Set 6 are taught 'a specialised curriculum to match their needs'. At School S, Set 6 had historically consisted of no more than ten pupils, all 'working well below national average' and the majority with special educational needs. However, at the time of his interview, pressures of finance and pupil numbers were meaning that Sanjiv was having to increase the size of Set 6 by including pupils who would previously have been in Set 5, with the effect that the curriculum needed to be modified. He felt this would mean that 'those pupils are not getting the curriculum that they need in order to make progress'.

Larry (mathematics, School Q) also supports the differentiation afforded via setting, explaining that as a new teacher he had thought 'expectations should be the same for all the classes', but found that when he 'set the bar so high in the lower set I find out there will be loads of arguments or sometimes even some confrontations. "Why are you so strict?" "Definitely I can't do that."' He went on to clarify that while 20 questions might be a reasonable expectation for the top set, 'in a lower set . . . none of them can do that'. Larry regarded reducing his expectation to ten questions for lower sets as a necessary 'compromise' based on his increasing experience, but nevertheless expressed the reservation that 'morally it may be wrong'.

Hence many teachers appeared to be struggling with what is a genuine dilemma in the principle and practice of attainment grouping. They are aware of and often subscribe to a discourse of 'high expectations for all', and of related principles of equitable provision, but simultaneously are working within the parameters of setting (and/or streaming), which is predicated on the notion that pupils in different set levels have different respective needs. Teachers were seeking to be conscientious, and in some cases clearly thoughtful about the differentiated pedagogy they could apply that was facilitated through setting, but this is necessarily in tension with (equally) high expectations for all. We return to this conceptual dilemma and the practical challenges it precipitates, in Chapter 9.

Prior research has found that teachers spent more time preparing for higher-attaining pupils (Oakes, 1990; Rosenbaum, 1976), although Hallam and Ireson's (2005) later study findings challenged this. In our survey, nearly half of maths teachers (48%) disagreed that they spent more time preparing for high-attaining pupils with a further 31% saying that they neither agreed nor disagreed. Findings were similar for English teachers with 46% disagreeing and 24% saying they neither agreed nor disagreed. By contrast, just over one-third of maths teachers (35%) and 41% of English teachers agreed that they spent more time preparing for low-attaining pupils. Hence our findings challenge earlier research, with the trend for teacher articulation suggesting that more preparation energy is directed at low attainers. Our findings may reflect recent policy priorities of supporting pupils with SEND and closing the attainment gap between disadvantaged pupils (who are more likely to be low-attaining) and their more affluent peers. Teachers also tended to disagree that there were differences between the amount of feedback given to high- and low-attaining pupils, with well over half of maths teachers (57%) and 43% of English teachers disagreeing that they gave more feedback to high-attaining pupils and 38% of maths teachers and 39% of English teachers disagreeing that they gave more feedback to low-attaining pupils. The only notable difference for these statements was between the proportion of mathematics teachers reporting that they did give more feedback to high-attaining pupils (14%) and the proportion reporting that they gave more detailed feedback to low-attaining pupils (20%). This may reflect the style of marking and feedback in mathematics, where correct answers (potentially more often given by high-attaining pupils) would attract less feedback than incorrect answers.

However, in terms of pedagogical differences, it is clear that teachers provide different experiences and have different expectations of pupils with different levels of prior attainment. The overwhelming majority of maths teachers (85%) and English teachers (79%) agreed that they provided extension activities to stretch high-attaining pupils. In the interviews, Rajiv (mathematics, School Y) describes how 'more able' pupils are stretched with extension activities:

> We have extension tasks for them which is not more of the same but it's moving them on in their understanding and applying the knowledge to problem-solving questions.

Similarly, Patrick (English, School Y) describes his approach for pupils who complete work quickly:

> You give them extension tasks which are not necessarily related to the topic but we kind of get them to think about something different so it might be something contextual or a social issue or a cultural issue which is related to that text.

These differentiated practices would of course be expected in most classrooms, including mixed attainment settings.

A somewhat related issue was that of levels of discussion with high-attaining pupils, wherein our findings were slightly more mixed. Teachers tended to agree that they encouraged more discussion with higher-attaining pupils in both maths (41%) and English (39%). On the other hand, nearly one-third of English teachers (29%) and a quarter of maths teachers (25%) disagreed with the statement. Nevertheless, this shows a significantly greater likelihood for teachers to say they engage in discussion more with high-attaining pupils.[2]

To summarise, these findings suggest that high-attaining pupils are still more likely than their lower-attaining peers to be offered additional activities, and potentially therefore access to additional curriculum areas, although extension activities could equally be about increasing depth rather than breadth. According to teachers, higher-attaining pupils are also more likely to be given the opportunity to discuss their learning and, as we saw above, more likely to be expected to show more analytical thought, implying again some differential access to learning opportunities based on prior attainment.

In turn, we also asked teachers about provision for lower-attaining pupils. Previous research has found that lower-attaining pupils were more likely to be offered repetition and rehearsal, and more structured tasks. Our research supported these patterns. Around two-thirds of maths and English teachers said they did more repetition and rehearsal with low-attaining pupils (68% for maths and 63% for English), provided more structured tasks for low-attaining pupils (69% for maths and 73% for English) and were slightly more likely to provide more practical activities (46% for maths and 43% for English).

These quantitative findings, then, speak to different pedagogical approaches and curricula being experienced by pupils in high and low sets. Many teachers also elaborated such distinct approaches in their interviews. For example, Charleen (English, School W) explains that writing tasks for Set 5 are 'very structured when we do them' and describes a directive approach to teaching her low attaining group: 'They have frames for writing and it's very much, "Right, we're going to do this one together on the board now and you're going to do it like this."' Similarly, Jamie (maths, School W) contrasts the 'open-ended' explorative approach in a top set with the 'very scaffolded, very structured, very rigid' approach in low sets, where the focus is on 'developing fluency – do this sum, let's practice it, let's get better at it'. Hayley (maths, School R) also associates structure and support for pupils. She reports that her top set 'don't get much support if they're doing an activity', while 'your bottom would be more structured'. A particularly illustrative explanation is provided by Danielle (maths, School U), who described top and bottom set Year 8 lessons as '100% completely different lessons'. She went on to explain that:

> Year 8 top set will have a lot more things they can put in their books. So they like having things on paper, whereas the bottom set will have a lot more interactive things, so they'll work on their white boards so they don't have to put things on paper if they get stressed by making mistakes. And they'll have more games and things going on just to keep them engaged. So quicker, smaller tasks, whereas the top set will love to just sit and work through questions on their own so a lot more independent in top sets than bottom sets. [. . .] So [with top sets] we encourage independent thought, discussion, and then sort of moving on, and they can stay focused on tasks for longer periods of time. So you can set them bigger chunks of work, whereas on a bottom set, your pace will be a lot quicker; it's ten minute activities throughout the lesson.

This is a very good expression of some of the open questions we raised above. On the one hand, this might be read from a differentiation lens (or within an argument for setting), as an example of a teacher conscientiously and creatively tailoring her pedagogy and curriculum to the differing needs of different attainment groups. Conversely, it might be read through a critical/social justice lens as risking privileging the top set and patronising the bottom set (with potential impacts of labelling, see Chapter 4); and also as risking depriving bottom set pupils of the opportunity to develop independent thinking and research skills.

As we have argued in this chapter it is very difficult to assess whether such adaptations are appropriate adjustments for pupil groups representing different broad levels of attainment, or whether the approaches directed at low attainment sets represent an inappropriate reduction in quality of pedagogy and curriculum. Nevertheless, our research has shed some light on how this has been received by pupils, with many pupils reading higher expectations of behaviour and progress in the higher sets as positive indicators of investment (and the reverse in the case of low sets), and some low-set pupils feeling frustrated, and/or raising objections to being 'babied'. We will return for more detailed discussion of this in Chapter 9.

Chapter summary

Prior research has found differences in the quality of teachers and teaching experienced by pupils in high- and low-attainment sets; as well as differences in the expectations and pedagogy applied to pupils in different groups. Our research has supported some of these findings. For example, we find that pupils in low sets are more likely to be taught by a teacher without a degree level qualification in the subject taught. Some pupils felt that teacher quality and – especially – pedagogy varied between sets, with low attainment sets getting worse quality teachers and teaching. We have also found that teachers continue to have very different expectations of pupils in different sets and, consequently, apply different pedagogical approaches when teaching. Our research also supports earlier findings of pupils in higher sets being encouraged to engage in more discussion and problem-solving activities and to develop more independence of thought, while pupils in lower sets and streams are given more structured and repetitive tasks.

On the other hand, our study has found little difference between the amount of time teachers report that they spend preparing for higher- and lower-attaining pupils. It is possible that this reflects changes in the priority given to disadvantaged pupils and those with SEND in English educational policy, meaning that the achievement of these, typically low-attaining, groups is more important to schools than it might have been in the past. In any case, this is an encouraging distinction from prior findings.

What remains clear is that the experience of a pupil in a low set still tends to stand in stark contrast to that of a pupil in a high set. Less likely to be taught by a subject expert, pupils in low sets are also likely to be exposed to very different expectations. Classroom activities are likely to be very different in character: delivered as a greater number of smaller chunks, but overall covering the curriculum at a slower pace. Low-attaining pupils are less likely to be expected to complete extended written tasks – and may be expected to completed fewer written tasks altogether than their higher-attaining peers. When written tasks are used, low-attaining pupils are likely to be given a more rigid, inflexible structure within which to write, inhibiting creativity and perhaps limiting the potential scope or quality of the outcome. In class, low-attaining pupils can expect to be closely monitored by their teacher or by a teaching assistant, while higher-attaining pupils might be offered more freedom to progress with tasks independently.

It is striking that in the years since the last major studies of attainment grouping that have examined pedagogy and practice in this level of detail (Dunne et al., 2007; Ireson & Hallam, 2001; Kutnick et al., 2005), so little progress has been made in increasing equity of provision for groups with different prior attainment. The pedagogical practices and differentiation of curriculum and expectations between sets today remains much as described in these older studies, and outcomes likewise continue to reflect longstanding trends, with a long tail of achievement reflecting slower progress for low attainers (Marshall, 2013), and a widening gap between disadvantaged pupils and their peers over the course of secondary education (Andrews et al., 2017; Clifton & Cook, 2012), begging important questions as to why the inequity of resources to low attainers remains, and whether the 'nurturing' pedagogies (Mazenod et al., 2019) frequently offered to them via attainment grouping are productive.

Notes

1 Here and throughout this chapter, when discussing the survey data, where we report numbers that 'agreed with' a proposition we are counting responses that slightly and strongly agreed; and where we report numbers that 'disagreed with . . .' we include responses that slightly and strongly disagreed.

2 The somewhat narrower gap for English teachers on the matter of engaging different attainment sets in different levels of discussion might possibly reflect the importance of discussion in English lessons.

References

Ainscow, M., Dyson, A., Goldrick, S., & West, M. (2012). *Developing equitable education systems.* London: Routledge.

Andrews, J., Robinson, D., & Hutchinson, J. (2017). *Closing the gap? Trends in educational attainment and disadvantage.* Retrieved from: https://epi.org.uk/wp-content/uploads/2017/08/Closing-the-Gap_EPI-.pdf.

Black, P. & Wiliam, D. (1998). Assessment and classroom learning. *Assessment in Education: Principles, Policy & Practice, 5*(1), 7–74.

Boaler, J., Wiliam, D., & Brown, M. (2000). Students' experiences of ability grouping-disaffection, polarisation and the construction of failure. *British Educational Research Journal, 26*(5), 631–648.

Boyd, D., Lankford, H., Loeb, S., Rockoff, J., & Wyckoff, J. (2008). The narrowing gap in New York City teacher qualifications and its implications for student achievement in high-poverty schools. *Journal of Policy Analysis and Management, 27*(4), 793–818.

Clifton, J. & Cook, W. (2012). *A long division: closing the attainment gap in England's secondary schools.* Retrieved from: www.ippr.org/publications/a-long-division-closing-the-attainment-gap-in-englands-secondary-schools.

Clotfelter, C. T., Ladd, H. F., & Vigdor, J. L. (2006). Teacher-student matching and the assessment of teacher effectiveness. *The Journal of Human Resources, 41*(4), 778–820.

Coe, R., Aloisi, C., Higgins, S., & Elliot Major, L. (2014). *What makes great teaching?* Retrieved from: www.suttontrust.com/wp-content/uploads/2014/10/What-makes-great-teaching-FINAL-4.11.14.pdf.

Dunne, M., Humphreys, S., Sebba, J., Dyson, A., Gallannaugh, F., & Muijs, D. (2007). *Effective teaching and learning for pupils in low attaining groups.* London: DCSF.

Francis, B., Hodgen, J., Craig, N., Taylor, B., Archer, L., Mazenod, A., & Tereshchenko, A. (2019). Teacher 'quality' and attainment grouping: the role of within-school teacher deployment in social and educational inequality. *Teaching and Teacher Education, 77,* 183–192.

Gamoran, A. (1992). Synthesis of research: is ability grouping equitable? *Educational Leadership, 50,* 11–11.

Gillborn, D. & Youdell, D. (2000). *Rationing education: policy, practice, reform, and equity.* Buckingham: Open University Press.

Good, T. L. & Marshall, S. (1984). Do students learn more in heterogeneous or homogeneous groups? In P. Peterson, L. C. Wilkinson, & M. T. Hallinan (Eds.), *Student diversity and the organization, process and use of instructional groups in the classroom.* New York: Academic Press.

Hallam, S. & Ireson, J. (2005). Secondary school teachers' pedagogic practices when teaching mixed and structured ability classes. *Research Papers in Education, 20*(1), 3–24.

Hallinan, M. T. (1994). Tracking: from theory to practice. *Sociology of Education, 67*(2), 79–84.

Hattie, J. (2012). *Visible learning for teachers: maximizing impact on learning.* Abingdon, New York: Routledge.

Husbands, C. & Pearce, J. (2012). *What makes great pedagogy? Nine claims from research.* Nottingham: NCSL.

Ireson, J. & Hallam, S. (2001). *Ability grouping in education.* London: Paul Chapman.

Ireson, J., Hallam, S., & Hurley, C. (2005). What are the effects of ability grouping on GCSE attainment? *British Educational Research Journal, 31*(4), 443–458.

Jackson, B. (1964). *Streaming: an education system in miniature.* London: Routledge and Kegan Paul.

Kelly, S. (2004). Are teachers tracked? On what basis and with what consequences. *Social Psychology of Education, 7*(1), 55–72.

Kutnick, P., Sebba, J., Blatchford, P., Galton, M., Thorp, J., MacIntyre, H., & Berdondini, L. (2005). *The effects of pupil grouping: literature review.* London: DFES.

Marshall, P. (2013). *The tail: how England's schools fail one child in five – and what can be done.* London: Profile Books Ltd.

Mazenod, A., Francis, B., Archer, L., Hodgen, J., Taylor, B., Tereshchenko, A., & Pepper, D. (2019). Nurturing learning or encouraging dependency? Teacher constructions of students in lower attainment groups in English secondary schools. *Cambridge Journal of Education, 49*(1), 53–68.

Murphy, J. & Hallinger, P. (1989). Equity as access to learning: curricular and instructional treatment differences. *Journal of Curriculum Studies, 21*(2), 129–149.

Oakes, J. (1985). *How schools structure inequality.* New Haven: Yale University Press.

Oakes, J. (1990). *Multiplying inequalities: the effects of race, social class, and tracking on opportunities to learn mathematics and science.* Santa Monica, CA: RAND.

Papay, J. & Kraft, M. (2014). Productivity returns to experience in the teacher labour market: methodological challenges and new evidence on long-term career improvement. *Journal of Public Economics, 130,* 105–119.

Rockoff, J., Jacob, B., Kane, T., & Staiger, D. (2011). Can you recognize an effective teacher when you recruit one? *Education Finance and Policy, 6*(1), 43–74.

Rosenbaum, J. (1976). *Making inequality: the hidden curriculum of high school tracking.* New York: Wiley.

Rubin, B. C. (2006). Tracking and detracking: debates, evidence, and best practices for a heterogeneous world. *Theory Into Practice, 45*(1), 4–14.

Slavin, R. E. (1990). Achievement effects of ability grouping in secondary schools: a best-evidence synthesis. *Review of Educational Research, 60*(3), 471–499.

Sutton Trust. (2011). *Improving the impact of teachers on pupil achievement in the UK – interim findings.* London: Sutton Trust.

7

WHY IS GOOD PRACTICE IN SETTING SO DIFFICULT TO ACHIEVE?

We showed in Chapter 2 that grouping by attainment remains the dominant practice in English schools, but is problematic given its negative effects on lower attaining pupils. We have discussed various findings from our own study that demonstrate ongoing inequity resulting from setting: in Chapter 4 we demonstrated the impact of attainment grouping on pupil self-confidence, showing the negative impact on lower attainers, and the cumulative impact over time. Chapter 5 outlined our findings concerning inequitable patterns in set allocation. And in the previous chapter we showed how low sets are less likely to be allocated subject expert teachers, and frequently complain of 'dumbed down' pedagogy reflecting low expectations. However, we have also argued that not all attainment grouping is equal: setting (grouping by attainment in individual subjects) is preferable to streaming (where pupils are grouping by a general notion of 'ability' and stay in the same group across the curriculum). Our 'Best Practice in Setting' intervention was premised on the idea of militating against some of the ways in which setting causes harm, to attempt to improve equity in setting practice.

In this chapter, we investigate the experience from our study that schools found many of the elements of our 'best practice' intervention – which were designed to ensure conceptual integrity and practical quality in setting practice – difficult to implement. In fact, as explained in Chapter 3, we had significant attrition from the intervention group over the course of the trial, suggesting that schools found our stipulations difficult. Even if pedagogic approaches are substantiated by research, if they are difficult to implement in practice this will impede efficacy and likely render such approaches fruitless. This chapter, then, explores the extent to which our intervention was fully subscribed to by schools, and the various reasons that many schools seemed to either dislike it, or to struggle to implement the various elements in totality. Our findings are important for informing further development (or otherwise) of future approaches, and provide important evidence on the potential and limits of improvement.

In Chapter 3, we outlined the stipulations of our 'Best Practice in Setting' (BPS) intervention, which draws on the research evidence to militate against the detrimental effects of attainment grouping. As a reminder, the elements of our intervention were:

- Sets organised in three or four 'levels'.
- Students allocated to sets by Key Stage 2 attainment only.
- Students moved between sets at regular points, by assessment results only.
- Teachers allocated to sets randomly, or according to 'Best Practice Principles'.
- Teachers applying high expectations for all pupils regardless of prior attainment (supported by teachers from each participating department attending professional development sessions that addressed this issue).

In this chapter we will consider each of the elements of the intervention in turn and examine the extent to which schools complied with each request and the various structural, political, and practical explanations we discovered for this, via our interview and survey data from teachers.[1] [2]

Sets organised in three or four 'levels'

The stipulation for schools in our intervention group to group their pupils into three or four set levels was designed to ensure that sets contained reasonably broad ranges of prior attainment; to minimise steep hierarchies; and to reduce the impact of labelling by 'ability'. We did not specify beyond the number of levels any detail of how schools should group their pupils: for example, schools had complete freedom to have different numbers or sizes of groups at each level.

Table 7.1 shows levels of adherence to this intervention requirement, calculated from schools' reports of their pupils' class membership. We can see that schools' adherence to this stipulation was moderate, with only 15% of schools in the maths intervention, and 11% in English, saying that they had not adopted this approach. And in spite of the large amount of missing data, nearly half of schools in the maths intervention and over 40% of those in the English intervention stated that they had grouped their pupils in the required three or four set levels. The number of sets reported in the intervention schools ranged from three to five in maths, and from two to six in English.

In our survey, we asked teachers in BPS intervention schools whether they felt that setting pupils in three or four set levels was practical or beneficial for all

TABLE 7.1 Sets organised in three or four 'levels', calculated from school class data

	Mathematics schools (n=60)		English schools (n=45)	
Yes	29	48.3%	19	42.2%
No	9	15.0%	5	11.1%
Missing	22	36.7%	21	46.7%

pupils. Responses are summarised in Tables 7.5 (maths teachers) and 7.6 (English teachers). Maths teachers were overwhelmingly negative about the practicality of this stipulation, with no one responding that they agreed[3] that it was practical to group pupils in this way. Moreover, only a minority of English teachers (20%) agreed that this form of grouping was practical to implement. Mathematics teachers were also sceptical about the benefits for pupils, with nearly two-thirds (63%) *dis*agreeing that it was beneficial for all pupils, although a portion (23%) felt that it was beneficial.[4] This lack of support may explain the difficulties for some schools to gain 'buy in' from staff, and/or why the intervention may have been experienced as difficult to implement, and it comprises an unexpected finding from our study – we had no inkling that somewhat constraining the number of set levels would be perceived as difficult or undesirable.

At the end of each interview with teachers in intervention schools, we asked them about their experiences of the intervention. School X was one of the schools that had not subscribed properly to the set number stipulation, as they had maintained five mathematics set levels, and maths teacher Ajda explained that to have reduced the number of levels would have been 'too much work'. She elaborated that her colleagues were 'happy' with how things were, because 'they kind of feel it works'. She also pointed out that there were workload implications to making a change to the number of set levels: 'it would have been changing the schemes of work slightly, doing extra work in that sense and, you know, I don't think the school would have been happy about it'. This begs a question about the extent to which teachers, individually and collectively, realise they need to take seriously particular stipulations in an intervention; and relatedly suggests we were not successful in communicating this importance.

By contrast, Larry from School Q felt that having three set levels was completely unproblematic, because it was 'pretty much what we're doing so far'. In fact, Larry's assessment was that three set levels was the approach used by '99% of schools' and he referred to this as 'the normal way' that he thought 'most of the teachers [would] be familiar with'.

The difference in response from Ajda and Larry gives us an indication of one of the barriers facing schools in changing setting practice, that *any change at all* is perceived as something that will create extra work, so the status quo is to be preferred. Although understandable, especially in a period of stretched resource for schools and where teacher workload is recognised even by the government to be problematic (DfE, 2019), this is a concern – as resistance to even a slight change to the scheme of work prohibits more equitable setting practice. It is notable as well that even where a change in practice is considered potentially beneficial, the (im) practicalities might be overwhelming.

Students allocated to sets by Key Stage 2 attainment only

The second stipulation of our intervention was to allocate pupils to sets based solely on Key Stage 2 assessment data. This was to avoid bias, ensuring that setting was consistent and focused exclusively on attainment. A summary of adherence to this point can be found in Table 7.2.[5] As we can see, schools appeared to find this stipulation more difficult than that of the number of set levels, with nearly a third of maths intervention schools, and over a quarter of English intervention schools, stating that they had *not* allocated pupils to sets using only attainment data, and only a similar number saying that they had. (Indeed, for English a smaller number stated they had applied the stipulation than had not: just over one-fifth of schools in the intervention for English, and less than one-third of mathematics schools, stated that they had allocated pupils to sets simply by attainment). Although we cannot know the approach adopted by the large number of schools that did not provide data, the active responses suggest low adherence generally on this measure.

Again this was an area where teachers were sceptical about the practicality of our request (see Tables 7.5 and 7.6). In the survey, intervention teachers tended to disagree that it would be practical to allocate pupils to sets exclusively according to Key Stage 2 results, with 77% of mathematics teachers and 57% of English teachers disagreeing with the statement. However, teachers were more positive about the potential benefits: Two-thirds of teachers in the English intervention agreed that setting only by KS2 attainment would be beneficial for all, while only 27% disagreed. Teachers in the maths intervention were a little less enthusiastic, with 47% agreeing that it would be beneficial. Nevertheless, only around a third of maths teachers (35%) disagreed.

One might wonder therefore what other information is being used to group pupils and why KS2 results are not being used as the exclusive mechanism, given that teachers seem positive about potential benefits. In our teacher survey we also asked teachers what information was used to group pupils into sets. We found that KS2 test data was the most popular choice reported by both maths (74%) and English (89%) teachers, however, a wide range of other sources of information were also reported. Maths teachers reported making use of tests devised by the school (46%), commercial tests (26%), and teacher judgement (25%). English teachers likewise subscribed to the same alternative methods, but among this group commercial tests were more likely to be adopted (42%), followed by school-devised tests (35%), and teacher judgement (18%). This finding on the extensive use of other sources to determine set level, even by the intervention group, is concerning on a number of fronts. KS2 data is widely available and provides a reliable and

TABLE 7.2 Pupils allocated to sets by Key Stage 2 attainment data only

	Mathematics schools (n=60)		English schools (n=45)	
Yes	19	31.7%	10	22.2%
No	19	31.7%	13	28.9%
Missing	22	36.7%	22	48.9%

Source: Taylor et al. (2019)

TABLE 7.3 Sources of information for allocation of pupils to sets in intervention schools, 2015/16*

	Mathematics teachers (n=134)		English teachers (n=66)	
KS2 test	99	74%	53	89%
KS2 teacher assessment	45	34%	24	42%
Commercial test	35	26%	26	42%
School's test	61	46%	20	35%
Teacher judgement	34	25%	18	30%
Teacher observation	10	7%	8	14%
Parental judgement	0	0%	0	0%
Feeder school information	8	6%	10	17%
Random allocation	1	1%	0	0%
I'm not sure	4	3%	9	14%
Total responses	297		168	

Source: Adapted from Taylor et al. (2019)

* More than one teacher may have responded per school and teachers were able to choose as many options as applicable.

valid source of information for predicting attainment at KS4 (Treadaway, 2013). The use of commercial tests is unlikely therefore to add value and may reflect a poor use of school funds for this purpose. Tests devised by the school are unlikely to meet the rigorous standards of either KS2 assessments or commercially available tests and so are not likely to be a reliable source of information for allocating pupils to sets on the basis of an assessment of current attainment. The use of teacher judgement is more worrying still, as this is a factor known to introduce bias into the attainment grouping process (Campbell, 2015; Gillborn & Youdell, 2000; Timmermans et al., 2015). It is heartening however to see that no schools in our intervention group were being swayed by parental judgement!

In fact, all of the teachers we interviewed reported that they were using KS2 results to group pupils, but the way in which they used them varied widely. In some schools they were used alone, for example Dominic (maths, School T) asserted that grouping was by 'Key Stage 2 prior attainment, of course, yes'. While in other schools they were used in combination with other data:

> [groups were initially] based on SATS and teacher-assessed work [. . .] And then after October half-term [. . .] we used the NFER reading tests and the graded 100 scores to allocate them into sets.
>
> *(Ellie, School T, English)*

Sources were combined in different ways, for example calculating an average score, or refining or triangulating decisions. Mark (English, School Q) wasn't sure how multiple sources of data were combined in his school:

So, the school policy in English is we set students by ability, so in Year 7 students come in and are given a spelling test and some writing tests where they have to do some creative writing and some non-fiction writing. We also have all of their Key Stage 2 data sent up from their primary schools, and using all of that information *we set students by ability.*

The approaches in some schools were highly complex. Teachers may have felt that they or their schools were executing a sophisticated and accurate grouping strategy, but by diverging from our stipulation of grouping by KS2 attainment only, participants were reducing the conceptual integrity of the intervention and introducing opportunities for biased judgements to influence the process.

So why are schools so reluctant to group based on KS2 attainment alone? We explored this question in our teacher interviews and there were some frequently recurring themes.

The most common concern cited was a belief that Key Stage 2 results lacked validity; that results 'don't really reflect that ability' (Dominic, maths, School T). Dawn (English, School R) articulated an unease with relying on a one-off performance as a measure:

> You know, they might have had an off-day. They might have had . . . you know, something might have happened around the time of the test that affected it. Then again, they might have had a very, very good day, or might have had a bit of a fluke or something like that.

However, of course one-off exam results are used as an indicator at other stages in the education system including secondary schools, for example at GCSE for access to study of subjects at A Level, and at A Level for access to universities. Other teachers were sceptical of the validity of results, illustrating the mistrust that some secondary school teachers have of primary school practices, such as teaching to the test. This narrative was reflected by Hayley (maths, School R) who blamed the accountability demands on primary schools:

> A lot of pupils just get hot-housed, so they just get trained and drilled for the SATs, sit the SATs, and then don't actually understand any of the maths; they are just trained to practice these few things, so that when they actually do come to do it, they've forgotten it, because they were only trained to remember it and they have forgotten it since they came to Year 7.

Other teachers cited practical problems with KS2 results: Dev (maths, School T) pointed out that not all pupils arrive with data:

> So if you've got somebody who's come with no Key Stage 2 data and they started in September, what have you put in place or what is your assessment or your starting point to analyse where that child should go?

However, retesting an entire year group may be considered an extreme solution to resolving the set allocation of a very few pupils without KS2 results.

Another practical problem experienced by schools was that 'somehow we don't have the Key Stage 2 data prior to the students entering the school' (Dominic, maths, School T). Inevitably, this poses a difficulty for schools, because they are unable to group pupils immediately. However, this is no different to other forms of testing applied by the host secondary school, which would take place after the beginning of the school year in September.

Finally, it was striking that in some schools even the heads of subject did not know for certain how pupils were grouped. For example, at School Q there was a high degree of disagreement between teachers as to how bands and sets were structured. All the teachers interviewed there had been in post for less than three years, high staff turnover being a factor that would prevent classroom teachers and subject leaders from engaging in the decision-making process about how pupils should be allocated to sets.

Overall, teachers' views on grouping by KS2 attainment are somewhat contradictory and this may underlie the difficulty schools had with this aspect of our intervention. Teachers see the benefit in setting by attainment, but some find the practicalities insurmountable, and perhaps in some schools teachers are not in the position to intervene in longstanding operational cultures.

Students moved between sets at regular points, by assessment results only

The third stipulation of our intervention was to have regular movement of pupils between groups at fixed points in the school year. We identified the Christmas break 2015, summer holiday 2016, and Christmas holiday 2016 as the three points for movement and requested schools only to move pupils at these times. In fact the purpose of this was to encourage movement, rather than to restrict it, as typically teachers overestimate the amount of movement between sets in their schools (Hallam & Ireson, 2005). We found it very difficult to draw conclusions about the extent of set movement between groups, because of issues with missing data. However, our teacher survey and interview data are helpful in understanding how set movement is regarded and carried out in schools.

In terms of teachers' views about whether the set movement stipulation was practical or beneficial, survey results revealed that again maths teachers were not enthusiastic, with over two-thirds (70%) disagreeing that it was practical to implement, and over half (54%) disagreeing that it was beneficial for all pupils. English teachers were also sceptical, with half disagreeing that it was practical and 60% disagreeing that it was beneficial.

In fact, our teacher interviews revealed that it was not just impractical but nigh on impossible to move pupils mid-year in some schools.

Practical and financial constraints on decisions around timetabling in some schools profoundly impeded the movement of pupils between sets. In some larger schools, timetable flexibility was achieved through banding: dividing a year group into two or more sub-groups that were then timetabled as a block. Banding permitted teachers to teach more than one class within a year group and was therefore an economical way of employing specialist teachers. Furthermore, in some schools the bands were set up at different 'ability' levels and operate as streams. Samira (School T, English) described the system within her school: '7A1, 7A2, I have 7A2 which is the A band, and then the B band, B1 and B2'. Students could not move between bands A and B during the school year. At School Y, Patrick likewise explained that he is unable to move pupils between bands, explaining that any such rare decisions would be 'down to "Pupil Progress"' ('Pupil Progress' is the function title referring to the middle leader responsible for pupil progress within a school year group). In other words, movement between streams was highly restricted and had to be negotiated with colleagues.

Further complexity was introduced by the fact that some intervention schools even appeared to be streaming rather than setting, or setting within streams (setting was supposed to be the only attainment method being applied in the intervention). Patrick, mentioned above, explained that at his school the banding extended across the entire curriculum. Ajda (mathematics, School X) reported that at her school 'in Year 7 and 8 maths and science are set together, they're timetabled together, so some kids in Year 7 will be having maths, some will be having science'. This particular subject combination wherein set levels were extended from maths across the sciences is especially common in English schooling. Likewise, at School R, English was timetabled against RE. This practice also introduces elements of streaming, compromising the integrity of the intervention and introducing difficulties for set movement. In fact, Ajda was clear that her colleagues in the maths department were unhappy about this arrangement 'because sometimes the science teachers are like, "this kid is really bright in science", but in maths they're not doing as well in terms of the results'. She reported that such situations would lead to the respective heads of department discussing individual pupil cases and 'trying to compromise', while both feeling that setting by attainment in their subject was important.

Hence, when subjects were timetabled together, this necessitated negotiations between subject teams for the initial placement of pupils, and also meant that renegotiation was required if pupils were to be moved between sets mid-year. But even without these arrangements between subjects, in some schools a highly complex timetable meant that for a pupil to move group for one subject would have serious consequences. Ellie (English, School T) told us, 'Year 7 are never all taught [English] at the, like, their classes aren't at the same time. [. . .] So to move them in, say, English would mean them moving in every subject'. She went on:

> When we've looked at maybe one student that was definitely out of place in English, but he was maybe fine in maths. There was no way of moving them in one subject without it affecting every other subject, and without them getting the full new timetable. So that's been my main logistical concern and what I can't really get my head round.

While Ellie could not think of a solution to this problem, it seems that it was an artefact of the 'completely erratic' Year 7 timetable. She told us that Year 8 was 'a little bit different' and had more flexibility, suggesting that more thoughtful timetabling could result in greater equity for pupils. Certainly, practices of banding – which often contain elements of, or equate to, streaming – appear problematic, both in impeding the fluidity required for fairness and efficacy in setting, and in introducing streaming.

Furthermore, movement was often not based solely on assessment. Indeed some teachers cautioned against the assessment-only approach required by our intervention. Chloe (School R, English) felt that summative assessments didn't give the 'full picture of everything [. . .] they might just have had a bad day' and stressed the importance of 'build[ing] up that picture over time' before moving a pupil. Dev (maths, School T) asserted that movement should be based on not just whether a pupil was at the top of their group, but that there 'should be a good firm overlap along with teacher assessment and commentary'. Larry (School Q, maths) suggested that 'attitude to learning' should be factor. The emphasis on teachers' subjective perceptions of pupils' performance and behaviour articulated in these teachers' preferences is perhaps understandable; yet research shows the importance of non-subjective approaches, given that teacher perceptions are shown to be influenced by pupil characteristics (e.g. Gillborn & Youdell, 2000; Archer & Francis, 2006; Connolly et al., forthcoming).

Compounding such views was an apparent resistance, for some teachers, to the idea of movement across sets as beneficial at all. For these teachers, there appeared a strong urge to keep pupils in the same groups. Dawn (School R, English) stated that 'we try to keep [movement] to a minimum'. Hayley (School R, maths) describes strategies her department used before moving set as 'the last option': 'if it's behaviour, they can go on report. If it's achievement, we have a discussion with them about what they can do'. Richard (School Q, English) argued that 'I think actually having the consistency in the setting is as important, in some ways, as being sure someone is in the right group', feeling that 'a good relationship with a teacher [. . .] can be far more powerful'. Patrick (English, School Y) explained that he would only seek to move pupils if they were moving up or down two English groups, rather than one, and Dev (maths, School T) described needing to see large gains or losses in attainment before considering moving a pupil, so that pupils didn't move from the top of one group to the bottom of the next or vice versa.

On the other hand, many teachers did not share such views. And indeed, it seemed that, on occasion, our stipulation of moving any pupils that were shown to be over- or underperforming in assessment between sets at three testing points across the two year period of the intervention, may have actually limited movement in some schools. Our assumption, based in the research literature, had been that set movement would be strongly limited and require encouragement (via our intervention stipulation). However, we also found some teachers who felt restricted by our intervention and would have moved pupils more frequently or at different times had they been permitted to. Larry and Sophie (maths, School Q) both felt that the intervention reduced the amount of movement that was permitted. Sophie in particular was frustrated because pupils 'weren't allowed to move' and she felt that there were pupils in the wrong groups as a result. Samira (English, School T) told us about her school's policy on set movement, which she considered to be 'best practice':

> There's been a push on ensuring, for instance, like the pupil premium students, are in the top sets moving them up. I've had, like, a few students moved up from Set 2 to Set 1 even though they're not as able as those in my Set 1, just for them to have that experience and be in the same classroom.

This demonstrates that some schools are thinking carefully about how they can increase the equity of their grouping practices. Nevertheless, we would suggest that the approach expounded by Samira remains problematic given the opportunity to move is only open to some pupils, and appears to undermine the conceptual basis of setting (i.e. if sets are not based on homogenous attainment levels, why practice it at all?). Our preference is for a systematic approach equally applied to all pupils in order to reduce any potential bias.

Despite this complex picture, it is clear that movement is frequently restricted in schools, either due to teachers' views, or – more frequently – because of practical arrangements, school policies and practices that contrive to keep pupils in the same set levels. These school-wide policies and practical arrangements often make it hard for individual teachers to intervene, and make good practice in pupil movement very difficult to achieve.

Teachers allocated to sets randomly, or according to 'Best Practice Principles'

We now turn our attention to the allocation, not of pupils but of *teachers* to sets. The fourth stipulation of our intervention was originally to allocate teachers randomly to sets, in order to remove any bias in teacher placement. Randomisation was to be carried out by the project team and not by schools. During our pilot and recruitment phase, we became aware that this option was likely to be very unappealing to schools. We were told both that schools would not want to relinquish control of this aspect of their practice, or that (and this seems a natural corollary of the issues with set movement above) constraints of timetabling would not allow teachers to be assigned to sets at random. As a result of this, we proposed a potential alternative stipulation to schools, should they not agree to randomisation of teachers to set groups: three 'Best Practice Principles' for the allocation of teachers to sets:

1. Newly qualified teachers and non-subject specialist teachers should not be generally allocated to the lowest set level.
2. Teachers should be allocated to the sets with a view to ensuring an equitable distribution both across year groups and year-on-year.

3. Teachers should not teach the same set in the Year 8 in the 2015/16 academic year as in Year 7 in the 2014/15 academic year.

In the event, only three schools were prepared for us to randomise teachers to sets in Year 7, so clearly the randomisation of teachers was unpalatable to schools, as predicted. In fact, one of the schools that requested randomisation for Year 7 later told us that they were unable to implement this; and no schools sent us details of their teachers for randomisation in Year 8.

Rather surprisingly, and despite the reluctance to take up randomisation of teachers as a practice, respondents to our survey were somewhat positive about the stipulation. While around half (49%) of mathematics teachers disagreed that random allocation of teachers to sets was *practical*, 58% declared that it would be *beneficial* for all pupils. A very similar pattern was found for English teachers, with 63% disagreeing that it was practical, but 57% asserting that it was beneficial.

We can see this contrast in the responses of teachers in interviews. Dinh (maths, School X) offered a common view: 'I think [random allocation] is fine for that because every teacher is able to teach different ability group'. Similarly, Ellie (English, School T) felt that 'it's nice that you've not always got the bottom sets' and enjoyed the variety in teaching different groups because it 'is nice because it just means you go from different things'.

In fact, the 'equitable distribution of classes' element of our Best Practice Principles seemed to be regular practice in some schools. Hayley (mathematics, School R) told us that 'We just, kind of, do it fairly, so we say "what have you got? Right, well you've got a top set in this year, so we should balance that out with a lower ability."' The rationale in Hayley's school was very much one of equity in terms of workload and behaviour management:

> So, we just, kind of, do it on fairness as well, because I think, sometimes, the best-behaved classes are your higher ability ones, so sometimes it's not fair to give somebody all the higher ability ones, and none of the lower ability ones. And, it would be unfair to give somebody all the lower ability ones, especially if you had a bottom set.

Likewise, Larry (maths, School Q) explains that the Best Practice Principles reflected business as usual in his department: 'what we do is we allocate the teachers to different sets. Every teacher has got some year of Set 1 and some of the Set 4 so we do it anyway'.

By way of contrast, Richard (English, School Q) identified that it was difficult to allocate teachers to sets, because 'we do have a relatively young department that the school is frequently getting more Teach First participants in, and School Direct trainees, and PGCEs, so it's hard to often know where to put those'. In fact, Richard notes that placing these teachers in Year 7 was a preference 'because it's in some ways the least impactful place'. Richard's comment brings to the fore the fact that the allocation of teachers to sets does not happen in isolation for a year group, instead it can be seen as part of a holistic picture for all year groups in the school.

Ellie (English, School T) identified an advantage of randomisation being that of teacher development. She suggests that because some teachers are 'maybe better with certain types of children', randomisation supports the broadening of skill sets. However, Dev (maths, School T) had a different view of best practice, arguing instead for stability of staffing, especially for the lowest group: 'I'd say the most stable staffing, if it's directed at your lowest-attaining group, if you are setting, will yield results in years to come'. Dev was of the opinion that this would work best if it could be extended over a two- or three-year cycle, especially at Key Stage 4.

It seems that for the allocation of teachers, as with the allocation and movement of pupils, there are some practical constraints that make randomisation difficult. Albeit, we remain intrigued as to how or why it is so prevalently received as insurmountable (especially given the equity imperative). However, some schools do seem to have a sense of allocating of sets to teachers based around ensuring that teachers get their fair share of higher and lower sets (though this also needs to be considered in the light of our findings about teacher quality, see Chapter 6). The purpose of this seems to be focused on giving teachers a balanced experience in terms of workload and pupil behaviour, as well as allowing for teacher development. It is notable that in teachers' above responses the emphasis is on the benefit for teachers, rather than pupils – suggesting that one reason why good practice in setting is difficult to achieve is that schools' attention could be more clearly focused on benefitting pupils.

Teachers applying high expectations for all pupils regardless of prior attainment

Attendance of the professional development sessions

The final stipulation of our intervention was that teachers from each participating department should attend professional development sessions on how to support and actualise high expectations for all pupils irrespective of set/attainment level, and then cascade their learning to colleagues in their department. There were four professional development events across the Best Practice in Setting intervention, with topics and timing summarised in Table 7.4.

While attendance at professional development sessions and the cascading of teachers' learning was initially enthusiastic, it tailed off later in the project. We

TABLE 7.4 Summary of professional development sessions

Session	Content	Date
1	Intervention overview	July 2015
2	High expectations and a flexible conception of 'ability'	October 2015
3	A rich curriculum for all; differentiation	February 2016
4	Review of the intervention and progress check	September 2016

were very aware of the burden of attending professional development on teachers and schools and took the following measures to make it as feasible as possible:

- Professional development was organised around six 'hubs', the locations of which were determined by the locations of schools in the intervention group.
- Professional development events were twilight sessions, i.e. they ran after the end of the school day, thus minimising the need for teachers' lessons to be covered.
- When teachers could not attend a particular session, we invited them to come to an alternative one (realistically, this only worked for the two London-based hubs) or to attend training via Skype.
- We sent out the professional development materials to all schools, regardless of whether they had attended the session or not (this is why in some cases the percentage of schools cascading learning is greater than the percentage attending professional development).

Despite these efforts, numbers reduced particularly significantly for session four. There seems to have been an effect here of the timing of this session at the beginning of the school year, which coincided with school open evenings for a number of schools. Given that the professional development sessions were the key way in which the realisation of high expectations in practice was supposed to be discussed, agreed, and cascaded for the intervention, the lack of full attendance, and significant reduction in attendance over time, presented a significant challenge, and likely reduced effective impact of this element. What, then, explained this reduced engagement?

In general, teachers were positive in their feedback about the professional development events. For example, teachers reported the benefits of an opportunity to discuss with teachers from different schools, and the reflection provoked by different opinions presented. Albeit, others had sometimes felt less engaged, and the lack of continuity in attendees, coupled with the lag between meetings, meant that key messages or assumptions of the intervention had not always been understood. Fundamentally, the 'after hours' nature of the provision, coupled with sometimes significant journeys necessary for attendance, seems to have been a key – and perhaps unsurprising – impediment to attendance of hardworking professionals in a national context of workload challenge.

High expectations for all pupils regardless of prior attainment

As we explained above, we were keen for teachers to attend the professional development event because our review of the literature had revealed key issues of expectations and curriculum that could only be addressed through training and development, rather than through structural changes to pupil grouping practices. Yet attendance at professional development had not been as strong as we had hoped, and this will likely have impacted the level to which high expectations for all were upheld and/or manifested *in practice* in intervention classrooms.

This element was assessed through the teacher survey conducted towards the end of the two-year trial. An average score was calculated for each school from teachers' responses to the survey item 'Colleagues have high expectations of all students regardless of prior attainment'. This is recognised to be a nebulous indicator, given that it is easy to state that one has high expectations of pupils, but often harder to enact these in the classroom, or to evidence this (Mazenod et al., 2019). In the schools that responded to the final teacher survey, approximately half of these met the above criterion for high expectations.

Clearly this survey measure is a limited and somewhat superficial indicator. In absence of systematic observational data in our study, or probing with teachers on this point in interviews, it is not possible for us to further explain this mixed result. However, we have already discussed in Chapter 6 some of the practical challenges around application of high expectations for all pupils. We found that there was substantial evidence of variation of teachers' expectations, as perceived by pupils in different sets. Teachers of higher sets were typically perceived as more strict than those teaching low sets and offered more challenging work to students in higher sets. Teachers tended not to agree with this perception, being more likely to say explicitly that their expectations were the same, but nevertheless describing quite different expectations as manifest in the curriculum and pedagogy provided to different groups.

Barriers to good practice in setting

We have summarised above the struggles that schools had with adhering to our intervention and some of the reasons they shared with us for this difficulty. Overall, schools had moderate success, and teacher support for the stipulations of our intervention was variable to say the least. Even when teachers broadly supported a stipulation, they had doubts as to how practical it might be to implement and this was borne out in the reflections of teachers on the specific requirements. The practical impediments listed were intriguing and often concerning from a research perspective – they often reflect longstanding organisational approaches within schools with which teachers feel powerless to intervene.

These issues were also reflected when we additionally asked teachers more generally about what barriers there might be to taking up the intervention practices. One key obstacle cited was the school timetable. Dominic's (maths, School T) observations were indicative of numerous responses:

> Timetabling is the biggest problem, definitely. I think senior leadership or whoever is in charge of that needs to rethink that and needs to rethink it in terms of best practice. I am not sure how they would do that but perhaps you need somebody who has got a better ability or someone who is much better at doing it in charge of it.

Dominic's words are telling in that achieving best practice is out of the hands of the classroom teacher. Good practice needs to be fully supported by the senior leadership team and planned for a long time in advance. Issues like impact on timetabling may not be intuitive (especially for those in both senior management and among the teaching staff who do not have to organise this), and we hope that our findings in this regard will make an important enabling contribution in highlighting the need to reflect on this issue. Typically the timetabling process will begin several months prior to the school year for which it is going to apply. As we heard from teachers in Chapter 6, planning will include considerations of available staff, pupil numbers and finance, all of which put constraints on the possibilities of the timetable. Unless a strong vision for equitable practice is incorporated at an early stage, schools will struggle to make retrospective changes for the better later on.

A related problem is that of *complexity* of the timetable, in terms of balancing sequencing and staff resource. Hayley (maths, School R) reported how problems arose when 'Year 7 were just completely all taught maths at a completely different time; there weren't even, like, two teachers that taught maths to Year 7 at the same time, it was completely different'. As we have discussed above, such complexity impacts on the flexibility of grouping and whether pupils can be moved between groups. More encouragingly, Hayley recounts that her school later resolved this issue, and reflects that, 'It just depends where you start this because, obviously, with the Year 7s, now, it will be completely fair and allocated'.

Getting a person with the right skills and vision to oversee the timetabling and ensuring availability of the requisite data are essential first steps to more equitable setting practices. Where movement is impeded or set placement dictated by the system, rather than by pupil needs, good practice in setting will be impossible to achieve.

Another challenge is to the improvement of equity is the necessary identification of issues within existing practice which potentially remain unrecognised. There was a notable paradox in teacher responses to our 'Best Practice in Setting' intervention, in that while many teachers regarded our intervention as impractical and even unachievable (see above); many other teachers indicated that our stipulations were unremarkable and even difficult to distinguish from what they were already doing. A quote from Larry (maths, School Q) is illustrative:

Interviewer: In terms of just what we've asked you to do for setting this year and last year, is that much different to what you would be doing anyway?

Larry: Not much difference, not much. We know what we need to do and we did do it, but in terms of the approach I can't see any difference so far.

It may be that some of the schools concerned were already implementing similar practices so that our intervention requirements did simply gel with this existing practice. Indeed we came across examples where, for example, highly expert and experienced teachers were placed with low sets (see Chapter 6), where schools did allocate solely on the basis of national test scores, and so on. However, this of course raises questions as to why other schools found the intervention requirements so countercultural and challenging to accommodate. It may also be that some schools believed their existing practice fitted our requirements when it didn't (as indicated by the significant portions of responses indicating a lack of compliance on certain measures). Achieving changes in practice is hard (Ruthven, 2009; Taylor et al., 2019), but in order to make a change, teachers have to be able to identify what they need to change. If they consider that their current practices are already 'good practice' then they are unlikely to be motivated to change.

Another barrier to good practice is staff turnover. Richard (English, School Q) told us that colleagues who had been leading on the intervention in his school had either gone on long-term sick leave, or had left for other reasons. It wasn't just the staff leading the intervention that had moved on: at School Q, none of the members of staff we talked to had been in post longer than three years. Hence the crisis in teacher recruitment and retention in Britain, ongoing at the time of writing (Syal, 2018), was having a detrimental impact here as in so many other areas of teaching and learning. With changes to practice and/or ethos requiring strong leadership to drive and maintain, schools with high staff turnover are at risk of not being able to embed improved attainment grouping practices.

In order for the harms of setting to be reduced, it would need to be feasible for schools to overcome the hurdles described above. Effecting change in schools and particularly in classrooms is challenging (Cuban, 1993), and the immediate pressures on teachers can further reduce the viability further (Hargreaves & Shirley, 2009). In a supportive policy climate, with reduced pressures on teachers, we think the problems we have raised above would not be insurmountable, but they would require schools to determinedly prioritise equity for pupils in their strategic planning.

Chapter summary

We have explored in this chapter some of the reasons why good practice in setting is so difficult to achieve. We have seen that adherence to our intervention was only moderate, and that teachers were often doubtful about how practical our stipulations were. Although teachers perceived the intervention requirements to be potentially beneficial, this scepticism, along with genuine practical obstacles, and difficulties with recognising where practices need to change, all stood in the way of improving setting practices in schools. In particular we found that very prosaic considerations such as timetabling, finance, and staffing were obstructing the possibility of more equitable grouping practices. We therefore suggest that schools need to prioritise the benefit for pupils if improvements in setting practices are going to be made.

TABLE 7.5 Maths BPS intervention teachers' views of the intervention (n=43)

	Strongly disagree	Slightly disagree	Neither agree/ disagree	Slightly agree	Strongly agree	Missing
Setting students at 3 to 4 set levels is practical to implement	24 55.8%	17 39.5%	2 4.7%	0 0.0%	0 0.0%	0 0.0%
Setting students at 3 to 4 set levels is beneficial for all students	11 25.6%	16 37.2%	6 14.0%	9 20.9%	1 2.3%	0 0.0%
Setting students exclusively on the basis of their KS2 results is practical to implement	13 30.2%	20 46.5%	4 9.3%	6 14.0%	0 0.0%	0 0.0%
Setting students exclusively on the basis of their KS2 results is beneficial for all students	3 7.0%	12 27.9%	7 16.3%	14 32.6%	6 14.0%	1 2.3%
Moving students between sets on the basis of assessment is practical to implement	12 27.9%	18 41.9%	2 4.7%	10 23.3%	0 0.0%	1 2.3%
Moving students between sets on the basis of assessment is beneficial for all students	4 9.3%	19 44.2%	6 14.0%	13 30.2%	0 0.0%	1 2.3%
The random allocation of teachers to sets is practical to implement	8 18.6%	13 30.2%	14 32.6%	5 11.6%	2 4.7%	1 2.3%
The random allocation of teachers to sets is beneficial for all students	4 9.3%	8 18.6%	6 14.0%	20 46.5%	5 11.6%	0 0.0%

TABLE 7.6 English BPS intervention teachers' views of the intervention (n=30)

	Strongly disagree	Slightly disagree	Neither agree/ disagree	Slightly agree	Strongly agree	Missing
Setting students at 3 to 4 set levels is practical to implement	11 36.7%	11 36.7%	2 6.7%	5 16.7%	1 3.3%	0 0.0%
Setting students at 3 to 4 set levels is beneficial for all students	4 13.3%	11 36.7%	3 10.0%	10 33.3%	2 6.7%	0 0.0%

(continued)

TABLE 7.6 *(continued)*

	Strongly disagree	*Slightly disagree*	*Neither agree/ disagree*	*Slightly agree*	*Strongly agree*	*Missing*
Setting students exclusively on the basis of their KS2 results is practical to implement	6 20.0%	11 36.7%	2 6.7%	4 13.3%	7 23.3%	0 0.0%
Setting students exclusively on the basis of their KS2 results is beneficial for all students	0 0.0%	8 26.7%	2 6.7%	10 33.3%	10 33.3%	0 0.0%
Moving students between sets on the basis of assessment is practical to implement	2 6.7%	13 43.3%	7 23.3%	4 13.3%	4 13.3%	0 0.0%
Moving students between sets on the basis of assessment is beneficial for all students	8 26.7%	10 33.3%	2 6.7%	4 13.3%	6 20.0%	0 0.0%
The random allocation of teachers to sets is practical to implement	8 26.7%	11 36.7%	5 16.7%	4 13.3%	2 6.7%	0 0.0%
The random allocation of teachers to sets is beneficial for all students	2 6.7%	4 13.3%	5 16.7%	12 40.0%	5 16.7%	2 6.7%

Notes

1 As part of a randomised controlled trial, typically data will also be collected regarding fidelity to the intervention programme. Fidelity analysis attempts to provide a measure of how closely participating schools adhered to the intervention: fundamentally, fidelity analysis is concerned with the extent to which the intervention was conducted as stipulated. This permits an 'on treatment analysis' to establish the impact of the intervention in schools where it was delivered as intended, alongside an 'intention to treat analysis' which includes all schools in the intervention group, regardless of whether they proceeded to apply the intervention or not (Connolly et al., 2018).

2 As noted in Chapter 3, the Education Endowment Foundation commissioned NFER to carry out an independent evaluation of the Best Practice in Grouping Students project. Their reports also include consideration of fidelity to the interventions (Roy et al., 2018a; Roy et al., 2018b).

3 Responded as agreeing slightly or strongly, here and throughout. Likewise, where 'disagreed' is used, we include those that disagreed slightly and disagreed strongly, unless otherwise stipulated.

4 English teachers were more divided on this point, with half disagreeing that applying three to four set levels was beneficial, and 40% agreeing.

5 This measure was calculated by computing the Spearman correlation coefficient for each school between Key Stage 3 reading or maths fine point score and the school-reported set level in English or maths respectively. Schools were deemed to have complied with the stipulation if the value of the correlation coefficient was 0.816 or higher, demonstrating that the variables share two-thirds of their variation in common. If the coefficient was lower than 0.816 the school was deemed not to have complied.

References

Archer, L. & Francis, B. (2006). *Understanding minority ethnic achievement: race, class, gender and 'success'*. London: Routledge.

Campbell, T. (2015). Stereotyped at seven? Biases in teacher judgement of pupils' ability and attainment. *Journal of Social Policy*, *44*(03), 517–547.

Connolly, P., Biggart, A., Miller, S., O'Hare, L., & Thurston, A. (2018). *Using randomised controlled trials in education*. London: Sage.

Connolly, P., Taylor, B., Francis, B., Archer, L., Hodgen, J., Mazenod, A., & Tereshchenko, A. (forthcoming, accepted). The misallocation of students to academic sets in maths: a study of secondary schools in England. *British Educational Research Journal*.

Cuban, L. (1993). *How teachers taught*. New York, NY: Teachers College Press.

DfE. (2019). New national strategy unveiled to boost teacher numbers. Retrieved from www.gov.uk/government/news/new-national-strategy-unveiled-to-boost-teacher-numbers.

Gillborn, D. & Youdell, D. (2000). *Rationing education: policy, practice, reform, and equity*. Buckingham: Open University Press.

Hallam, S. & Ireson, J. (2005). Secondary school teachers' pedagogic practices when teaching mixed and structured ability classes. *Research Papers in Education*, *20*(1), 3–24.

Hargreaves, A. & Shirley, D. (2009). The persistence of presentism. *Teachers College Record*, *111*(11), 2505–2534.

Mazenod, A., Francis, B., Archer, L., Hodgen, J., Taylor, B., Tereshchenko, A., & Pepper, D. (2019). Nurturing learning or encouraging dependency? Teacher constructions of students in lower attainment groups in English secondary schools. *Cambridge Journal of Education*, *49*(1), 53–68.

Roy, P., Styles, B., Walker, M., Morrison, J., Nelson, J., & Kettlewell, K. (2018a). *Best Practice in Grouping Students Intervention A: Best Practice in Setting evaluation report and executive summary*. London: Education Endowment Foundation.

Roy, P., Styles, B., Walker, M., Bradshaw, S., Nelson, J., & Kettlewell, K. (2018b). *Best Practice in Grouping Students Intervention B: Mixed Attainment Grouping pilot report and executive summary*. London: Education Endowment Foundation.

Ruthven, K. (2009). Towards a naturalistic conceptualisation of technology integration in classroom practice: the example of school mathematics. *Education & Didactique*, *3*(1), 131–159.

Syal, R. (2018, 31 January 2018). Teacher shortage leaves English schools in crisis, watchdog says. *The Guardian*. Retrieved from www.theguardian.com/education/2018/jan/31/teacher-shortage-leaves-english-schools-in-crisis-watchdog-says.

Taylor, B., Francis, B., Craig, N., Archer, L., Hodgen, J., Mazenod, A., Tereshchenko, A., & Pepper, D. (2019). Why is it difficult for schools to establish equitable practices in allocating students to attainment 'sets'? *British Journal of Educational Studies*, *67*(1), 5–24.

Timmermans, A. C., Kuyper, H., & van der Werf, G. (2015). Accurate, inaccurate, or biased teacher expectations: do Dutch teachers differ in their expectations at the end of primary education? *British Journal of Educational Psychology*, *85*(4), 459–478.

Treadaway, M. (2013). *An analysis of Key Stage 2 reliability and validity*. FFT Research Paper No. 2. London: Fischer Family Trust.

8

DOING MIXED ATTAINMENT GROUPING WELL

So far we have mainly focused on setting practice ('tracking by subject'), and challenges with equity. This chapter turns to the alternative to grouping by attainment; mixed attainment practice – or 'mixed ability',[1] as it tends to be known. We draw on our work with those schools in our study conducting successful mixed attainment practice, including schools in our pilot study and from the 'Best Practice in Mixed Attainment' trial. We will begin the chapter by exploring why teachers tend to perceive mixed attainment grouping to be difficult, considering some of the barriers to this practice. Next we will present some key aspects of good practice in mixed attainment grouping, gleaned from the literature, from interviews and focus groups with teachers and pupils, and from our classroom observations. Drawing out these features of good practice, we will also consider implications and needs for schools if they are to expand mixed attainment teaching.

What is mixed attainment grouping?

In the previous chapters we have considered some of the challenges relating to setting: the impact on pupil attainment and self-confidence outcomes, the inequitable distribution of high quality teaching, the differences in expectations, pedagogy, and curriculum experienced by pupils in different sets, and the overwhelming difficulty of mitigating these unintended detrimental practices associated with setting. One potential solution to these challenges is to consider adopting mixed attainment grouping, where classes are formed with a broad range of prior attainment in each group, and which may be a 'better bet' in terms of equity outcomes (EEF, 2018; OECD, 2013).

We characterise fully mixed attainment grouping as an approach where classes are formed with a range of prior attainment in each group broadly representative of the attainment range of the cohort as a whole. However, where secondary schools describe their practices as mixed attainment or 'mixed ability' they can be describing a number of different practices. These include fully mixed across the cohort (as with our definition); mixed attainment for the majority of the cohort but with an additional bottom set or nurture group; mixed attainment with a top set or stretch/challenge group; and/or even arrangements involving a large 'mixed middle' with both a top and bottom group (Taylor et al., forthcoming). Furthermore, within a mixed attainment class there may be formal or informal within-class grouping based on some measure of attainment or perception of 'ability'. Versions of mixed attainment grouping that are not actually completely mixed are of course seeking to address the principal perceived difficulty of mixed attainment grouping: how to teach pupils with a broad range of prior attainment effectively in the same classroom. And despite this proliferation of types of grouping described as mixed attainment, overall these approaches are less used than setting in key curriculum subject areas: why?

Why is mixed attainment grouping seen as difficult?

As we heard in Chapter 2, only a very small minority of secondary schools in England adopt mixed attainment grouping for the core subject of maths, and setting remains a popular grouping strategy for English and many other subjects as well. As we have described in detail elsewhere (Taylor et al., 2017) we found it a real challenge to find schools that were willing to change their practices and teach maths and English to mixed attainment groups following randomisation in our RCT study. Perhaps this is unsurprising, as moving from setting to mixed attainment grouping is a significant shift in practice and for many teachers of maths, a completely new experience. Tellingly, the majority of the 13 schools we were able to recruit to the Best Practice in Mixed Attainment trial were already using mixed attainment grouping and at least two of these joined the trial in order to share their strong commitment to mixed attainment grouping with other schools. We had determined that, in order to make recruitment possible, operation of a 'nurture group'[2] would not comprise an exclusion criterion in our trial. While we decided to allow use of this practice in our trial, this was in order to support recruitment. We consider that the inclusion of nurture groups is a potential limitation of our approach and that significant further research is needed on this form of practice. What was apparent from our recruitment experience, was that schools operating comprehensive mixed attainment grouping are hard to find. This, in conjunction with our troubles recruiting to the trial, paints a picture of schools perceiving mixed attainment grouping as difficult.

Considering why this might this be, responses from practitioners in our pilot study shed some light. We asked the teachers participating in the pilot project to complete a short survey about their views on grouping and on the development process, receiving 16 completions, and also interviewed the Head of English and Head of Maths in one of our pilot schools (School F). A strong theme emerging was the perceived difficulty of mixed attainment grouping. Teachers' explanations are summarised in Table 8.1, where we attempt to group the concerns articulated by theme. Numbers indicate the number of times a theme or concern was mentioned.

The most frequently mentioned difficulties related to stakeholder opinions, workload, and pedagogy. There was particular concern about resistance from colleagues and lack of time to do the work necessary to teach mixed attainment groupings. For example, asked in the short pilot year survey about the challenges of mixed attainment teaching, teachers responded:

> Getting the department teachers on board; changing mindsets of established teachers.

> The biggest challenge was to get the team on board with the idea of mixed ability teaching in maths as experienced members in the team had no exposure to any such practices.

The teachers seemed to believe that only a minority of their colleagues would have positive feelings about changing to mixed attainment teaching. The dominance of attainment grouping as a method of organising teaching groups over such a prolonged period of time may mean that, particularly in maths, there are relatively few teachers with experience of mixed attainment teaching. Teachers tend not to change their classroom practices much over time, making only superficial adjustments (Cuban et al., 2001; Ruthven, 2009; Stigler & Hiebert, 1999). Hence, adapting to a wholly new approach, such as mixed attainment pedagogy, provides a major challenge. Experienced teachers are a resource that schools rely upon to deliver quality teaching and to act as models to new teachers, so when they are unsettled the system can be undermined. And in a period of recruitment and retention challenge, any such destabilisation or discontent may be seen as a particularly undesirable risk. Previous research has found that inexperienced and very long-experienced teachers are most averse to the ideas of mixed attainment practice: Reid et al. (1981) found that teachers in their first year, or with more than ten years' teaching experience, were least likely to be see the advantages of mixed attainment teaching. By contrast, those with prior experience of teaching across the full attainment range, and/or of teaching mixed attainment groups, and those whose initial teacher training placements included mixed attainment teaching, are more likely to perceive more advantages to mixed attainment (Reid et al., 1981). Teachers are also more likely to hold positive attitudes to mixed attainment teaching when they have some control over whether and how it is introduced (Reid et al., 1981). Welner and Burris (2006) suggest that teachers should be eased into teaching mixed attainment groups and provided with support and encouragement.

It is well-documented that teachers feel their workload is a source of great pressure (Banning-Lover, 2016; DfE, 2015). The teachers involved in our pilot feared

TABLE 8.1 Difficulties anticipated and experienced by pilot teachers

Stakeholder opinions		Workload factors		Pedagogic factors		Change factors		Accountability	
Colleagues	6	Time	6	Differentiation	4	Resisting change until certain	3	Results	1
Parents	3	Workload	4	Used to setting rather	4	Interpreting policy for the context	1	Judgements	1
Students	2	Resource development	2	than mixed attainment	2	Lack of exemplars	1		
School leaders	1	Need for training	1	Pace	1	Departmental autonomy	1		
Governors	1			Nature of maths	1				
				High attaining pupils	1				
				Low attaining pupils					
Total count of use of explanations	13		13		13		6		2

Source: Reproduced from Taylor et al. (2017)

that mixed attainment teaching would add to that burden, as illustrated by the questionnaire responses regarding challenges of mixed attainment:

Time is always an issue in teaching.

Time for teachers to participate/ facilitate/ develop principles and materials.

Time pressure!

Part of the reason a move to mixed attainment teaching is considered time-consuming is due to the need to develop entirely new lesson plans and resources: teachers were acknowledging that they could no longer use the materials they were accustomed to using with set groups. However, there is also a perception that it is almost always much more time-consuming to prepare for a mixed attainment group than for a set. This is because many teachers assume that multiple activities must be prepared in order to meet all learners' needs. This has resulted in some teachers claiming that mixed attainment teaching is unfeasible (Delisle, 2015). For example, from our own data, Daniel (maths, School S) told us about his experience, 'because it was mixed, I had to be planning for extension, core and support because they were all in there. It was just impossible'. We suggest that differentiation is better achieved through carefully designed, stimulating tasks that all pupils are able to make a start on. This type of task enables the teacher to offer rich feedback to pupils and allows pupils at all levels of prior attainment to progress (Hodgen & Marshall, 2005; Hodgen & Wiliam, 2006; Marshall & Wiliam, 2006). A gradual approach to the introduction of mixed attainment groups, focusing on specific year groups may also help with the impact on workload (Welner & Burris, 2006). We will discuss later in this chapter some of what we have gleaned about successful mixed attainment grouping.

Connected with concerns about time and workload, pedagogy was the third area of concern, particularly the perceived difficulty of meeting the needs of all pupils in the classroom. This was framed in a number of different ways in responses to the questionnaire, including with reference to issues such as 'differentiation', 'high attaining students, 'low attaining students', and 'pace':

Differentiation to a wide range and to stretch and challenge more able without causing disappointment to less able in the same class seems challenging.

If many of the students have weaker prior attainment it can be very easy to slip and have lowered expectations.

Research shows that when teaching attainment groups (streaming, or setting), teachers tend to view pupil attainment and capabilities within groups as homogenous (Hallam & Ireson, 2005; Hodgen, 2011) and thus feel that differentiation is not a concern. In fact the treatment of pupils within an 'ability' set as homogeneous is widely criticised (Boaler, 1997; Hallam & Ireson, 2005; Hodgen, 2011) and there is an adage that 'every class is a mixed ability class'. Nevertheless, encountering pupils with a diverse range of prior attainment within the same classroom is constructed as unfamiliar and intimidating, and a concern that mixed attainment groups are harder work to teach predominates. Fear of failing to meet the needs of lower attaining learners can be alleviated through the provision of a range of support, both in and out of the classroom, for those pupils struggling in a mixed group (Rubin & Noguera, 2004).

These themes, such as differentiation, workload, and stakeholder opinions, were echoed in the more detailed responses in interviews with the Heads of Maths and English at School F. These middle leaders' accountability for departmental results and responsibility for leading their colleagues also introduced two new areas: issues relating to the management of change and to accountability.

> [The teachers] do genuinely want their kids to do really, really well in the class and they don't want anything at the cost of the results.
>
> *(Head of Maths)*

> The teachers are measured on progress so they are going to be worried about trying something new, which would be the biggest barrier. Every school is being measured, the measures are changing every day. So I think it's the worry about trying something new where it may cost them. Or may not cost them but it's the worry.
>
> *(Head of Maths)*

The head of subject has responsibility for managing these fears on the part of her team and ensuring that teachers are in a position to teach mixed attainment groups confidently and successfully. As we have already observed, the climate is one of 'high stakes' both for the teacher through the appraisal process (DfE, 2013) and for the school via Ofsted and through parent choice (Ball et al., 1996; Gewirtz et al., 1995; Perryman, 2012). As Jackson (2010) has specifically argued, this climate of heightened accountability, closely coupled to pupil attainment expressed by performance indicators, generates and perpetuates a set of fears for teachers and senior leaders, with both emotional and behavioural consequences. This climate militates against pedagogic and curriculum innovation, resulting in conservatism and risk-aversion in spite of the theoretical autonomy notionally enjoyed by schools in England (Academies Commission, 2013).

In the case of pupil grouping practice, it appears that a vicious circle arises. The perception of mixed attainment teaching as risky and difficult means that few schools take up the challenge – for maths in particular. This may make it even more difficult for schools to adopt mixed attainment practices, for reasons described above. In both the questionnaires and interviews, resource development was mentioned as a barrier to mixed attainment practice. As there is a relatively small market for teaching resources tailored to mixed attainment teaching, there are very few off-the-shelf resources available and so teachers would need to develop all or nearly all their own resources. Similarly, there are few exemplars for schools to draw on:

I would have loved my teachers to get more opportunities to go out and see different schools. We couldn't find schools. . . . The majority of [the ones we found] were not really mixed ability because they were either grammar schools or selective schools and that's not a real mixed ability. That's something similar to Set 1 and Set 2 teaching.

(Head of Maths)

What is intriguing is that we have found such explanations of a lack of exemplars and materials to be frequently used by maths teachers within School F where other departments teach mixed attainment as standard (such as History, Geography, and Philosophy and Religious Studies, in addition to creative subjects such as Art and Music). Nevertheless, a shortage of exemplars and resources – whether due to reality or to levels of awareness – means that teachers used to segregation by attainment lack evidence that mixed attainment teaching can be successful, thus reproducing fear of mixed attainment grouping and deterring schools – and our perception is that this effect is stronger for maths than for English. The vicious circle is summarised in Figure 8.1.

The action of the vicious circle is in spite of the research evidence that mixed attainment teaching may be beneficial to many pupils, with fears resulting in detrimental consequences, particularly for pupils in low attaining sets (EEF, 2018).

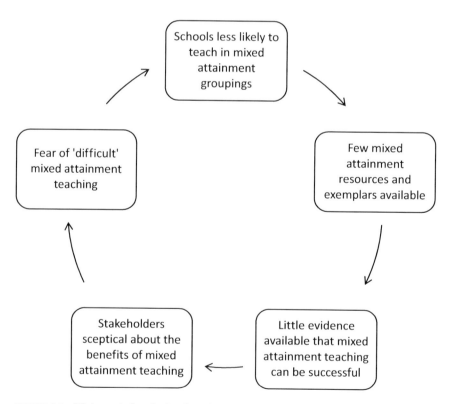

FIGURE 8.1 Vicious circle of mixed attainment grouping

Support for the feasibility of mixed attainment grouping

Nevertheless, mixed attainment practice is attractive to some, and has some passionate school and teacher advocates. As with the difficulties identified above, we analysed the mini questionnaire responses of pilot teachers for the factors that attract them to mixed attainment teaching. These are summarised in Table 8.2. Benefits to pupils were identified most often, with these including increased confidence, unlocking potential and mutual support. Teachers also perceived that mixed attainment teaching made them into better teachers. Some colleagues had been directed to switch to mixed attainment and were sceptical to begin with but were won over; an interesting counter to the caution of cf. Reid et al. (1981), who suggest that a directive approach to introducing mixed attainment can be counterproductive. Collegiate working practices and a fairer, more inclusive education were also perceived to be attractive features of mixed attainment teaching.

Teachers are not the only stakeholders whose views are of relevance here, of course. In our focus groups with pupils in mixed attainment schools, we asked about their views of mixed attainment pedagogy, and students told us that there were many things they liked about learning in mixed attainment groups (see Chapter 5). A number of benefits to the learning process were identified. Students who liked mixed attainment classes from all levels of attainment appreciated the modelling offered by higher attaining pupils. Being in a mixed attainment group also allows for successful work to be used as exemplars for others to follow. Students also told us that not only do they appreciate the help they get from their peers, but they also enjoy being able to help others. Interestingly, pupils themselves made the distinction between attainment and ability.

> I think it's good for most people because say in like maths or English there would be the lower achieving people trying to become better by using the higher achieving people's work as a guide.
>
> *(Killian, high attainment, School M)*

> Because you have the people to help you around you, but then you also have the people you can help, so it's easier.
>
> *(Joey, low attainment, School M)*

TABLE 8.2 Reasons given in support of mixed attainment practice

Reason for mixed attainment practice	Number of occurrences
Benefits to pupils	6
Passion for/benefits of mixed attainment	4
Improving teaching	4
Decision made by a more senior colleague	3
Developing shared resources/teamwork	3
Inclusion/equality	2

Source: Reproduced from Taylor et al. (2017)

I find it helps me a lot with my dyslexia, people helping out, explaining it in a different way – the teachers can't explain to you like that. It's nice to learn some stuff off them as well and then write it down and then remember you've learnt something new off someone else.

(Nikita, low attainment, School K)

Furthermore, as we saw in Chapter 5, pupils recognised that mixed attainment provides a situation of greater equity for all pupils, including with access to the curriculum, and helped with narrowing the attainment gap. Kian's response is indicative:

I don't think it's fair to like split people because of their ability because then some people won't learn the things that they need to learn to get to university and go pass their GCSEs and A Levels.

(Kian, middle attainment, School L)

There was also a recognition by pupils that teachers adapted their pedagogy when teaching mixed attainment groups, and that tasks could be taken to different lengths when differentiation by outcome was employed. For example:

It's quite good because in English, like if it's a writing task you can write to your ability.

(Killian, high attainment, School M)

Students also identified classroom diversity as an advantage: they enjoyed the opportunity to work alongside people with different backgrounds, strengths, and interests. Furthermore, pupils enjoyed and appreciated the diverse peer relationships that were given the opportunity to blossom within mixed attainment groups.

In the world that we live in today, there are different people and people aren't always going to be on the same wave length as you . . . when you go into the real world, there are going to be people who don't like you and people who are different to you so you've got to get used to that at a young age so when you finish your GCSEs, you're just able to go into the wide world and think, 'What should I do now?'

(Jeremy, high attainment, School K)

My friend that I sit next to now, I didn't know her until I sat next to her and then we worked together and then we're really good friends now, which I find also quite good about mixed classes and having seating plans and sitting next to people that you don't really talk to.

(Nikita, low attainment, School K)

Students identified a number of ways in which mixed attainment grouping supported them in developing important traits. For example, practices pupils experienced in the context of mixed attainment teaching was felt to encourage independence, self-confidence, and perseverance.

> But usually the teachers make you think yourself, then ask your buddy and then ask your table and then the teacher. They like you to do that before you ask them.
>
> *(Brooke, high attainment, School M)*

We have seen in this section that, an addition to the research evidence presented in Chapter 5, where mixed attainment grouping is used teachers and pupils perceive many advantages and benefits. Teachers perceive potential benefits for pupils, as well as seeing mixed attainment as improving their own teaching practice. Some experienced teachers also identified that, rather than increasing workload, mixed attainment grouping can help with sharing the burden of planning and preparation between staff. Students perceived a range of benefits, including being able to work with others and help their peers, and appreciating the diversity in the classroom. Of course, simply grouping pupils in mixed attainment groups will not of *itself* yield positive outcomes. So the next section shares what we have we learned about the effective practice of mixed attainment grouping.

Doing mixed attainment teaching well

As we have noted above, what constitutes good mixed attainment grouping and teaching is an under-researched area. Research has tended to focus on the effects of mixed attainment teaching (or 'detracking' as it is referred to in the US literature) on pupil outcomes, rather than the actual practices deployed.

As we saw in Chapter 2, research suggests that mixed attainment grouping provides an equitable alternative to setting or streaming. For example, Jo Boaler found improved academic outcomes and self-confidence in mixed attainment maths classes, compared with attainment sets (Boaler, 2008; Boaler et al., 2000). Slavin (1990) found no advantage to 'ability grouping', when compared with heterogeneously grouped classes, and a trend towards higher outcomes for heterogeneously grouped social studies classes. It therefore appears that mixed attainment grouping can be employed without causing detriment to academic outcomes, and potentially with improved outcomes for lower-attaining pupils, as some of the equity issues with setting are addressed. (See Chapter 2 for further elaboration of the evidence).

Mixed attainment grouping should eliminate the negative effects associated with misallocation and lack of fluidity, as pupils are not allocated to classes on the basis of prior attainment. Furthermore, organising pupils in mixed attainment groups may address issues such as quality of teaching, curriculum, pedagogy, and qualifications, as these will be offered equitably to all pupils.

However, it is not *inevitable* that the elimination of these detrimental effects associated with setting will lead to improved outcomes (Good & Marshall, 1984), or that resources will be allocated more equitably to pupils in the same classroom. Mixed attainment grouping has been criticised for practices such as 'teaching to the middle', and failing to stretch higher-attaining pupils or to support lower-attaining pupils (Kulik & Kulik, 1987; Loveless, 1998; Reid et al., 1981). In fact, inequitable classroom practices may be reproduced in mixed attainment groups because, while the allocation of pupils to classes is straightforward, fundamental changes to teaching practices and school structures are more difficult for teachers to achieve (Rubin, 2003; and see our findings about the difficulties of mixed attainment grouping above). Hence it is very important that these matters are addressed in mixed attainment practice, to successfully aid equity.

Given the scarcity of existing research closely focused on pedagogic practice in mixed attainment grouping, one of our goals in setting up the 'Best Practice in Mixed Attainment' trial was to address this gap by identifying and characterising good practice in mixed attainment teaching. To do this, we drew on the support of four secondary schools that were using mixed attainment grouping in English and maths in Year 7. All of these schools were graded 'Good' or 'Outstanding' by Ofsted, with results above the national average. We met with teachers from these schools over several months, including making visits to their schools where we observed lessons and endeavoured to understand what made their mixed attainment grouping successful. Notably, the four schools had quite different approaches to pedagogy and curriculum, which both demonstrates that a wide variety of approaches to mixed attainment teaching are possible, and provided us with a significant challenge in distilling their practices! However we endeavoured to combine our findings in our pilot schools with what we could glean from the literature around mixed attainment grouping.

Drawing on the experiences of our pilot school teachers, and on our review of the literature, we distilled four principles of Best Practice in Mixed Attainment (Francis et al., 2017a; Taylor et al., 2015). These principles formed the backbone of our mixed attainment teaching intervention.

The first principle we established is that *teaching groups should be established such that there is a broad range of prior attainment in each group.* As noted above, this not only prevents pupils from being allocated to the wrong set, or from being unable to move from a set, but also prevents the inequitable practice of allocating specialist teachers, or those considered more effective, to higher attaining sets (Ireson & Hallam, 2001; Kutnick et al., 2005; Slavin, 1990).

As noted above, one key area that requires further research is the use of 'nurture groups' (Cooper & Whitebread, 2007; Mazenod et al., 2019). As noted above, our expectation had been that all pupils within a year group would be included in mixed attainment classes, but some schools wanted to provide separately for the very lowest-attaining pupils. The Head of Maths in one of our pilot schools told us:

We did pick a very small group from each half of the Year 7 who were below level 3, and we thought that it is probably not best for them to be sitting in mixed ability because those students could have lots of SEN needs. And they could find themselves being much more timid in the classroom because they see everybody else being able to get the work at how it is being taught, and they might be really worried with lots of expectations from them.

(Interview with Head of Maths, School F)

However, there are alternative strategies for managing the integration of very low-attaining pupils into mixed attainment groups. For example, checking pupils' prior knowledge before starting a topic and ensure that key knowledge is put in place through pre-teaching can be a successful approach.

The second principle of mixed attainment grouping is that, where used, *within-class grouping should be flexible and established for specific activities*, rather than inflexible and based on pupils' general attainment in a subject. It is likely that when pupils are assigned to relatively inflexible within-class groups (cf. the 'ability' tables commonly used in primary schools, Towers et al., 2019) then some of the same effects on pupils are created as in setting, such as inequitable effects on teacher expectations, pupil perceptions, the creation of learner identities and the self-fulfilling prophecy. Indeed, Marks has found exactly this in her studies of within-class 'ability' grouping in primary schools (Marks, 2013, 2014). However, other studies, focusing on intervention activities and flexible grouping for catch-up teaching, have found positive effects of small group teaching (Slavin, 1987) and of pupils explaining their learning to peers (Slavin, 1996) and so a best practice approach must not exclude these strategies. Indeed, this approach is supported by the most recent update to the EEF Teaching and Learning Toolkit (EEF, 2018).

Our pilot school teachers suggested a number of practices that support flexible grouping; for example, grouping pupils randomly as they enter the classroom. In fact, a strategy preferred in many classrooms that we observed was to create deliberately mixed subgroups within the classroom. In an English classroom in School M, pupils were seated in pairs of either two pupils with middle prior attainment or one pupil with high prior attainment and one with low prior attainment. When pupils worked together within the lesson, they could work with their seat partner, or turn around so that they were in mixed threes with one high, one middle and one low prior attaining pupil. In an English classroom in School N, pupils sat in table groups of four to six. Each group was established to have a broad mixture of prior attainment. Another strategy, described by teachers but not observed, was to group based on assessment of prior knowledge. For example, one teacher described how she had assessed pupils' current understanding of punctuation and then grouped pupils accordingly. This enabled her to consolidate learning with one group of pupils and introduce new material with another group. Another teacher described how she would group in this way and give the more confident subgroup an activity to get on with straight away, while she worked with the other group. Once she had finished her input, the groups would change places and she would teach the more confident group while the less confident group consolidated the material that she had just introduced.

Closely linked to the above is our third principle, that *differentiation should mainly be by feedback (or response) and by outcome*, avoiding any differentiation practices that encourage the labelling of pupils by 'ability' or which differentiate the curriculum accessed by pupils working from different levels of prior attainment. Bloom (1971) had the insight that the same teaching methods and approaches are not always appropriate for all pupils. He argued that adapting teaching approaches to pupils' learning needs should enable almost all pupils to reach a high level of attainment and would thus reduce the attainment gap through 'mastery learning'. The concept of differentiation as good practice gained traction in England in the 1970s and 1980s, when a series of reports from Her Majesty's Inspectorate observed that teaching did not cater sufficiently to the needs of all pupils (Hart, 1996). Fundamentally different approaches to differentiation exist (Coffey, 2011), whereby some practitioners seek to differentiate between pupils, while others seek to make the common curriculum accessible to all, regardless of prior attainment (Hart, 1996). Practices that differentiate between pupils typically offer a range of tasks to a class (e.g. Tomlinson, 2005) but this risks increasing teacher workload (Delisle, 2015) and encouraging fixed labelling of pupils (Hart, 1996; Hart et al., 2004), in turn encouraging self-fulfilling prophecy and failing to challenge low teacher expectations of pupils labelled as 'low-attaining' (Francis et al., 2017b; Marks, 2013; Oakes, 1985). Instead, we advocate the use of tasks accessible to all pupils, with a range of entry points and support and challenge provided through differentiated teacher responses. Such tasks are sometimes characterised as 'low threshold, high ceiling' (Nrich, nd). All pupils can be facilitated to access tasks through the use of scaffolding (Wood et al., 1976), which involves approaching a concept or task by breaking it into discrete elements, and then supporting students to learn each part according to their needs before they move forward to the next. Combining rich classroom tasks with personalised questioning and feedback from peers and from the teacher (Hodgen & Webb, 2008) creates opportunities for all pupils to be supported and challenged. The provision of a single, scaffolded activity also prevents inequity of curriculum quality, which can arise where differentiation by task is practised.

The benefits of talk in the classroom are well-documented: pupils benefit from feedback on their learning and from the opportunity to explain their learning to each other (Slavin, 1996). Teachers should be careful not to depend too far on higher attaining pupils to do the explaining: teaching another pupil is beneficial to all pupils regardless of prior attainment and, furthermore, higher attaining pupils can become disillusioned and lower attaining pupils patronised if high attainers are used too often in this way (Tereshchenko et al., 2018). This constructive talk requires a supportive classroom climate, where all pupils feel able to articulate their ideas and listen to the ideas of others (Rubie-Davies, 2007).

During our visits to schools we saw a number of examples of this approach to differentiation. In a Year 7 maths lesson at School M, pupils were exploring three-dimensional shapes and learning to draw them using isometric paper. The activities used in the lesson: analysing nets, making tetracubes, and drawing shapes on isometric paper were accessible to all pupils. Students were encouraged to talk to one another as they worked and the teacher walked around the classroom prompting their explorations through questioning. In this way, all pupils could be challenged appropriately without being labelled by 'ability'. In an English lesson at School N, the lesson began with all pupils reading a text together, before the teacher modelled a writing activity for pupils to complete. All pupils worked on the same written task, with the teacher providing support through questioning and through the provision of support sheets. These sheets, providing scaffolding for the task, were not directed towards particular pupils, but were available for pupils to choose to use if they wished. This meant that there was no labelling of pupils in the classroom. In a maths lesson at School N, pupils worked in small, mixed attainment groups to consider whether a series of statements were true or false. For example, 3×4 is a quarter of 12×4. Students were encouraged to discuss each statement and they wrote down their explanations for their answers as well as 'True' or 'False'. Throughout, the teacher circulated, prompting pupils and encouraging their discussion. For groups that finished quickly, an extension task was provided.

It is worth reiterating the criticism that some teachers do not address the challenge of differentiation, with the consequence that their lessons lack challenge for some of their pupils. 'Teaching to the middle' is something we counsel strongly against, in fact teachers who worked with us on the pilot phase of Best Practice in Mixed Attainment recommended 'teaching to the top' and then putting in place appropriate scaffolding or support in order to enable all pupils to access and succeed on the tasks (Taylor et al., 2015). It is of course essential that appropriate support is in place if teachers take this approach, otherwise the lesson will be inaccessible to lower-attaining pupils.

Our fourth and final principle builds on this point: *teachers should have high expectations of all pupils regardless of prior attainment and should take a flexible view of 'ability'*. As we have seen, research suggests that teachers' expectations of pupils are inequitable, with lower expectations of progress held for pupils perceived as lower 'ability' (Boaler et al., 2000; Ireson et al., 2005; Mazenod et al., 2019; Sukhnandan & Lee, 1999). There is a tendency for teachers to regard ability as 'fixed' (Hamilton & O'Hara, 2011; Hart & Dixon, 2004), and to adjust pedagogy (Hallam & Ireson, 2005; Oakes, 1985) and curriculum (Boaler, 2002; Gillborn & Youdell, 2000; Oakes, 1985) accordingly. A mixed attainment class group, wherein all pupils are expected to engage with one common task, enables the same high expectations to be held for all pupils. It also permits the teacher to expect that all pupils, including those with low prior attainment, can achieve at the highest levels.

As we have described above, when we visited schools we observed a number of lessons where all pupils were expected to engage with the same, challenging task. Teachers provided support and stimulation in order for this to work. Support and challenge were offered through conversations with peers, teaching assistants, and the teacher, through additional structure provided in the form of support sheets, through the provision of additional resources such as dictionaries or aide-memoires around the classroom, and through extension tasks for those who had completed work and were ready to move on to something new.

School N had put a particular emphasis on 'growth mindset' (Dweck, 2008) and the classrooms in which we observed lessons displayed growth mindset posters. In fact, teachers linked the move to mixed attainment grouping in maths at School N to the emphasis on growth mindset:

> I think it's quite driven by our school promotes growth mindset and it really supports that and I think if they're taught in Year 7, 'Right, you're in set three', or whatever, then they automatically get that feeling of, 'I'm never going to be very good at maths'. It [setting] creates that [negative attitude?] that we were trying to combat.
>
> *(Eleanor, maths, School N)*

An English teacher in School F, one of our pilot schools, reported how her approach to teaching meant that there was no ceiling on what might be achieved by any of her pupils. Every member of her class could potentially achieve the highest possible marks. This contrasts with setting, where potential outcomes for lower attaining sets are sometimes capped, and with mixed attainment teaching where rigid within-class groups or differentiation by task or resource are used. In fact, this teacher told us how pupils with low prior attainment were sometimes the highest attainers in the class – an outcome only possible because of the approach to mixed attainment teaching employed in her classroom.

We have described in this section the principles of Best Practice in Mixed Attainment that we have developed, based on observations in schools, conversations with teachers, and our review of the literature. Our intervention was deliberately 'light touch', as we wanted schools to be able to adapt it to their own contexts and schemes of work, as well as wanting the intervention to be feasible to enact. Our intervention entails four principles: pupils grouped in broad mixed attainment classes, flexible within class grouping, differentiation through questioning and outcome, and high expectations for all pupils. We will now go on to consider how mixed attainment teaching can be better facilitated in schools.

Making mixed attainment teaching possible

We have described in this book some of the detrimental effects of setting and some of the ways that mixed attainment grouping and teaching may address these. We have gone on to explain our 'Best Practice in Mixed Attainment' intervention and how it draws on the research literature and the practices of good schools to describe principles for successful, impactful mixed attainment grouping. At this stage, we feel it is important to offer a cautionary note. As we have illustrated in the first section of this chapter, mixed attainment teaching is perceived as difficult by teachers and, in maths, it is used in a minority of schools. Of the schools that participated in our intervention, not all succeeded in making mixed attainment grouping work over the longer term: while most schools were successful in sustaining mixed attainment grouping in English, three of the six schools taught maths to set groups in the second year of the intervention. Although we continue to believe that the negative and discriminatory effects of setting need to be addressed, we need to exercise appropriate caution in our claims for mixed attainment grouping. Evidence shows it can be done well (and indeed Scandinavian education systems illustrate feasibility at scale), with successful outcomes for all; but there will likely be challenges in encouraging and facilitating take-up by inexperienced teachers. However, our research so far has provided useful insights about making mixed attainment work and we share these now.

As we have noted, teachers are anxious and fearful of mixed attainment teaching. In our earlier article on this subject (Taylor et al., 2017), we used Carolyn Jackson's (2010) analysis of 'fear in education' to theorise this problem. Jackson challenges the education community to consider how to address these fears; and we turn now to potential strategies for addressing fear of mixed attainment.

As we identified in our model of the vicious circle of mixed attainment grouping (Figure 8.1) one difficulty for mixed attainment is the lack of exemplification and models of successful practice. However, the disinclination of schools towards mixed attainment teaching, despite research evidence that is already encouraging, suggests that provision of such exemplification will not necessarily be sufficient on its own to effect a significant change.

Some useful insights are available from the USA, where Welner and Burris (2006) recommend a strategy of 'winning them over', based on their experience of 'detracking' in two case study schools. Welner and Burris identify a problem of 'resistance tied to beliefs and values (known as normative resistance)' (p. 91), which we recognise as having parallels with fear-based resistance in the English case. Indeed Welner and Burris write specifically about parents' fears, teachers' apprehension, and the perceived threat to children's education.

Welner and Burris (2006) advise that parental concerns should be addressed directly, perceiving that parents are concerned with the achievement of their own child above equity. Schools can address these concerns by explaining clearly how the needs of all pupils will be met effectively in the classroom. It also appears that the personal commitment of the relevant middle leader is necessary to implement mixed attainment. The importance of supportive leadership is emphasised by Welner and Burris (2006) who identify a commitment by leaders to outstanding outcomes and equity as fundamental to reform. This was also our experience of those intervention schools and their departments that proceeded with mixed attainment grouping in the second year. The significance of the relevant middle leader, as well as senior leaders, is reinforced by a project note about the school unable to move to mixed attainment grouping in time for the start of the trial. This note, made following one of the initial professional development sessions, also raises the issue of two other constraints, namely timetabling and teacher preparation.

The deputy head was quite clear that it was impossible for them to do any-thing for September, because their timetabling would not allow it (they operate attainment-based banding in both maths and English in Year 7) and they will not be ready to make such a big shift in practice in that time. The Head of Maths did not attend and it was clear that he or she was not on board with moving to mixed attainment teaching.

(Project team professional development log)

Another difficulty for schools is the lack of experience of some teachers with mixed attainment teaching. This is particularly likely to be an issue for maths. As we saw above, teachers are more likely to hold positive attitudes to mixed attainment teaching when they have some control over whether and how it is introduced. Reid et al. (1981) suggested that dialogue and discussion around the introduction of mixed attainment teaching is likely to be facilitative, rather than a top-down approach when it is imposed by a senior leader. Welner and Burris (2006) suggest that teachers should be eased into teaching mixed attainment groups and provided with support and encouragement as they begin on this jour-ney. Our professional development sessions aimed to provide this kind of support and we adapted them to meet teachers' needs and address their questions and challenges as we went along. In addition, this approach worked extremely well in one of our pilot schools in adopting mixed attainment maths teaching. Support was secured from senior leadership at the school, as well as from the project team, and department members visited other settings and carried out peer observations with feedback and coaching.

Welner and Burris also suggest strategies for making the introduction of mixed attainment grouping manageable for staff in terms of the additional workload. As we have already observed, the introduction of a new approach inevitably brings extra work, although ultimately there is no reason why mixed attainment grouping should be more labour-intensive than setting. A gradual approach to the introduc-tion of mixed attainment groups, focusing on specific year groups may also help with the impact on workload (Welner & Burris, 2006).

Overall, Welner and Burris advise 'steady, determined progress' (p. 94) rooted in committed leadership. They recommend that each step towards 'detracking' should be taken assertively, with clear communication to all stakeholders and mitigating actions taken to reduce any potential additional stresses. We have shown above that their recommendations for supporting teachers and pupils, directly engaging all stakeholders and maintaining a relentless focus on excellence and equity would address many of the fears raised by the schools engaged in our research.

In our own research we additionally found the role of the middle leader to be particularly significant in driving change. We found in successful mixed attainment schools, middle leaders who were passionate proponents of mixed attainment grouping, as they perceived it as contributing to a 'wider project' (Hodgen, 2017) to which they were committed. For example, in School K, the Head of Maths observed:

In my previous school, we had had mixed ability grouping in Year 7, and what was interesting was the change of perspective. It was in a grammar school area, so some students when they came, they hadn't managed to get into the grammar school, hadn't done well in their Eleven Plus, already had this idea 'I'm not good at maths', and they came with that fixed idea. And the reason why I so believe in mixed ability definitely for Year 7, is that you can change, it just seems so much easier to change that perception. And we had two students that went from being level, I think it was borderline three/four, when they arrived, who got level eight at the end of Year 9. Now in theory, that shouldn't be possible but once you get students, 'Oh, I can study maths' – and it's possible.

As a result, she was a passionate advocate of growth mindset and the possibility of transforming pupils' attitude towards learning maths. We have already described how this was likewise one of the motivating factors for mixed attainment in School N. At this school, the Head of Maths had an additional purpose to develop deeper understanding in all the pupils in the context of mastery maths learning:

How can we instil a positive maths mindset in all our students . . . a fixed mindset was quite prevalent in this school . . . but how can we instil that positive mindset for students across the attainment spectrum . . . and with the new curriculum . . . and with mastery . . . it was about how, as a head of department, how could I develop the teaching in my department . . . for that deeper understanding.

(Head of Maths, School N)

And like many other mixed attainment advocates, this Head of Maths was also driven by a concern for equity and social justice:

And what used to happen was that they [the low attainers] would access a support curriculum, a curriculum that was very different from what many of the other students were actually accessing. . . . and, of course, what you've got is this gap that widens. They stay in the bottom set because this gap widens and they can't manage to sort of crawl their way up to a better set . . . and it was how we can try and change that cycle of poor achievement. . . . How do we combat that massive effect of the rich getting rich and the poor staying where they are and that gap getting wider?

This powerful impetus of effective pedagogy for all appeared to lend the necessary commitment middle leaders needed to drive mixed attainment practice forward in the 'steady, determined' way proposed by Welner and Burris (2006, p. 94).

In addition to the above, we suggest that if mixed attainment practice is to be more widely adopted, a supportive policy climate will need to be created. Moreover, teachers will additionally need access to exemplars of effective mixed attainment practice and teaching materials to draw on in developing their own curricula. Indeed, we would suggest that high quality mixed attainment resources, lesson plans, and other materials need to be developed urgently if the development of mixed attainment practice is to be a serious proposition. Mixed attainment practice should also be something that teachers get to see in action, as part of their initial teacher education or continuing professional development. Importantly, these will need to happen in the context of a professional climate that facilitates rather than hinders change. Central to this is the liberation of teachers' time, currently too over-scheduled to allow for innovation; the further development of a genuine commitment to evidence based practice on the part of the English schools' regulator Ofsted; and the movement towards a professionalised, research-engaged, confident teaching profession.

Chapter summary

In this chapter we have provided an overview of our findings about mixed attainment grouping: examining what it is, and why so many schools find it difficult to implement in core subjects, especially maths. We have outlined what is currently known about good practice in mixed attainment grouping from the limited research literature, and how we have added to that from our own work with schools, highlighting also the positive impacts noted by many teachers and pupils. We have described our principles of 'Best Practice in Mixed Attainment' and made suggestions as to how mixed attainment can be approached successfully in schools. We have recognised that more work needs to be done to support the successful uptake and implementation of mixed attainment practice, including resources and modelling of effective practice for teachers inexperienced in these approaches.

Notes

1 Again, we try to avoid using this term, due to the problematic implications of reference to 'ability'.
2 'Nurture groups' and/or 'transition groups' are a frequently used strategy that enables specialist provision to be made available for the very lowest attainers in a year group. The approach is especially common in Year 7, at the start of secondary schooling, to address the needs of those pupils that are deemed not 'secondary school ready', and are anticipated to struggle with transition. Hence these groups are conceived as having both a protective ('nurture') and compensatory 'catch up' function. Nurture groups can be problematic because, while they are often used in supporting the transition from primary to secondary school, they are strongly associated with equity issues, such as restricted curricula and pedagogies, low teacher expectations and lack of access to subject specialist teaching (Mazenod et al., 2019; Webster & Blatchford, 2017). As an example of a school endeavouring to implement nurture groups with integrity, School N was one of our participating schools which had a nurture group. Their intention was to reduce this group in size over Years 7–9, gradually moving pupils into mainstream classes as they had caught up sufficiently with their learning in order to be able to study alongside their peers.

References

Academies Commission. (2013). *Unleashing greatness: getting the best from an academised system*. London: Pearson/RSA.

Ball, S. J., Bowe, R., & Gewirtz, S. (1996). School choice, social class and distinction: the realization of social advantage in education. *Journal of Education Policy*, *11*(1), 89–112.

Banning-Lover, R. (2016, 22 March 2016). 60-hour weeks and unrealistic targets: teachers' working lives uncovered. *The Guardian*. Retrieved from www.theguardian.com/teacher-network/datablog/2016/mar/22/60-hour-weeks-and-unrealistic-targets-teachers-working-lives-uncovered.

Bloom, B. S. (1971). Mastery learning. In J. H. Block (Ed.), *Mastery learning: theory and practice*. New York: Holt, Rinehart & Winston.

Boaler, J. (1997). When even the winners are losers: evaluating the experiences of 'top set' students. *Journal of Curriculum Studies*, *29*(2), 165–182.

Boaler, J. (2002). Learning from teaching: exploring the relationship between reform curriculum and equity. *Journal for Research in Mathematics Education*, *33*(4), 239–258.

Boaler, J. (2008). Promoting 'relational equity' and high mathematics achievement through an innovative mixed-ability approach. *British Educational Research Journal*, *34*(2), 167–194.

Boaler, J., Wiliam, D., & Brown, M. (2000). Students' experiences of ability grouping – disaffection, polarisation and the construction of failure. *British Educational Research Journal*, *26*(5), 631–648.

Coffey, S. (2011). Differentiation in theory and practice. In J. Dillon & M. Maguire (Eds.), *Becoming a teacher* (pp. 197–209). Maidenhead: Open University Press.

Cooper, P. & Whitebread, D. (2007). The effectiveness of nurture groups on student progress: evidence from a national research study. *Emotional and Behavioural Difficulties*, *12*(3), 171–190.

Cuban, L., Kirkpatrick, H., & Peck, C. (2001). High access and low use of technologies in high school classrooms: explaining an apparent paradox. *American Educational Research Journal*, *38*(4), 813–834.

Delisle, J. R. (2015). Differentiation doesn't work. *Education Week*. Retrieved from www.edweek.org/ew/articles/2015/01/07/differentiation-doesnt-work.html?r=72617547&preview=1.

DfE. (2013). New advice to help schools set performance-related pay. Retrieved from www.gov.uk/government/news/new-advice-to-help-schools-set-performance-related-pay.

DfE. (2015). *Government response to the workload challenge*. DFE-00058-2015. London: DfE.

Dweck, C. S. (2008). *Mindset: how you can fulfil your potential*. New York: Random House.

EEF. (2018). *The Sutton Trust – Education Endowment Foundation Teaching and Learning Toolkit*. London: Education Endowment Foundation.

Francis, B., Archer, L., Hodgen, J., Pepper, D., Taylor, B., & Travers, M-C. (2017a). Exploring the relative lack of impact of research on 'ability grouping' in England: a discourse analytic account. *Cambridge Journal of Education*, *47*(1), 1–17.

Francis, B., Connolly, P., Archer, L., Hodgen, J., Mazenod, A., Pepper, D., Sloan, S., Taylor, B., Tereshchenko, A., & Travers, M-C. (2017b). Attainment grouping as self-fulfilling prophecy? A mixed methods exploration of self confidence and set level among year 7 students. *International Journal of Educational Research*, *86*, 96–108.

Gewirtz, S., Ball, S. J., & Bowe, R. (1995). *Markets, choice, and equity in education*. Buckingham: Open University Press.

Gillborn, D. & Youdell, D. (2000). *Rationing education: policy, practice, reform, and equity*. Buckingham: Open University Press.

Good, T. L. & Marshall, S. (1984). Do students learn more in heterogeneous or homogeneous groups? In P. Peterson, L. C. Wilkinson, & M. T. Hallinan (Eds.), *Student diversity and the organization, process and use of instructional groups in the classroom*. New York: Academic Press.

Hallam, S. & Ireson, J. (2005). Secondary school teachers' pedagogic practices when teaching mixed and structured ability classes. *Research Papers in Education, 20*(1), 3–24.

Hamilton, L. & O'Hara, P. (2011). The tyranny of setting (ability grouping): challenges to inclusion in Scottish primary schools. *Teaching and Teacher Education, 27*(4), 712–721.

Hart, S. (Ed.) (1996). *Differentiation and the secondary curriculum: debates and dilemmas*. London: Routledge.

Hart, S. & Dixon, A. (2004). *Learning without limits*. Maidenhead: Open University Press.

Hodgen, J. (2011). Setting, streaming and mixed ability teaching. In J. Dillon & M. Maguire (Eds.), *Becoming a teacher: issues in secondary education* (pp. 210–221). Maidenhead: Open University Publishing.

Hodgen, J. (2017). *How some schools buck the trend and implement mixed attainment teaching: reconstructing subject culture*. Paper presented at the BERA Annual Conference, University of Sussex, Brighton.

Hodgen, J. & Marshall, B. (2005). Assessment for learning in English and mathematics: a comparison. *Curriculum Journal, 16*(2), 153–176.

Hodgen, J. & Webb, M. (2008). Questioning, dialogue and feedback. In S. Swaffield (Ed.), *Unlocking assessment* (pp. 73–89). New York: Routledge.

Hodgen, J. & Wiliam, D. (2006). *Mathematics inside the black box: assessment for learning in the mathematics classroom*. Slough: nferNelson.

Ireson, J. & Hallam, S. (2001). *Ability grouping in education*. London: Paul Chapman.

Ireson, J., Hallam, S., & Hurley, C. (2005). What are the effects of ability grouping on GCSE attainment? *British Educational Research Journal, 31*(4), 443–458.

Jackson, C. (2010). Fear in education. *Educational Review, 62*(1), 39–52.

Kulik, J. A. & Kulik, C. L. C. (1987). Effects of ability grouping on student achievement. *Equity and Excellence in Education, 23*(1–2), 22–30.

Kutnick, P., Sebba, J., Blatchford, P., Galton, M., Thorp, J., MacIntyre, H., & Berdondini, L. (2005). *The effects of pupil grouping: literature review*. London: DFES.

Loveless, T. (1998). The tracking and ability grouping debate. Retrieved from www.edex-cellence.net/foundation/publication/publication.cfm?id=127&pubsubid=804.

Marks, R. (2013). 'The blue table means you don't have a clue': the persistence of fixed-ability thinking and practices in primary mathematics in English schools. *FORUM: for Promoting 3–19 Comprehensive Education, 55*(1), 31–44.

Marks, R. (2014). Educational triage and ability-grouping in primary mathematics: a case-study of the impacts on low-attaining pupils. *Research in Mathematics Education, 16*(1), 38–53.

Marshall, B. & Wiliam, D. (2006). *English inside the black box: assessment for learning in the English classroom*. London: GL Assessment.

Mazenod, A., Francis, B., Archer, L., Hodgen, J., Taylor, B., Tereshchenko, A., & Pepper, D. (2019). Nurturing learning or encouraging dependency? Teacher constructions of students in lower attainment groups in English secondary schools. *Cambridge Journal of Education, 49*(1), 53–68.

Nrich. (nd). Low threshold high ceiling tasks. Retrieved from https://nrich.maths.org/8769.

Oakes, J. (1985). *How schools structure inequality*. New Haven: Yale University Press.

OECD. (2013). Selecting and grouping students. In *Pisa 2012 results: What makes schools successful? Resources, policies and practices* (Vol. IV, pp. 71–92). Paris: OECD Publishing.

Perryman, J. (2012). Inspection and the fabrication of professional and performative processes. In B. Jeffrey & G. Troman (Eds.), *Performativity in UK education: ethnographic cases of its effects, agency and reconstruction*. Stroud: E&E.

Reid, M., Clunies-Ross, L., Goacher, B., & Vile, C. (1981). *Mixed-ability teaching: problems and possibilities*. Windsor: NFER-Nelson.

Rubie-Davies, C. M. (2007). Classroom interactions: exploring the practices of high- and low-expectation teachers. *British Journal of Educational Psychology*, 77(2), 289–306.

Rubin, B. C. (2003). Unpacking detracking: when progressive pedagogy meets students' social worlds. *American Educational Research Journal*, 40(2), 539–573.

Rubin, B. C. & Noguera, P. A. (2004). Tracking detracking: sorting through the dilemmas and possibilities of detracking in practice. *Equity & Excellence in Education*, 37(1), 92–101.

Ruthven, K. (2009). Towards a naturalistic conceptualisation of technology integration in classroom practice: the example of school mathematics. *Education & Didactique*, 3(1), 131–159.

Slavin, R. E. (1987). Ability grouping and student achievement in elementary schools: a best-evidence synthesis. *Review of Educational Research*, 57(3), 293–336.

Slavin, R. E. (1990). Achievement effects of ability grouping in secondary schools: a best-evidence synthesis. *Review of Educational Research*, 60(3), 471–499.

Slavin, R. E. (1996). Research on cooperative learning and achievement: what we know, what we need to know. *Contemporary Educational Psychology*, 21(1), 43–69.

Stigler, J. W. & Hiebert, J. (1999). *The teaching gap: best ideas from the world's teachers for improving education in the classroom*. New York: Free Press.

Sukhnandan, L. & Lee, B. (1999). *Streaming, setting and grouping by ability*. Slough: NFER.

Taylor, B., Francis, B., Archer, L., Hodgen, J., Pepper, D., Tereshchenko, A., & Travers, M-C. (2017). Factors deterring schools from mixed attainment teaching practice. *Pedagogy, Culture & Society*, 25(3), 327–345.

Taylor, B., Hodgen, J., Tereshchenko, A., & Gutierrez Cofre, G. (forthcoming). Attainment grouping in English secondary schools: a national survey of current practices.

Taylor, B., Travers, M-C., Francis, B., Hodgen, J., & Sumner, C. (2015). *Best practice in mixed attainment grouping*. London: Education Endowment Foundation/King's College London.

Tereshchenko, A., Francis, B., Archer, L., Hodgen, J., Mazenod, A., Taylor, B., Pepper, D., & Travers, M-C. (2018). Learners' attitudes to mixed attainment grouping: examining the views of students of high, middle and low attainment. *Research Papers in Education*, 1–20.

Tomlinson, C. (2005). This issue: differentiated instruction. *Theory Into Practice*, 44(3), 183–184.

Towers, E., Taylor, B., Mazenod, A., & Tereshchenko, A. (2019). 'The reality is complex': teachers' and school leaders' accounts and justifications of grouping practices in the English Key Stage 2 classroom. *Education 3–13*.

Webster, R. & Blatchford, P. (2017). *The Special Educational Needs in Secondary Education (SENSE) study final report: a study of the teaching and support experienced by pupils with Statements and Education, Health and Care Plans in mainstream and special schools*. London: UCL Institute of Education/Nuffield Foundation.

Welner, K. & Burris, C. C. (2006). Alternative approaches to the politics of detracking. *Theory Into Practice*, 45(1), 90–99.

Wood, D., Bruner, J. S., & Ross, G. (1976). The role of tutoring in problem solving. *Journal of Child Psychology and Psychiatry*, 17(2), 89–100.

9

REFLECTIONS

We have presented much evidence – new and old – on attainment grouping, and shown how our own project has added important new findings to the already huge corpus of research on this topic. But what is the significance, and connotation for practice going forward? In this chapter we reflect on what we have learnt from our own study and from distillation of the prior research literature on attainment grouping and social in/justice. Especially, we want to focus on the implications of the findings for social in/justice, and the longstanding socio-economic gap for educational attainment.

So we begin with a summary of key findings, and then continue with an analysis of the leading issues raised. We consider conceptual implications, but especially, implications for educational practice.

Key findings

As we explained at the outset, the identification of attainment grouping as an issue for social justice is very long-established. Our research not only reiterates this, but also adds significantly to the literature with new findings, and by drawing on experimental, quantitative, and qualitative data to show why this is the case. And a further key puzzle which motivated our own project was the reason that attainment grouping remains so prevalent *in spite of* this longstanding research. We feel that our research has helped to shed light on this, and will recap our findings on this point too.

So, to summarise:

We have rehearsed the evidence that attainment grouping is found to have no overall impact on pupil attainment outcomes, but has a detrimental impact on the outcomes for low attainers. Given that low attainment groups tend to disproportionally represent pupils from socially disadvantaged backgrounds, and from certain minority ethnic groups, this has clear implications for social (in)justice, suggesting that education systems are reinforcing and perpetuating disadvantage. Our 'Best Practice in Setting' intervention, designed to mitigate inequitable practices in setting, was not found to improve attainment outcomes. This may be explained by two elements established. Firstly, inequalities in pedagogy offered to different sets. This reflected in the finding of a slight trend for high sets to be taught by more subject-specialist teachers (albeit the intervention group demonstrated slight evidence of improved equitable distribution of teachers), and by differences in pedagogy and expectation for students in different sets. Secondly, the impact of labelling on students' engagement with schooling and their perception of themselves as learners.

This latter suggestion is strongly supported by our study findings that pupil self-confidence is affected by set placement, both in relation to the curriculum subjects in which they are set, and in relation to general self-confidence in learning. We have shown that these significant effects are evident shortly after pupils are placed in sets. Importantly and worryingly, we have also found that these trends are exacerbated over time, with the self-confidence of low-set pupils decreasing, and that of high set pupils increasing. These new findings, facilitated by the longitudinal nature of our study, must concern all educationalists. Our qualitative interviews with students shows their strong articulation of the impact that attainment grouping and the associated labelling has on self-confidence, and worrying distress and internalisation demonstrated by some responses.

As with prior studies, we found that young people from working class (low socio-economic status) backgrounds, and from certain minority ethnic groups, were over-represented in low attainment groups in our school sample, illustrating how consequences of attainment grouping particularly impact certain social groups, with implications for in/equity. These findings show how attainment grouping leads to social segregation within schools by building on the different starting points which pupils begin schooling, which are patterned by social background. This hampers the social mixing which the research shows to be beneficial to all (see e.g. Willms, 2006; OECD, 2013), and which is a principle of a comprehensive education system. On top of this, we have provided new evidence to support the long-established finding that set allocation is unjust, with a startling finding that a third of pupils in the 'business as usual' control group schools were allocated to sets that would not have been predicted based on their Key Stage 2 SAT test results. Unlike many prior studies, we did not identify trends of misallocation according to pupil socio-economic background, but we did find strong trends in relation to gender and (especially) ethnicity (see Chapter 5). These deeply troubling findings appear to illustrate longstanding discriminatory stereotypes about particular pupil groups, reflected in allocation bias.

In Chapter 5, drawing on longitudinal survey data, we found that pupils in all sets become significantly more negative about setting over two years in secondary school, with young people in low sets predictably displaying the most negative attitudes. Unsurprisingly we found that pupils often have strong views about attainment grouping and mixed attainment classes. Young people in low sets frequently felt confused, embarrassed, and disappointed. Some also candidly discussed the negative impact of attainment grouping within peer social hierarchies. We identified a strong preference for mixed attainment among pupils with low prior attainment. However, not only low prior attainers, but also the majority of young people in mixed attainment classes, felt the practice supported equity and promoted learning opportunities for all. Nevertheless, young people's views on grouping practices were also shaped by wider messages about their 'ability' identity. For example, our analysis demonstrated how a small number of low-attaining students felt anxious about their potential to succeed in a mixed attainment class due to their prior experiences with 'ability' grouping that shaped their learner identities, and conversely, some of the high prior attainers felt entitled to preferential treatment. Discourses of 'natural' talent, 'ability', and meritocracy remain prevalent.

In Chapter 6, we demonstrated the profound impact of attainment grouping on pedagogy and practice. We showed that injustices in the allocation of subject-qualified teachers still persist, with lower-attaining sets less likely to have a highly subject-qualified teacher. We also found differences in teachers' expectations of students in different attainment groups, and discuss how this is perhaps unavoidable where attainment grouping is practiced, given that these distinctions in expectation provide the rationale for segregated practices in the first place. Students felt that teachers were stricter and more demanding with students in higher groups, reflecting higher expectations; while pupils often characterised lower groups as being 'babied' with dumbed down pedagogy and curriculum. Teachers themselves felt that there was no difference even though they expected to spend more time keeping lower attaining students on task. Furthermore, we showed that students perceived differences in the work provided for higher and lower sets, with higher sets being given more challenging work and granted more autonomy. We also found evidence that the curriculum differed for higher and lower sets, with lower attaining students not expected to do all of the same topics as their higher-attaining peers.

In Chapter 7 we explored some of the practical reasons that improvements in setting practice for equity appear to be so difficult to achieve. We showed the strong resistance to performing set allocation exclusively based on Key Stage 2 results alone. The majority of schools in our study used other information in addition to or instead of Key Stage 2 data to allocate students to sets, including subjective information such as teacher perceptions or reports from primary schools. Yet this begs the question, if we cannot use national test results as a basis for track placement, on what basis is this elusive (and problematic) notion of 'ability' to be decided? Our findings on misallocation are a disturbing reminder that once subjective decision-making creeps in, so too does prejudice and stereotyping. We also showed that schools struggled to comply with all the requirements of our intervention. A number of intervention schools had more than four set levels. A large proportion of students were not allocated according to attainment and not all schools moved students regularly between groups. And only a small proportion of teachers reported that their colleagues had high expectations of all students regardless of prior attainment. We considered some of the cultural and practical impediments to improving equity in attainment grouping, which included issues such as complexities of timetabling and the difficulty of changing longstanding school structures.

In Chapter 8 we showed that, while teachers frequently perceive mixed attainment teaching as difficult and time-consuming to establish, there are schools in England that have made it work and where students are articulate about the benefits it affords them. We have made a significant contribution to the literature around what constitutes successful mixed attainment teaching, drawing on our work with four secondary schools using mixed attainment grouping in English and/ or maths, and finding that broad mixed attainment grouping, high expectations, flexible within-class grouping and differentiation by feedback and outcome within a discussion-rich classroom context are central to a research-informed approach. We have also been able to demonstrate the elements of leadership and support that facilitate mixed attainment grouping in practice. We have found that, while senior leaders are able to shape which grouping practices are possible through timetabling and resource allocation, the effective promotion of mixed attainment grouping is often driven by a middle or senior leader following a broad improvement and/or equity agenda. We have shown that collaboration between teachers in schools and professional development centred around discussion, practice, and feedback can help teachers make rapid progress with mixed attainment teaching.

However, what is also clear is that mixed attainment ('mixed ability') teaching is not a panacea. Our own study shows that not *all* students enjoy or appreciate it – and this includes some low attainers (albeit fewer of these than the proportion disliking setting). The recent film *H is for Harry* (Owles & Taylor, 2018) illustrates effectively how mixed attainment grouping is not necessarily welcomed by all low attaining pupils, as well as the challenges teachers face to engage the lowest attainers in *any* classroom environment. We have repeatedly made the point in this book that there is little research evidence on effective strategies in mixed attainment teaching, which we urgently need if the approach is to be responsibly encouraged. But this also extends to a lack of research on *pupils' experiences* of mixed attainment grouping (for exceptions, see Francome & Hewitt, 2018; Hallam & Ireson, 2006, 2007). Our findings make a contribution here, and present i) broad support for mixed attainment practice among pupils experiencing it; but ii) that some pupils across attainment levels were ambivalent about the approach, and that this was especially true for middle attainers who appeared to be preoccupied with their status and asserting their position in the academic hierarchies (see Chapter 5).

Implications

Conceptually and practically, then, attainment grouping in school remains a crucial issue for social justice. Nancy Fraser (1997) delineates two elements of social justice: distributive and recognitive justice. Distributive justice is concerned with issues of economic inequality and disadvantage, i.e. the distribution of material goods, and the control of resources. Recognition, on the other hand, concerns symbolic or cultural inequality, where particular social groups are relatively privileged or devalued within a cultural hegemony.[1] Pupils in low sets are being subject to distributive injustice, as they are shown to receive poorer resources (less well qualified teachers, for example). And, ironically, pupils from some disadvantaged groups are shown themselves to be potentially prey to erroneous distribution *to* low attainment groups. Again, as we have highlighted throughout, it is pupils from socially disadvantaged groups, and certain minority ethnic groups, who are over-represented in low attainment groups and hence most likely to be subject to these inequities of distribution; a *double-disadvantage*. In terms of recognitive justice, labelling pupils as 'low attainers' (or 'low ability'), and the consequent impact on peer, self, and teacher perception, arguably comprises a strong example of recognitive injustice; shown to have consequences for pupils' self-confidence, and for their experiences of schooling and level of dis/engagement with it.

Reflections

So given all this, why then does setting remain so prevalent? We have identified in prior policy documents and ministerial statements a strong (albeit unevidenced) association between attainment grouping and 'high standards', which presents segregation by attainment – and, by proxy, segregation by socio-economic background – as 'natural' and 'rigorous' (Francis et al., 2017a). Nevertheless, while potentially indicative, these are nationally situated, whereas segregation by attainment is an international phenomenon (see Chapter 2). More research is needed to explore whether the discourses justifying and supporting attainment grouping in the UK are mirrored or distinct elsewhere. Meanwhile, subscription to setting should not necessarily prevent it being performed with greater fairness, so why did so many schools struggle to subscribe to our 'Best Practice in Setting' intervention? A significant contribution from our study has been the identification of the various practical issues that impeded engagement with, and fidelity to, the intervention stipulations. These were outlined in Chapter 7. Key among them were i) practical, environmental impediments, such as timetabling systems, pupil enrolment numbers and staffing, the availability of leadership time and 'joined-up thinking' required to make changes, and the various 'knock on' difficulties of moving pupils between sets; and ii) cultural issues such as suspicion of the validity of KS2 test outcomes, trust in subjective perceptions, belief in predictable pupil attainment trajectories and in the notion of fixed 'ability'.

These latter points of course speak to some of the ongoing 'dilemmas' of the education system (see Francis et al., 2017b). Comprehensive provision and practices are shown to best serve the needs of the many overall (Alegre & Ferrer, 2010; Willms, 2006; OECD, 2013), and this is vital for policymakers and school leaders to keep in mind. Yet comprehensive practices can never satisfy the needs of each and every individual family or student, who have diverse preferences, needs, affiliations (religion), and so on. And in a system tightly constrained by economic parameters, meeting the needs of the majority often involves compromise and sacrifice of some individual needs. These are challenging dilemmas for policymakers, school leaders and teachers, wherein stakes for individual pupils are high – as indeed are the stakes for the collective at a regional and national level (we are thinking here of our nationally poor record for the progress and attainment of low attaining pupils,[2] and the scale of the attainment gap for social background). So, given these challenges and the acknowledgement of an inevitably imperfect system, what do our findings tell us that may inform best practice going forward?

What we have found out about promoting more equitable practice

One of the things we have clearly shown is that *it is very difficult to improve equity in attainment grouping*. Of the various attainment grouping practices, our project focused on setting ('tracking by subject' – see Chapter 2). That is – at least in theory – a relatively equitable and flexible approach to attainment grouping which, if applied strictly in relation to prior attainment levels in each discrete subject concerned, provides high conceptual fidelity as an attainment grouping method. As we discussed in Chapter 2, setting is less detrimental than 'streaming' or 'banding', because it facilitates the necessary flexibility for students to be in different attainment level classes for different subjects; hence avoiding the deeply problematic, generalised approach of streaming/banding (with its associated 'ability thinking', and categorisation of pupils overall, rather than in discrete subject areas), and facilitating higher levels of the social mixing that is shown by the OECD and UNESCO (Willms, 2006; OECD, 2001, 2013) to be so beneficial for overall attainment. We consider that it is important to recognise that different *types* of tracking (attainment grouping) can be more or less detrimental to overall attainment and social justice. Our study supports that 'high integrity' setting is certainly preferable to streaming and banding. And of course, far preferable to between-school tracking.

Nevertheless, we have shown how many schools practising setting are *not* practising this with high integrity, and are frequently melding setting with elements of streaming (e.g. by using attainment group allocation in one subject [such as maths] as a proxy to apply set designation in other subjects [such as the sciences]); or over-laying streaming with setting (e.g. operating broad 'ability' streams/bands for most subjects and then adding additional attainment hierarchisation by setting in certain subjects).

Moreover, our study has shown clearly, and for the first time, how and why it is very difficult for schools to operate setting with high fidelity. We have catalogued in Chapter 7 the many practical, structural, and cultural reasons that 'optimal' practice in setting is so challenging for schools to achieve. We also discussed how our findings concerning teachers' offering of different pedagogy and curricula for different set levels actually reflect the basic premise of setting: the logic of setting is that it addresses the different paces/needs of different student groups. But then the dilemma is that in that case it is hard to argue that there is an 'equal' offer for all – or indeed that expectations are the same for all students (as patently they are not). Of course, we have recognised that pupils have different needs according to prior attainment, and that in any classroom this must be recognised and addressed. But in applying assumptions to whole class groups of pupils, clearly there is more temptation for stereotyping and suboptimal practices.

The implication here is clear. If it is too difficult for schools to improve setting practices to improve equity, then setting ought to be minimised – indeed, in an ideal world, phased out. As we argued at the outset, it is a key principle of our state school system that pupils are equally entitled to schooling, and by extension they ought to be equally entitled to high quality provision. There is clear evidence that often attainment grouping is undermining this tenet, in practice.

We are, however, pragmatists. One of us has written elsewhere about the importance of maintaining a pragmatic approach to improving equity, simultaneous to utopian calls for radical social change (Francis & Mills, 2012): while more profound innovations may take a long time to realise (if ever), every day millions of pupils sit in classrooms experiencing present educational practice and its consequences, and incremental improvement for these children is better than none. While it would be wrong to cast comprehensive mixed attainment teaching as utopian, given that this is widely practiced across Scandinavian countries, and in pockets elsewhere (including in some schools in the UK), it is also the case that in many nations attainment grouping is so firmly and enduringly inscribed that rapid change would likely be impossible (even irresponsible). In our conversations on this matter in numerous different countries where attainment grouping is long entrenched (including, for example, the UK, Hong Kong, and the US), we have noticed that many educators are aware of and somewhat concerned about the iniquitous implications of attainment grouping, but feel at a loss as to how to address this. Done badly, a turn to mixed attainment grouping could have detrimental consequences for pupils experiencing the unsupported change of pedagogical approach, and also provide negative experiences for teachers, potentially discouraging their further pursuit of mixed attainment methods. Moreover, given that high quality teaching is especially impactful on the attainment of pupils from disadvantaged backgrounds, it is possible that poorly managed change would impact this group most.

We therefore feel that the role of research should be to support the movement *towards* mixed attainment grouping, recognising that different schools (and at a higher level, different international systems) will be at different stages on this journey, and will need support to move forward. Further, we recognise that this development needs to be led by teachers and school leaders, supported by research evidence focused on practitioner needs and pedagogic impacts of different approaches.

What we need to be able to improve practice further and support pupil outcomes and experiences

To be clear, we feel absolutely legitimised by the depth and longevity of the research evidence to say that any schools practising streaming (or the related practice of banding) ought to desist this poor and inequitable practice. Likely for schools that have been reliant on these approaches, a turn to 'high integrity setting' will comprise a preferable approach which delivers somewhat better flexibility and nuance (and therefore somewhat more equitable practice), and begins the journey away from 'fixed ability' assumptions and associated practices. (This is of course not to rule out the *possibility* of a whole-school direct move from banding to mixed attainment grouping, but this would likely require *very significant* planning and preparation, and capacity and resource to this end).

We also feel it warranted to assert that attainment grouping (including 'high integrity setting') should be minimised so far as possible. Many schools in the UK, including secondary schools, are already practising mixed attainment grouping in certain subjects such as the humanities and arts. There *may* be pedagogical reasons why attainment grouping is more prevalent in some areas of the curriculum than others, but this is not well evidenced. On the one hand, schools within existing networks such as Mixed Attainment Maths[3] are demonstrating that even in subjects wherein attainment grouping is most prevalent, excellent outcomes for young people can be delivered by mixed attainment grouping. And certainly it is puzzling to consider why some subjects (say, Biology) are more frequently taught in attainment groups than others (say, History). Yet here we know little either about the relative proportions of mixed attainment practice versus attainment grouping in specific subject areas, nor why this is the case. More research is needed.

Meanwhile, albeit research on good practice in mixed attainment grouping remains relatively scant, the evidence that lower attainers make better progress in such environments than when subject to attainment grouping is long-standing. Hence the need to support schools to move towards this practice and increase it is clear from a social justice perspective. The success of systems like Finland and some other systems where attainment grouping is less prevalent (such as regions in Canada) demonstrates clearly that mixed attainment grouping does not imply a drop in standards. Nevertheless, precisely *how* these education systems achieve the success for all pupils and the appropriate meeting of diverse needs in a mixed attainment classroom needs urgent attention. Findings may have resource implications – for example, in Finland very high numbers of pupils are provided with additional learning support.

Nevertheless, our project has generated clear evidence and guidance that can support teachers to these ends, both in improving equity in setting, and in supporting and improving mixed attainment teaching practice. These are outlined in the next chapter. We hope that these, in conjunction with the findings reported in this book, will help support a move towards more equitable grouping practice in schools – a move that we have demonstrated is urgently needed to secure equitable life chances, and the equal chance of a high quality education for all pupils.

Notes

1 For elaboration, see e.g. Fraser (1997); Choudhry (2000).
2 See Marshall et al. (2012).
3 www.mixedattainmentmaths.com.

References

Alegre, M. À. & Ferrer, G. (2010). School regimes and education equity: some insights based on PISA 2006. *British Educational Research Journal*, *36*(3), 433–461.

Choudhry, S. (2000). Distribution vs. recognition: the case of anti-discrimination laws. *George Mason Law Review*, *9*(1), 145–178.

Francis, B., Archer, L., Hodgen, J., Pepper, D., Taylor, B., & Travers, M. (2017a). Exploring the relative lack of impact of research on 'ability grouping' in England: a discourse analytic account. *Cambridge Journal of Education*, *47*(1), 1–17.

Francis, B., Mills, M., & Lupton, R. (2017b). Towards social justice in education: contradictions and dilemmas. *Journal of Education Policy*, *32*(4), 414–431.

Francis, B. & Mills, M. (2012). What would a socially just education system look like? *Journal of Education Policy*, *27*(5), 577–585.

Francome, T. & Hewitt, D. (2018). 'My math lessons are all about learning from your mistakes': how mixed-attainment mathematics grouping affects the way students experience mathematics. *Educational Review*. September.

Fraser, N. (1997). *Justice interruptus: critical reflections on the 'post-socialist' condition*. London: Routledge.

Hallam, S. & Ireson, J. (2006). Secondary school pupils' preferences for different types of structured grouping practices. *British Educational Research Journal*, *32*(4), 583–599.

Hallam, S. & Ireson, J. (2007). Secondary school pupils' satisfaction with their ability grouping placements. *British Educational Research Journal*, *33*(1), 27–45.

Marshall, P. (2012). *The tail: how England's schools fail one child in five – and what can be done*. London, Profile Books Ltd.

OECD. (2001). *Knowledge and skills for life: first results from the OECD Programme for International Student Assessment (PISA) 2000*. Paris: OECD Publishing.

OECD. (2013). Selecting and grouping students. In *PISA 2012 results: what makes schools successful? Resources, policies and practices* (Vol. IV, pp. 71–92). Paris: OECD Publishing.

Owles, E. & Taylor, J. (2018). *H for Harry* [Documentary Film]. United Kingdom: Mercurial Pictures.

Willms, J. D. (2006). *Learning divides: ten policy questions about the performance and equity of schools and schooling systems*. Montreal: UNESCO Institute for Statistics.

10
RECOMMENDATIONS

Having reflected on the implications of our findings in the previous chapter, in this chapter we set out our recommendations accordingly, for moving towards more effective and fairer practice for realising educational outcomes for all young people, and for equality of opportunity in pupils' access to high quality educational provision, and positive experiences of school.

The negative impacts of attainment grouping for educational equity and the outcomes of low attainers have been plainly shown, as has the resulting social injustice, given the lack of equality of opportunity, and the 'double disadvantage' for the disproportionally large numbers of pupils from socially disadvantaged and/or particular minority ethnic backgrounds placed in low attainment groups. As such, our principles for recommendations going forward are as follows:

- A need to collectively reflect on attainment grouping.
- 'High integrity setting' is preferable to other forms of tracking – much more can be done here, both in replacing 'harder' forms of tracking with high integrity setting in those schools that presently maintain streaming, and in improving the 'integrity' of setting for schools that are using this approach.
- Social mixing is established as a social and educational good, and should be facilitated.
- Setting should be minimised.
- Research has a role in supporting with the necessary evidence on good practice in moves towards mixed attainment grouping.

In order to facilitate collective reflection, we have instigated a 'pledge' at our 'Best Practice in Grouping Students' webpage, wherein educators can commit to engaging professional conversations about attainment grouping and its impact, and what improvements might be made in their own school contexts. Effective and impactful change will be teacher-led, and these professional conversations will be vital to that end – whether conducted through professional associations and networks, unions, subject associations, social media, or individual class and staffrooms.

Recommendations for practitioners

We have discussed at length the prevalence of 'fixed ability thinking' in schools, and the anxiety about mixed attainment grouping of mixed attainment practice in relation to perceived additional workload and the potential impact on accountability measures. In the face of such powerful narratives and institutional constraints, and furthermore in the current climate of heavy teacher workloads and burdens on schools, significant changes to grouping and pedagogy pose a real challenge. Indeed our research findings have led us to question whether many schools have the capacity for large-scale change at the present time (Taylor et al., 2017; 2019). Furthermore, although the overall benefits are clear, the evidence base for good practice in mixed attainment grouping is still limited (Francis et al., 2017). However, the need for increased equity is urgent for pupils currently undergoing schooling, so a pragmatic response must be found. It is insufficient for us as researchers merely to critique policy and practice without providing constructive suggestions as to alternative and socially just actions (Francis & Mills, 2012), so our approach is to draw on the key principles of equitable grouping to propose a number of adaptations to practice that are manageable for schools. With this in mind we developed our resource *Dos and Don'ts of Attainment Grouping* (Francis et al., 2018), summarised in Table 10.1. The *Dos and Don'ts* draw on the research literature, including our own empirical findings outlined in this book, to support teachers and school leaders in reflecting on current practices, and identifying improvements that should increase equality of opportunity and mitigate present injustice.

Our intention with the *Dos and Don'ts of Setting* is to draw on the research evidence and on practical findings from our study to identify feasible 'tweaks' to setting practice that can improve equity. Likewise, our *Dos and Don'ts of Mixed Attainment Grouping* may support those already using mixed attainment grouping in improving practice, and we hope will additionally assist schools new to mixed attainment teaching to implement it productively. The following sections present the rationale and research findings that underpin our recommended *Dos and Don'ts* in both setting and mixed attainment grouping. Note that we don't include streaming, as the practice is both socially unjust and conceptually flawed, and therefore not justifiable (Boaler & Wiliam, 2001).

Setting: how to group pupils

Our advice around grouping pupils in sets is that allocation to a set in a particular curriculum subject should be based exclusively on a pupil's prior attainment in that subject only, and that sets should not be extrapolated across subjects or arranged for timetable convenience. Furthermore, where there are pupils on the borderline

TABLE 10.1 Dos and don'ts of attainment grouping

Dos and don'ts of setting	
Do make setting as subject specific as possible	**Don't** set by timetable convenience
Do group students by attainment only	**Don't** extrapolate setting across subjects
Do retest regularly and move students between groups	**Don't** assign subject expert teachers only to top sets
Do use a lottery system when assigning borderline students to sets	**Don't** give less homework to low sets
Do make sure all students have access to a rich curriculum	**Don't** provide low sets with a 'dumbed' down curriculum
Do apply high expectations to all sets	**Don't** leave students in sets without regular testing
Dos and don'ts of mixed attainment grouping	
Do practice differentiation	**Don't** teach to the middle
Do change in-class groupings regularly	**Don't** establish fixed within-class 'ability' groups
Do have high expectations of all students in the class	**Don't** plan three lessons for every class
Do plan rich tasks that students can access at different levels and receive feedback	**Don't** over-rely on high attainers explaining to others
Do encourage a classroom climate where students support one another	

between sets we recommend that they should be allocated by lottery, to avoid emergent bias in allocation and support equity and transparency. We also suggest that pupils are tested regularly and moved between sets where appropriate.

The evidence behind these stipulations is as follows. A consistent finding in earlier research is that pupils in low sets and streams are more likely to be from disadvantaged backgrounds and from certain ethnic groups (e.g. Muijs & Dunne, 2010). Our research has found a similar pattern (Archer et al., 2018; Connolly et al., forthcoming), although we found that the allocation of pupils from disadvantaged backgrounds to low sets was explained by their prior attainment. However, we also found that where pupils were on the border of two mathematics groups, they were more likely to be placed in a lower group if they were Black, Asian or female and more likely to be placed in a higher group if they were White or male. This finding underpins our recommendation that schools should use a lottery system when assigning borderline pupils to sets. We also retain the recommendation to group only by attainment that formed part of our 'Best Practice in Setting' intervention (Taylor et al., 2019), as research suggests that when other factors are taken into account, this can introduce unintentional bias (Gillborn & Youdell, 2000; Timmermans et al., 2015).

The detrimental effects of streaming – grouping by a notion of general 'ability' – are well-documented (Boaler & Wiliam, 2001) and so our *Dos and Don'ts* include a number of injunctions to avoid this practice, which sometimes takes place inadvertently. We found that frequently the planning of the school timetable can distort subject-based setting and introduce elements of streaming, for example where two subjects are timetabled 'against' each other and must share groupings (Taylor et al., 2019) or where sets operate within 'ability' bands. Sets therefore should be established separately for each subject and the timetable written for the benefit of pupils.

Another area where the timetable can impede grouping arrangements is where it obstructs the movement of pupils between groups. Prior research has found that teachers tend to overestimate the amount of movement between groups (Hallam & Ireson, 2005) and we found that movement was difficult or impossible in some schools because of timetabling arrangements or the requirement to negotiate movement with numerous members of staff (Taylor et al., 2019). Furthermore pupils reported that they felt demoralised when they worked hard and yet did not move up a group, showing that the opportunity to move group is motivational for pupils (Francis et al., 2019).

Setting: curriculum and teaching

It is well-established that pupils in lower sets are often offered a lower-quality curriculum and pedagogy, frequently characterised by reduced curriculum content, less homework, and repetitive activities (Gillborn & Youdell, 2000; Oakes, 1985). Our study has shown how and why this can manifest. But the impoverished curriculum of the lower sets can make it difficult for pupils to succeed if they are moved up a set level, and as we have seen, the restricted pedagogy is often experienced as patronising, boring, and frustrating by pupils (Francis et al., 2019; Mazenod et al., 2019). We recommend therefore that all pupils are offered a rich curriculum and a range of classroom activities that facilitate the stretching development of knowledge and skills. Homework is an important part of this, with pupils in lower sets potentially falling further behind as they are not offered the same home learning opportunities as their peers in higher sets.

Previous research has found that pupils in lower sets tend to be taught by teachers who are less experienced and less highly qualified, and our research has confirmed this, with pupils in the lowest sets being less likely to have a teacher with a degree in the subject taught, and more likely to be taught by a teacher with just a GCSE in that subject (see Chapter 6; Francis et al., 2019). In fact, subject expertise is likely to be of great benefit to pupils in lower sets and our recommendation is that pupils in low sets should be just as likely to have a subject expert teacher. Low sets have also been found to be more likely to experience changes of teacher through the year (Kutnick et al., 2005). So considering issues of equity in teacher allocation (or where possible, taking a randomised approach to allocation across sets) is clearly important. An encouraging finding from our intervention was that there did seem to be an improvement in equitable distribution of subject expertise across set levels among the intervention schools, suggesting it is possible to improve practice here.

Mixed attainment: strategies for differentiation

Alongside our recommendations for setting we also make recommendations for successful mixed attainment grouping. A significant challenge when teaching pupils with a broad range of prior attainment in the same class is how to adapt or differentiate the lesson to enable all pupils to make progress. This is a matter of significant concern to teachers (see Chapter 8). However, some traditional strategies for managing this bring their own difficulties. Sometimes practitioners attempt to solve the problem of differentiation essentially by teaching as if they have three (or more) sets to teach simultaneously and differentiating by task or by resource. This may quickly become unsustainable (Delisle, 2015) and so our recommendation is to differentiate through questioning, feedback, and outcome (Hodgen & Webb, 2008), planning rich tasks that scaffold different levels of understanding and success, and that provide ample opportunity for feedback from peers and from the teacher.

Some teachers do not address the challenge of differentiation, with the consequence that their lessons lack challenge for some of their pupils. 'Teaching to the middle' is something we counsel strongly against, in fact teachers who worked with us on the design phase of the 'Best Practice in Mixed Attainment' intervention recommended 'teaching to the top' and then putting in place appropriate support in order to enable all pupils to access and succeed on the tasks (Taylor et al., 2015); though it is worth noting that this support is absolutely essential if pupils with low prior attainment and barriers to learning are to succeed.

Mixed attainment: managing the class

Teachers often report that it is difficult to manage a diverse group of pupils in a mixed attainment classroom. We therefore make some recommendations as to classroom strategies that can assist with this.

In the primary school classroom it is often the case that children in a mixed attainment class are divided onto 'ability tables' (Marks, 2013). The recent revision of the Education Endowment Foundation Toolkit (EEF, 2018) separated out the effect of within-class grouping from setting and streaming. The Toolkit finds a small overall positive effect of within-class grouping under specific circumstances, namely, where grouping is established flexibly and for specific purposes. Where within-class grouping is fixed, many of the negative effects of setting and streaming have been found to occur (Marks, 2013). We advise therefore that within-class groups are established based on specific learning objectives, for example grouping together pupils who all need to practise a particular aspect of the curriculum.

The benefits of talk in the classroom are well-documented: pupils benefit from feedback on their learning and from the opportunity to explain their learning to each other (Slavin, 1996). Teachers should be careful not to depend overly on higher attaining pupils to do the explaining: teaching another pupil is beneficial to all pupils regardless of prior attainment and, furthermore, higher attaining pupils can become disillusioned and lower attaining pupils patronised if used too often in this way (Tereshchenko et al., 2018). This constructive talk requires a supportive classroom climate, where all pupils feel able to articulate their ideas and listen to the ideas of others (Rubie-Davies, 2007).

High expectations for all pupils

Where pupils are labelled as 'high' or 'low ability', this can influence the expectations that teachers have of the class and that pupils hold of themselves. Our research has clearly demonstrated the impact of labelling through set placement, on the development of self-confidence in the specific curriculum subject concerned, and in general self-confidence in learning. So this is a particular issue for setting. Our research found that teachers of low sets often inadvertently taught in such a way as to create dependency and prevent pupils from developing into self-motivated, self-sufficient learners (Mazenod et al., 2019). Setting by attainment can invite very different expectations across groups: one teacher told us that the same lesson taught to a higher and a lower set would be 'unrecognisable', and pupils repeatedly reported that teachers of high sets were 'strict' and those of lower sets were 'laid back' (Francis et al., 2019). Within a mixed attainment class it should be easier to communicate the same high expectations to all pupils, but nevertheless, teacher expectations can influence learning in mixed attainment groups too (Dunne & Gazeley, 2008; Weinstein, 2002). So regardless of grouping strategies, teachers need to be mindful of what expectations they communicate to pupils and self-question to ensure that expectations are sufficiently and equitably high.

And additionally . . .

A few further points, not mentioned in our 'dos and don'ts'.

- Starting a research-informed conversation

Something else that was evident to us in our conversations with teachers was that schools are typically conservative in their attainment grouping practices: long-standing historical practices are often deeply embedded, practically and culturally, and can be hard to shift. Change is infrequently embarked upon and there can be many barriers to changing what schools do (see Chapter 7). We recommend therefore that teachers commit to starting conversations with one another about their grouping practices: reflecting on what does and doesn't work, and most importantly doing this informed by research. We hope that the present book, as well as our *Dos and Don'ts of Attainment Grouping* and other resources such as *Developing Best Practice in Mixed Attainment English* (Taylor & Yandell, 2017) will be supportive of such conversations; as will our 'pledge' initiative, mentioned above. We are very keen to hear from teachers additional ideas and tested approaches that facilitate equitable and high quality practice.

- Limiting the number of sets

It is worth saying that while not included in our 'dos and don'ts of setting', we also think that it is beneficial to limit the number of set levels. This facilitates social mixing (as fewer 'tiers' creates broader groupings), and somewhat reduces the impact of labels and potential stigma given that hierarchies are less steep.

- Ways are found to make labels less overt

Although our own and other research shows clearly that even very young children are aware of attainment grouping, however much teachers think they are avoiding transparency (Marks, 2013), given the issues we have raised about social stigma there is likely benefit in avoiding 'rubbing it in'. So, ensuring that the phrase 'ability grouping' (and/or 'high ability', 'low ability' etc) is not used, including within group titles. Likewise, the above recommendation to minimise set tiers, and hence social distinction.

- Minimising setting

We also reiterate that our findings justify a recommendation that setting is *minimised*. Good practice in mixed attainment grouping is available to model more readily in some subjects than others, from some subjects wherein attainment grouping is unusual, to those where in contrast mixed attainment grouping is rare. But we encourage practitioners to seek out good practice to model, as well as the supply of more resources and evidence on good practice.

Recommendations for policymakers

The English education system is notoriously driven by accountability measures, which for decades have been used by policymakers as effective levers via which to influence and drive the system. School leaders are therefore encultured to be sensitised to policy 'mood music' as well as directives, and especially to the views of Ofsted, the schools inspectorate, given the importance of Ofsted inspection results for a school's reputation and consequent future success. We have analysed elsewhere the very frequent pronouncements from policymakers (individual ministers, Government, and Ofsted) on the benefits of setting for pupil outcomes (Francis et al., 2017). Clearly, these statements were not based on research evidence (or any other sort), but spoke to a set of assumptions – deeply resonant in our cultural psyche – about 'natural order', different 'types' of student, and a conflation between 'academic rigor' and segregation (see Francis et al., 2017). This has thankfully died away of late, at least in relation to within-school segregation – while the debate about between school segregation has been reinstigated by the present Conservative Government's support for grammar schools.

So our recommendation to policymakers is to be open to research evidence; to be clear on available research evidence before making pronouncements on particular arrangements for teaching and learning; and not to support problematic approaches – especially those that could widen our existing yawning gaps for socio-economic attainment and for the outcomes for young people with different levels of prior attainment.

More positively, professional organisations such as subject associations, unions, and professional bodies such as the Chartered College of Teaching and international equivalents, have a role to play in facilitating professional debate and discussion of attainment grouping and in/equity, and in curating good practice.

For further research

We have discussed how, while some aspects of research on attainment grouping are saturated, clear gaps remain. The most glaring of which is research on effective mixed attainment practice – methods, and impact. As we have said, with teachers cautious about change, and schools having very limited capacity given the funding environment and the challenge to recruit and retain staff, schools need support if they are to respond to research evidence. In this case, teachers will need exemplars and materials from which to draw, as well as clear evidence on what will be fruitful in their contexts. We especially need more evidence on how the best international mixed attainment systems succeed, including how they manage differentiation at scale, and the respective resource implications.

Other evident areas for research exploration include:

- The relative impact of different numbers of set levels.
- The relative impact of attainment grouping/mixed attainment in different curriculum subject areas.
- The impact of nurture groups – on educational attainment and on experience of school.
- How to best support different vulnerable learners, in both setted and mixed attainment contexts (again, there is likely much to be learnt from other systems).

So, there is a great deal of work to be done, on the part of both education professionals and researchers. However, we hope that this book has demonstrated the importance of this work, to ensure that, rather than reproducing social inequality as attainment grouping is presently shown to do, schooling practices support social justice. We want to work collectively to ensure that all pupils – irrespective of background – have an equal chance to access high quality, stretching, engaging, and affirming educational opportunities.

References

Archer, L., Francis, B., Miller, S., Taylor, B., Tereshchenko, A., Connolly, P., Hodgen, J., Mazenod, A., Pepper, D., Sloan, S., & Travers, M.-C. (2018). The symbolic violence of setting: a Bourdieusian analysis of mixed methods data on secondary students' views about setting. *British Journal of Educational Research, 44*(1), 119–140.

Boaler, J. & Wiliam, D. (2001). Setting, streaming and mixed-ability teaching. In J. Dillon & M. Maguire (Eds.), *Becoming a teacher* (2nd ed., pp. 173–181). Maidenhead: Open University Press.

Connolly, P., Taylor, B., Francis, B., Archer, L., Hodgen, J., Mazenod, A., & Tereshchenko, A. (forthcoming, accepted). The misallocation of students to academic sets in maths: a study of secondary schools in England. *British Educational Research Journal*.

Delisle, J. R. (2015). Differentiation doesn't work. *Education Week*. Retrieved from www.edweek.org/ew/articles/2015/01/07/differentiation-doesnt-work.html?r=72617547&preview=1.

Dunne, M. & Gazeley, L. (2008). Teachers, social class and underachievement. *British Journal of Sociology of Education, 29*(5), 451–463.

EEF. (2018). *The Sutton Trust – Education Endowment Foundation teaching and learning toolkit*. London: Education Endowment Foundation.

Francis, B., Archer, L., Hodgen, J., Pepper, D., Taylor, B., & Travers, M.-C. (2017). Exploring the relative lack of impact of research on 'ability grouping' in England: a discourse analytic account. *Cambridge Journal of Education, 47*(1), 1–17.

Francis, B., Hodgen, J., Craig, N., Taylor, B., Archer, L., Mazenod, A., & Tereshchenko, A. (2019). Teacher 'quality' and attainment grouping: the role of within-school teacher deployment in social and educational inequality. *Teaching and Teacher Education, 77*, 183–192.

Francis, B. & Mills, M. (2012). What would a socially just education system look like? *Journal of Education Policy, 27*(5), 577–585.

Francis, B., Taylor, B., Hodgen, J., Tereshchenko, A., & Archer, L. (2018). *Dos and don'ts of attainment grouping*. London: UCL Institute of Education.

Gillborn, D. & Youdell, D. (2000). *Rationing education: policy, practice, reform, and equity*. Buckingham: Open University Press.

Hallam, S. & Ireson, J. (2005). Secondary school teachers' pedagogic practices when teaching mixed and structured ability classes. *Research Papers in Education, 20*(1), 3–24.

Hodgen, J. & Webb, M. (2008). Questioning, dialogue and feedback. In S. Swaffield (Ed.), *Unlocking assessment* (pp. 73–89). New York: Routledge.

Kutnick, P., Sebba, J., Blatchford, P., Galton, M., Thorp, J., MacIntyre, H., & Berdondini, L. (2005). *The effects of pupil grouping: literature review*. Retrieved from https://core.ac.uk/download/pdf/15171799.pdf.

Marks, R. (2013). 'The blue table means you don't have a clue': the persistence of fixed-ability thinking and practices in primary mathematics in English schools. *FORUM: for Promoting 3–19 Comprehensive Education, 55*(1), 31–44.

Mazenod, A., Francis, B., Archer, L., Hodgen, J., Taylor, B., Tereshchenko, A., & Pepper, D. (2019). Nurturing learning or encouraging dependency? Teacher constructions of students in lower attainment groups in English secondary schools. *Cambridge Journal of Education, 49*(1), 53–68.

Muijs, D. & Dunne, M. (2010). Setting by ability – or is it? A quantitative study of determinants of set placement in English secondary schools. *Educational Research, 52*(4), 391–407.

Oakes, J. (1985). *How schools structure inequality*. New Haven: Yale University Press.

Rubie-Davies, C. M. (2007). Classroom interactions: exploring the practices of high- and low-expectation teachers. *British Journal of Educational Psychology, 77*(2), 289–306.

Slavin, R. E. (1996). Research on cooperative learning and achievement: what we know, what we need to know. *Contemporary Educational Psychology, 21*(1), 43–69.

Taylor, B., Francis, B., Archer, L., Hodgen, J., Pepper, D., Tereshchenko, A., & Travers, M.-C. (2017). Factors deterring schools from mixed attainment teaching practice. *Pedagogy, Culture & Society, 25*(3), 327–345.

Taylor, B., Francis, B., Craig, N., Archer, L., Hodgen, J., Mazenod, A., Tereshchenko, A., & Pepper, D. (2019). Why is it difficult for schools to establish equitable practices in allocating students to attainment 'sets'? *British Journal of Educational Studies*, 67(1), 5–24.

Taylor, B., Travers, M.-C., Francis, B., Hodgen, J., & Sumner, C. (2015). *Best practice in mixed-attainment grouping*. London: Education Endowment Foundation/King's College London.

Taylor, B. & Yandell, J. (2017). *Developing best practice in mixed attainment English*. London: UCL Institute of Education.

Tereshchenko, A., Francis, B., Archer, L., Hodgen, J., Mazenod, A., Taylor, B., Pepper, D., & Travers, M.-C. (2018). Learners' attitudes to mixed-attainment grouping: examining the views of students of high, middle and low attainment. *Research Papers in Education*, 1–20.

Timmermans, A. C., Kuyper, H., & van der Werf, G. (2015). Accurate, inaccurate, or biased teacher expectations: do Dutch teachers differ in their expectations at the end of primary education? *British Journal of Educational Psychology*, 85(4), 459–478.

Weinstein, R. S. (2002). *Reaching higher: the power of expectations in schooling*. Cambridge, MA: Harvard University Press.

INDEX

Printed in Great Britain
by Amazon

67183439R00108